'This book is a very valuable source for modeling
follows a non-technical but mathematically rigorous
examples help readers develop a solid understanding o
Especially remarkable are the various parts of the bool
In this way the book provides clearly elaborated tool
engineering.'– *Dr. Christian Bluhm, Chief Risk Officer* .... *of the Executive Board,*
FMS Wertmanagement

'Copula functions have been controversial mathematical tools in financial modeling. The example of CDOs is still hot in the public perception and has been debated for several years even in mainstream press. We discussed this ourselves in the 2010 book *Credit Models and the Crisis*. It is good to see CDOs discussed here at the end of the book. More generally the authors, whose high technical standing in statistical distributions and copula functions is well known, take a middle path between hostility to copulas, stemming mostly from the abovementioned CDO case, and copula enthusiasts, who would like to employ copulas every time a dependence problem shows up.

The wrong way risk pattern for CVA on CDS epitomizes the problems one has when blindly using copula functions without investigating the setting first, as we pointed out with Chourdakis in 2008, and again it is good to see it reported here. Overall, the book is concise but well written, addressing the key questions in copula functions from the start, with a rigorous mathematical approach that does not sacrifice accessibility, and with good reference examples from financial engineering. It is an ideal book to start looking at copula functions for financial engineering with a balanced and technically rigorous perspective, as such it is recommended.'– *Damiano Brigo, Chair in Mathematical Finance, Department of Mathematics, Imperial College London, and Director of the Capco Institute*

'This book provides a well explained and broadly accessible introduction to copula models in financial engineering. It joins a rigorous mathematical explanation of the main aspects of copula theory with a series of illustrations, examples and practical aspects that is sure to be appreciated by practitioners. A must-read book to understand the role of dependence in the financial and insurance industry.'– *Fabrizio Durante, Free University of Bozen-Bolzano*

'This book is an excellent first choice and easy-to-read-introduction for all starting the journey into the realm of copulas. But it will be a great second choice for the many who have found this journey and the theoretical foundations of copulas too complex and intimidating the first time they tried it.' – *Frank Romeike, Managing Director and founder RiskNET*

Financial Engineering Explained

About the series

Financial Engineering Explained is a series of concise, practical guides to modern finance, focusing on key, technical areas of risk management and asset pricing. Written for practitioners, researchers and students, the series discusses a range of topics in a non-mathematical but highly intuitive way. Each self-contained volume is dedicated to a specific topic and offers a thorough introduction with all the necessary depth, but without too much technical ballast. Where applicable, theory is illustrated with real world examples, with special attention to the numerical implementation.

Series Editor:
Wim Schoutens, Department of Mathematics, Catholic University of Leuven.

Series Advisory Board:
Peter Carr, Executive Director, NYU Mathematical Finance; Global Head of Market Modeling, Morgan Stanley.
Ernst Eberlein, Department of Mathematical Stochastics, University of Freiburg.
Matthias Scherer, Chair of Mathematical Finance, Technische Universität München.

Titles in the series:
Equity Derivatives Explained, Mohamed Bouzoubaa
The Greeks and Hedging Explained, Peter Leoni
Smile Pricing Explained, Peter Austing
Financial Engineering with Copulas Explained, Matthias Scherer and Jan-Frederik Mai
Interest Rates Explained Volume 1, Jörg Kienitz

Forthcoming titles:
Interest Rates Explained Volume 2, Jörg Kienitz

Submissions: Wim Schoutens – wim@schoutens.be

Financial Engineering Explained series
Series Standing Order ISBN: 978–1137–32733–8

You can receive future titles in this series as they are published by placing a standing order. Please contact your bookseller or, in case of difficulty, write to us at the address below with your name and address, the title of the series and the ISBN quoted above.

Customer Services Department, Macmillan Distribution Ltd, Houndmills, Basingstoke, Hampshire RG21 6XS, England

Financial Engineering with Copulas Explained

Jan-Frederik Mai

XAIA Investment, Munich, Germany

and

Matthias Scherer

Technische Universität München, Germany

First published 2014 by
PALGRAVE MACMILLAN

Palgrave Macmillan in the UK is an imprint of Macmillan Publishers Limited,
registered in England, company number 785998, of Houndmills, Basingstoke,
Hampshire RG21 6XS.

Palgrave Macmillan in the US is a division of St Martins Press LLC,
175 Fifth Avenue, New York, NY 10010.

Palgrave Macmillan is the global academic imprint of the above companies
and has companies and representatives throughout the world.

Palgrave® and Macmillan® are registered trademarks in the United States,
the United Kingdom, Europe and other countries

ISBN: 978–1–137–34630–8

This book is printed on paper suitable for recycling and made from fully
managed and sustained forest sources. Logging, pulping and manufacturing
processes are expected to conform to the environmental regulations of the
country of origin.

A catalogue record for this book is available from the British Library.

A catalog record for this book is available from the Library of Congress.

To the new generation: Paul, Fabian, and Lara.

Contents

List of Figures

List of Tables

Preface and Acknowledgments

What can you expect from this book? We aim to provide you with an easy-to-read introduction to current problems (and solutions, of course) in the field of dependence modeling as it is required in today's financial and insurance industry. If you enjoy reading a chapter of the book after a long day at work or during a continental flight, and understand the essence of the exposition, then we have succeeded. Clearly, 'easy-to-read' strongly depends on your mathematical training. We take as granted familiarity with probability calculus and elementary statistics.[1] Aimed at readers from the financial industry, we try to illustrate the theory with real world examples. We are always mathematically precise, but we do not aim at being complete with respect to proofs and the latest generalizations of the presented results. Instead, we visualize the results and explain how they can be applied. Finally, we direct the interested reader to deeper literature, where proofs and further results are given. The field of dependence modeling has grown impressively in recent years.[2] Having said this, it is clear that this introduction has to prioritize certain aspects, but we provide many references for those readers with an appetite for further material.

The Importance of Dependence

Both authors strongly believe that the role of dependence has been underestimated for a long time (and still is) in the financial and insurance industry. A bank or insurance company hardly runs into substantial trouble if individual options or insurance contracts are mis-priced by a few basis points. Events where many things go wrong at the same time are those that create true financial distress. Think of an event that causes multiple stocks to fall jointly or multiple insurance claims to trigger simultaneously. Or, even more severe, consider events that affect prices across different markets (stocks, credit, FX, ...) at the same time. Many financial institutions have a very high level of sophistication inside each of their specialized trading desks, but might not have the simplest model available for how these different markets and trading desks interact. So the question of risk aggregation within such an institution is difficult to answer – if it is possible at all. As a different example, the reader might

---

[1] In particular, we always work on a probability space $(\Omega, \mathcal{F}, \mathbb{P})$ with event space Ω, σ-algebra $\mathcal{F}$, and probability measure $\mathbb{P}$. We write $\mathbb{E}[X]$ for the expectation value of a random variable $X : \Omega \to \mathbb{R}$. Moreover, we use '$\sim$' for 'is distributed according to', that is, $X \sim F$ means that the random variable X has distribution function F.

[2] A bibliographic study on the use of copulas in finance is given in [Genest et al. (2009)].

collect all univariate families of probability distributions (or stock-price models on the level of stochastic processes) she or he is aware of and compare this collection to all multivariate probability distributions (or multivariate stock-price models) she knows. Most likely, the former set is much bigger. The same clearly holds true for the number of scientific papers. Hence, we feel the need to provide tools that explain how risks can be aggregated and how multivariate stochastic models can be designed. In this introduction we focus on random vectors. Due to the lack of space we hardly touch multivariate stochastic processes, as this subject could easily fill another volume. So this book focuses on the concept of copulas, which allows us to link many univariate distribution functions to a single multivariate one.

To All the Quants Out There

We expect that many of you actually implement the presented methodologies. To simplify this task, we list useful R, see [R (2013)], packages during the exposition and at the end of selected chapters. We have decided on R due to its extensive functionality and the simple fact that it is open source software, so we do not have a conflict of interest as we would if we recommended a specific commercial software. Even if programming is not part of your daily business, we strongly recommend implementing the material; it will, for sure, be an eye-opener. For those of you not familiar with basic commands in R, a good introduction is [Venables, Smith (2012)].

Further Literature

This book serves as a first introduction to the huge field of copula modeling, with a focus on applications in financial engineering. To study the topic in more detail, good textbooks are: [Schweizer, Sklar (1983)] – the seminal book on the topic; [Joe (1997)] – very comprehensive with a strong focus on estimation; [Nelsen (2006)] – a classical analytical study of copulas; [Mai, Scherer (2012)] – a probabilistic treatment of copulas with a focus on simulation strategies; [Kurowicka, Joe (2010)] – an introduction to the field of pair–copula constructions. Textbooks with further applications in finance and insurance are: [Cherubini et al. (2004), McNeil et al. (2005), Cherubini et al. (2012), Rüschendorf (2013)].

Acknowledgments

Many thanks go to Fabrizio Durante (the living encyclopedia of copulas), Marius Hofert (R-expert and co-author of the `copula` package), and Aleksey Min (expert in all areas of statistics) for providing us with feedback, references, and many more. We also thank German Bernhart and Steffen Schenk for preparing and presenting the exercises in our lecture 'Simulating copulas'. Some of these problems found their way into this book. Moreover, we received valuable feedback from Giovanni Puccetti (one of the inventors of the rearrangement algorithm and editor of the journal *Dependence Modeling*) on an earlier version of Section 7.1 and from Axel Bücher (well known for his contributions to the estimation of copulas and to hypothesis testing) on Chapter 6.

Moreover, we thank Christian Genest and Hannes Haferkorn for very useful 'last minute' feedback. Last but not least, we thank Wim Schoutens (responsible editor of the book series), Pete Baker (publisher and head of business of Palgrave Macmillan), and Sam Hartburn (Quick Black Fox – Proofreading and editing of mathematics) for many useful comments on earlier versions of the manuscript, as well as Susanne Deuke and Bettina Haas for helping us to organize the bibliography.

1   **What Are Copulas?**

This chapter introduces a concept for describing the dependence structure between random variables with arbitrary marginal distribution functions. The main idea is to describe the probability distribution of a d-dimensional random vector by two separate objects: (i) the set of univariate probability distributions for all d components, the so-called '*marginals*', and (ii) a '*copula*', which is a d-variate function that contains the information about the dependence structure between the components. Although such a separation into marginals and a copula (if done carelessly) bears some potential for irritations (see Section 7.2 and [Mikosch (2006)]), it can be quite convenient in many applications. The rest of this chapter is organized as follows. Section 1.1 presents two examples which motivate the necessity for the use of a copula concept. Section 1.2 presents Sklar's Theorem, which can be seen as the '*fundamental theorem of copula theory*'.

1.1   Two Motivating Examples

The following examples illustrate situations where it is convenient to separate univariate marginal distributions and dependence structure, which is precisely what the concept of a copula does.

1.1.1   Example 1: Analyzing Dependence between Asset Movements

We consider three time series with daily observations, ranging from April 2008 to May 2013: the stock price of BMW AG, the stock price of Daimler AG, and a Gold Index. Intuitively, we would expect the movements of Daimler and BMW to be highly dependent, whereas the returns of BMW and the Gold Index are expected to be much more weakly associated, if not independent. But how can we measure or visualize this dependence? To tackle this question, we introduce a little bit of probability theory by viewing the observed time series as realizations of certain stochastic processes. For the sake of notational convenience, we abbreviate to $B = \text{BMW}$, $D = \text{Daimler}$, and $G = \text{Gold}$. First, each individual time series $\{s_{t_i}^{(*)}\}_{i=0,1,2,\ldots,n}$, for $* \in \{B, D, G\}$, is transformed to a return time series $\{r_{t_i}^{(*)}\}_{i=1,2,\ldots,n}$ via $r_{t_{i+1}}^{(*)} := (s_{t_{i+1}}^{(*)} - s_{t_i}^{(*)})/s_{t_i}^{(*)}$, $i = 0, 1, 2, \ldots, n-1$. Next, we assume that the returns are realizations of independent and identically distributed (iid) random variables.[1] More precisely, the vectors $(r_{t_i}^{(B)}, r_{t_i}^{(D)}, r_{t_i}^{(G)})$, $i = 1, \ldots, n$, are iid realizations of the random vector $(R^{(B)}, R^{(D)}, R^{(G)})$.

---

[1] Reality is not as simple as this first example suggests. Returns of financial time series are typically not iid. Reasons are, for example, periods with different market activity and thus different volatility of the returns.

We want to analyze the dependence structure between the components of this random vector. Under these assumptions, the dependence between the movements of the BMW stock, the Daimler stock, and the Gold Index are completely described by the dependence between the random variables $R^{(B)}$, $R^{(D)}$, and $R^{(G)}$. For the mathematical description of this dependence there exists a rigorous theory, part of which is introduced in this book. We now provide a couple of intuitive ideas of what to do with our data.

(a) **Linear correlation:** The notion of a '*correlation coefficient*' is the kind of dependence measurement that is omnipresent in the literature as well as in daily practice. Given the two time series of BMW and Gold Index returns, their empirical (or historical) correlation coefficient is computed via the formula

$$\hat{\rho}_n := \frac{\sum_{i=1}^{n} \left(r_{t_i}^{(B)} - \frac{1}{n}\sum_{j=1}^{n} r_{t_j}^{(B)} \right)\left(r_{t_i}^{(G)} - \frac{1}{n}\sum_{j=1}^{n} r_{t_j}^{(G)} \right)}{\sqrt{\sum_{i=1}^{n} \left(r_{t_i}^{(B)} - \frac{1}{n}\sum_{j=1}^{n} r_{t_j}^{(B)} \right)^2}\sqrt{\sum_{i=1}^{n} \left(r_{t_i}^{(G)} - \frac{1}{n}\sum_{j=1}^{n} r_{t_j}^{(G)} \right)^2}}.$$

Intuitively speaking, this is the empirical covariance divided by the empirical standard deviations. This number is known to lie between -1 and $+1$, which are interpreted as the boundary values of a scale measuring the strength of dependence. The value -1 is understood as negative dependence, the middle value 0 as uncorrelated, and the value $+1$ as positive dependence. Statistically speaking, the number $\hat{\rho}_n$, which is computed only from observed data, is an estimate for the theoretical quantity

$$\rho := \mathrm{Cor}(R^{(B)}, R^{(G)}) := \frac{\mathbb{E}[(R^{(B)} - \mathbb{E}[R^{(B)}])(R^{(G)} - \mathbb{E}[R^{(G)}])]}{\sqrt{\mathbb{E}[(R^{(B)} - \mathbb{E}[R^{(B)}])^2]}\sqrt{\mathbb{E}[(R^{(G)} - \mathbb{E}[R^{(G)}])^2]}}.$$

Generally speaking, the correlation coefficient ρ is one dependence measure (among many), and it is by far the most popular one. However, it has its shortcomings (see Chapter 3). Copula theory can help to overcome these limitations, because it provides a solid ground to axiomatically define dependence measures.

(b) **Scatter plot:** One of the most obvious approaches to visualize the dependence between the return variables, say $R^{(B)}$ and $R^{(G)}$, is to plot the observed historical data into a two-dimensional coordinate system, which is done in Figure 1.1. Such an illustration is called a '*scatter plot*'. In the same figure the scatter plots for the observed values of $R^{(B)}$ vs. $R^{(D)}$ and $R^{(D)}$ vs. $R^{(G)}$ are also provided in order to judge on the qualitative differences between the dependence structures. All scatter plots appear to be centered roughly around $(0,0)$; only the two automobile firms exhibit a scatter plot which is more elliptically shaped and appears to be more diagonal than the scatter plot of Gold vs. BMW or Gold vs. Daimler. This impression is made more precise by the idea of concordance measurement, which plays a fundamental role in copula theory. Picking two arbitrary points in the scatter plot, we call the two points concordant if one point lies north east of the other point. If not, then we call the two points discordant. If many points are concordant, as is the case for the scatter plot BMW vs. Daimler, intuitively one would say that there is a strong positive dependence because it means that high values of one variable are likely to imply a high value of the other variable, and vice versa. What is important to notice about the idea of concordance measurement is the fact that the information about the location of the points is totally discarded. Only the information about the relative location of one point with respect to another point is used. With regards to our initial idea of measuring the *'diagonality'* of the shape of the scatter plot, the unnecessary information is discarded, and only the essential information is used. This idea is made precise in Chapter 3.

(c) **Rank transformation**: We have argued that the shape of the scatter plot in Figure 1.1 gives us valuable information about the dependence structure. This intuition led to the idea of concordance measurement. Having a closer look at the idea of concordance measurement, we observe that for each and every pair of points in the scatter plot we discarded the information about its location. The only information we used was whether the two points were concordant or discordant. So, implicitly, we got rid of the axes of the scatter plot. This implicit step is made explicit by the idea of *'rank transformation'* and underlies the fundamental idea of the copula concept. Loosely speaking, the data is transformed in such a way that no information regarding the dependence is lost, but after the transformation the x- and y-axes are identical. For each time series $r_{t_i}^{(*)}$, $i = 1, \ldots, n$, the idea is to replace the smallest of these numbers with the value $1/(n+1)$, the second smallest number with the value $2/(n+1)$, and so on, until the largest number is replaced with the value $n/(n+1)$. This provides one ordering of the numbers $1/(n+1), 2/(n+1), \ldots, n/(n+1)$ for each time series. In particular, the transformed time series now live on a range between zero and one and can be plotted into a new scatter plot, which is done in Figure 1.2. Since the ranges of the time series are bounded in $[0, 1]$, the new scatter plot does not contain outliers like the original plot, and is therefore more convenient to look at. The essential observation is that the relative orderings are maintained, that is, if two points in the original scatter plot were concordant, so are the two newly assigned points. Hence, for pure dependence–concordance measurement it does not matter whether we apply the original plot in Figure 1.1 or the transformed plot in Figure 1.2. It is now intuitively clear that measuring dependence with an eyeball check from the transformed plot might be more convenient than measuring dependence from the original scatter plot. What the performed transformation did mathematically was to standardize the marginal distributions to the uniform distribution on $[0, 1]$. The marginals were discarded, and only the pure dependence structure is maintained. Speaking statistically, the original probability distribution of the vector $(R^{(B)}, R^{(D)}, R^{(G)})$ was transformed to the probability distribution of a new vector $(U^{(B)}, U^{(D)}, U^{(G)})$ which takes values in $[0, 1]^3$. However, the *'dependence structure'* remains unaltered under this transformation.

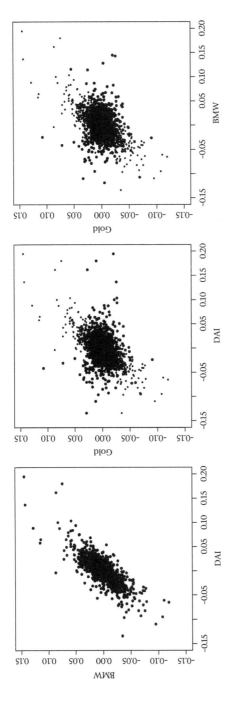

Figure 1.1 Left: daily stock returns of the BMW stock, plotted against daily stock returns of the Daimler stock. Their empirical correlation is around 79.6%. Middle: daily stock returns of the Daimler stock, plotted against daily returns of a Gold Index. Right: daily stock returns of the BMW stock, plotted against daily returns of a Gold Index. Both stock returns have an empirical correlation to Gold Index returns of about 4.4%. The time series comprise business days between April 2008 and May 2013. The R command used to create this figure is plot ().

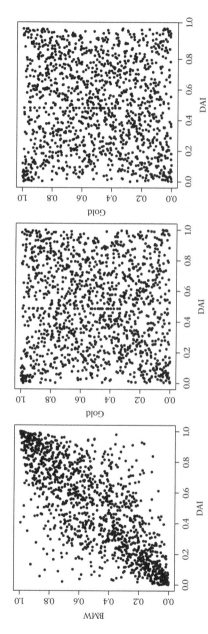

Figure 1.2 Left: transformed daily stock returns of the BMW stock, plotted against transformed daily stock returns of the Daimler stock. Middle: transformed daily stock returns of the Daimler stock, plotted against transformed daily returns of a Gold Index. Right: transformed daily stock returns of the BMW stock, plotted against transformed daily returns of a Gold Index. The time series comprise business days between April 2008 and May 2013. The rank transformation was done using the command pobs() from the R-package copula.

1.1.2   Example 2: Modeling the Dependence between Default Times

Assume we create a portfolio consisting of two bonds with identical maturity T. If the issuers of both bonds do not default until T, we know exactly what the portfolio is worth at time T. However, we face the risk of a default event during the bonds' lifetimes. Denoting by X_1, X_2 the future time points when the issuers go bankrupt, we hope that $X_1 > T$ and $X_2 > T$. Otherwise, with probability $1 - \mathbb{P}(X_1 > T, X_2 > T)$, our investment suffers a severe loss. Consequently, a sound estimate for the joint survival probability $\mathbb{P}(X_1 > T, X_2 > T)$ is of importance for us. From our credit analysts' exposés we have a strong opinion about the idiosyncratic survival probabilities $\mathbb{P}(X_1 > T)$ and $\mathbb{P}(X_2 > T)$, because the financial analysts number-crunched both firms to the core. However, we will see below that in order to compute the joint survival probability, we require additional information about the dependence structure between X_1 and X_2. Unfortunately, unlike in the previous example, we do not have empirical data available, simply because neither issuer has ever defaulted before, and there may not be any data available that provides useful information about the dependence between both default times. Now we require a bivariate stochastic model for the random vector (X_1, X_2) that is consistent with our opinions about the idiosyncratic survival probabilities. This is a modeling task which is far from trivial. For instance, the well-known bivariate normal distribution should not be applied, since its marginal (normal) laws are typically not consistent with the given ones. The given marginals are distributions on $[0, \infty)$, and the normal law is not. Copula theory can help to build such tailor-made models. Moreover, it allows us to provide model-independent upper and lower bounds for the joint survival probability.

1.2   Copulas and Sklar's Theorem

In the following, all random variables and random vectors are defined on some probability space, which we always denote by $(\Omega, \mathcal{F}, \mathbb{P})$. Having motivated the use of a concept to isolate the dependence structure of a random vector from its univariate marginal laws, it is now appropriate to introduce the formal definition of a copula. Loosely speaking, the probability distribution of a random vector is completely determined by its copula and its marginal laws. Recall that a random variable U is said to have a uniform distribution on the interval $[a, b]$ for some $-\infty < a < b < \infty$, we write $U \sim \mathcal{U}[a, b]$, whenever its distribution function is given by

$$\mathbb{P}(U \leq u) = \int_a^u \frac{1}{b - a} \, du = \frac{u - a}{b - a}, \quad u \in [a, b].$$

Intuitively, U takes values only in the interval $[a, b]$ and the probability mass is evenly distributed between a and b.

Definition 1.2.1 (Copula)
A function $C : [0, 1]^d \to [0, 1]$ is called a 'copula' if there is a random vector $(U_1, \ldots, U_d)$ such that each component U_k has a uniform distribution on $[0, 1]$,

$k = 1, \ldots, d$, and

$$C(u_1, \ldots, u_d) = \mathbb{P}(U_1 \leq u_1, \ldots, U_d \leq u_d), \quad u_1, \ldots, u_d \in [0,1].$$

FAQ 1.2.2 (Is there an alternative definition?)

Yes. Instead of the probabilistic definition via distribution functions, one can equivalently define copulas purely analytically. In fact, this is just analytically writing down the properties of a d-dimensional distribution function with standardized marginals. Which definition is more useful or more convenient depends on the situation, so knowing both is clearly an advantage. More precisely, a copula is a function $C : [0,1]^d \to [0,1]$ that satisfies the properties:

(i) **Groundedness:** Whenever at least one argument $u_j = 0$, then $C(u_1, \ldots, u_d) = 0$. This reflects $0 \leq \mathbb{P}(U_1 \leq u_1, \ldots, U_j \leq 0, \ldots, U_d \leq u_d) \leq \mathbb{P}(U_j \leq 0) = 0$.

(ii) **Normalized marginals:** $C(1, \ldots, 1, u_j, 1, \ldots, 1) = u_j$, for $u_j \in [0,1]$. This reflects the uniform marginals property, since $\mathbb{P}(U_1 \leq 1, \ldots, U_j \leq u_j, \ldots, U_d \leq 1) = \mathbb{P}(U_j \leq u_j) = u_j$.

(iii) **d-increasingness:** For each d-dimensional rectangle $\times_{j=1}^d [a_j, b_j]$, being a subset of $[0,1]^d$, one has:

$$0 \leq \sum_{(c_1, \ldots, c_d) \in \times_{j=1}^d \{a_j, b_j\}} (-1)^{|\{j : c_j = a_j\}|} C(c_1, \ldots, c_d) \leq 1.$$

This corresponds to the fact that the probability of $(U_1, \ldots, U_d) \sim C$ falling in the rectangle in question must be non-negative, see Exercise 8 in Chapter 2. Providing a small example in the bivariate case, consider the cube $[a_1, b_1] \times [a_2, b_2] := [0.1, 0.5] \times [0.2, 0.8]$. Then

$$0 \leq \underbrace{+C(0.5, 0.8)}_{(-1)^0 C(b_1, b_2)} \underbrace{+C(0.1, 0.2)}_{(-1)^2 C(a_1, a_2)} \underbrace{-C(0.5, 0.2)}_{(-1)^1 C(b_1, a_2)} \underbrace{-C(0.1, 0.8)}_{(-1)^1 C(a_1, b_2)} \leq 1.$$

FAQ 1.2.3 (Where does the word '*copula*' come from?)

The word '*copula*' was first used in [Sklar (1959)]. In [Sklar (1996)] he provides interesting historical background on the development of copula theory, including, among other things, that he felt this word (usually linking subjects and predicates) to be appropriate for a function linking marginal laws to a joint probability distribution.

Generally speaking, the focus of this book is the description of the probability distribution of some random vector $(X_1, \ldots, X_d)$. Mathematically speaking, this probability distribution is a finite measure on $\mathbb{R}^d$, that is, a function assigning a probability to an (almost) arbitrary subset of $\mathbb{R}^d$. Unfortunately, such functions that take sets as arguments are rather inconvenient to work with in many situations. Therefore, mathematicians put considerable effort into describing probability distributions by simpler objects, for example probability density functions, characteristic functions, survival functions, or distribution functions. The distribution function of $(X_1,\ldots,X_d)$ is defined as

$$F(x_1,\ldots,x_d) := \mathbb{P}(X_1 \leq x_1,\ldots,X_d \leq x_d), \quad x_1,\ldots,x_d \in \mathbb{R},$$

that is, it equals the probability law of $(X_1,\ldots,X_d)$ evaluated only on rectangles of the form $\times_{j=1}^{d}(-\infty,x_j]$. It is an object that is more convenient to work with compared to the full measure, because it is a function taking only d numbers as arguments, and therefore it can be studied by means of classical calculus. Luckily, it is well known that the distribution function characterizes the probability law of $(X_1,\ldots,X_d)$ completely, that is, we do not lose essential information by considering only rectangles of the form $\times_{j=1}^{d}(-\infty,x_j]$. However, a distribution function is still a complicated object, because it is a d-dimensional function that has to be of a very special form. What copulas basically do is separate a distribution function into two further mathematical objects, with the intention of simplifying its handling. The mathematical statement which accomplishes this simplification is known[2] as 'Sklar's Theorem' and is formulated as follows.

Theorem 1.2.4 (Sklar's Theorem)
A function $F : \mathbb{R}^d \to [0,1]$ is the distribution function of some random vector $(X_1,\ldots,X_d)$ if and only if there are a copula $C : [0,1]^d \to [0,1]$ and univariate distribution functions $F_1,\ldots,F_d : \mathbb{R} \to [0,1]$ such that

$$C(F_1(x_1),\ldots,F_d(x_d)) = F(x_1,\ldots,x_d), \quad x_1,\ldots,x_d \in \mathbb{R}. \qquad (1.1)$$

In this case, the distribution function of component X_j equals F_j, $j = 1,\ldots,d$, and the correspondence between F and C is one-to-one if all functions $F_1,\ldots,F_d$ are continuous.

The one-dimensional distribution functions $F_j(x) := \mathbb{P}(X_j \leq x)$, $x \in \mathbb{R}$, of the components X_j, $j = 1,\ldots,d$, are also called '(one-dimensional) marginals' or '(one-dimensional) margins' of the distribution function of the random vector $(X_1,\ldots,X_d)$. Summarizing, Sklar's Theorem (respectively copula theory) allows us to subdivide the handling of the probability law of a random vector $(X_1,\ldots,X_d)$ into two subsequent tasks: (i) handling of the one-dimensional marginal distribution functions, and (ii) handling of the isolated dependence structure in the form of a copula. In this sense, understanding copulas is an important step towards understanding the dependence structure behind random vectors.

FAQ 1.2.5 (What if the marginals $F_1,\ldots,F_d$ are not continuous?)
In this case, the copula C in Sklar's Theorem is not unique, that is, there exist at least two copulas C_1, C_2 which are different for at least one point $(u_1,\ldots,u_d) \in [0,1]^d$ but

---

[2] The result is originally due to [Sklar (1959), Schweizer, Sklar (1974)], see [Schweizer, Sklar (1983), Chapter 5] or [Mai, Scherer (2012), Theorem 1.2, p. 16] for a proof.

both satisfying

$$C_1(F_1(x_1),\ldots,F_d(x_d)) = F(x_1,\ldots,x_d) = C_2(F_1(x_1),\ldots,F_d(x_d))$$

for all $x_1,\ldots,x_d \in \mathbb{R}$. In most financial applications of copulas the marginals are continuous, so this ambiguity is not an issue. If one nevertheless is willing to use copula modeling with non-continuous marginals, some difficulties arise, and the interested reader is referred to the articles [Marshall (1996), Genest, Nešlehová (2007)].

1.2.1   The Generalized Inverse

In the case of continuous marginals, the proof of Sklar's Theorem is much simpler than in the general case and for almost all practically relevant applications it is sufficient to consider continuous marginals. Using the notation from Theorem 1.2.4 and assuming the marginals to be continuous,[3] it holds that the random vector

$$(U_1,\ldots,U_d) := (F_1(X_1),\ldots,F_d(X_d)) \tag{1.2}$$

takes values in $[0,1]^d$ and has the joint distribution function C. In particular, each component U_k is uniformly distributed on the unit interval $[0,1]$. This shows (on the level of random vectors) how to get from the distribution function F to the copula C. What about the inverse direction? Assume we are given an arbitrary random vector $(U_1,\ldots,U_d)$ with joint distribution function C. Can we transform each component individually to obtain a random vector with joint distribution function F? Having a look at Equation (1.2) it is natural to assume that the desired transformation is precisely given by

$$(X_1,\ldots,X_d) := (F_1^{-1}(U_1),\ldots,F_d^{-1}(U_d)). \tag{1.3}$$

In many situations, this is indeed the case. However, Equation (1.3) suffers from a small technical problem: the inverse functions F_j^{-1} might not exist! Recall from basic calculus that the inverse f^{-1} of a real-valued function f exists only if f is strictly increasing. Although they are non-decreasing, the marginals F_j need not be strictly increasing but can be constant on some intervals. However, the concept of an inverse function can be generalized in order to make Equation (1.3) valid. This means that the symbol $\cdot^{-1}$ is more generally defined for arbitrary (one-dimensional) distribution functions so that its definition agrees with the usual definition of an inverse in calculus for the subfamily of strictly increasing distribution functions. It is given as follows.

---

[3] For the general case including non-continuous marginals a more advanced transformation must be applied, see [Mai, Scherer (2012), p. 14, Lemma 1.4] for details.

Definition 1.2.6 (Generalized inverse)
The 'generalized inverse' $F^{-1} : (0,1) \to \mathbb{R}$ of a one-dimensional distribution function $F : \mathbb{R} \to [0,1]$ is defined by

$$F^{-1}(u) := \inf\{x \in \mathbb{R} : F(x) \ge u\}, \quad u \in (0,1).$$

Figure 1.3 illustrates a distribution function and its generalized inverse, as well as their concatenations. One can observe that, unlike in the case of usual inverses in basic calculus, it is not true that $F \circ F^{-1}$ and $F^{-1} \circ F$ are the identity function. This only holds in the case F is continuous and strictly increasing. A detailed reference to generalized inverses is [Embrechts, Hofert (2013a)].

While Equation (1.3) shows how to move from C to F on the level of random vectors, the generalized inverse can also be used to transform F to C on the analytical level, namely by

$$C(u_1,\ldots,u_d) = F(F_1^{-1}(u_1),\ldots,F_d^{-1}(u_d)), \quad u_1,\ldots,u_d \in (0,1),$$

which is the inverse equation to the statement (1.1) in Sklar's Theorem.

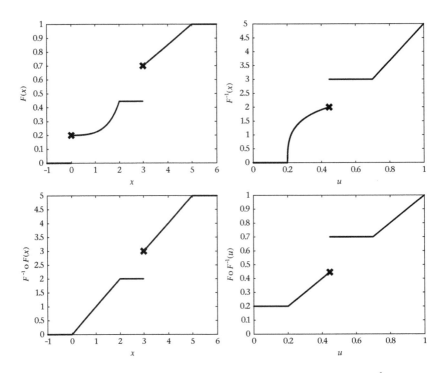

Figure 1.3 Plot of a distribution function F, its generalized inverse F^{-1}, and their concatenations $F^{-1} \circ F$ and $F \circ F^{-1}$ in the case where F is not continuous.

1.2.2 Sklar's Theorem for survival functions

The survival function of a random vector $(X_1, \ldots, X_d)$ is defined by

$$\bar{F}(x_1, \ldots, x_d) := \mathbb{P}(X_1 > x_1, \ldots, X_d > x_d), \quad x_1, \ldots, x_d \in \mathbb{R},$$

that is, it equals the probability law of $(X_1, \ldots, X_d)$ evaluated only on rectangles of the form $\times_{j=1}^d (x_j, \infty)$. In comparison with the distribution function, all '$\leq$'-signs are simply replaced by '$>$'-signs. Similarly, the components' one-dimensional survival functions are denoted by $\bar{F}_j(x) := \mathbb{P}(X_j > x) = 1 - F_j(x)$, $x \in \mathbb{R}$. It is quite intuitive that from a purely mathematical viewpoint an access to the probability distribution of $(X_1, \ldots, X_d)$ via the survival function is analogous to an access via the distribution function. Indeed, Sklar's Theorem can be reformulated for the survival function as follows.

Corollary 1.2.7 (Sklar's Theorem for survival functions)
A function $\bar{F} : \mathbb{R}^d \to [0,1]$ is the survival function of some random vector $(X_1, \ldots, X_d)$ if and only if there are a copula $\hat{C} : [0,1]^d \to [0,1]$ and univariate survival functions $\bar{F}_1, \ldots, \bar{F}_d : \mathbb{R} \to [0,1]$ such that

$$\hat{C}(\bar{F}_1(x_1), \ldots, \bar{F}_d(x_d)) = \bar{F}(x_1, \ldots, x_d), \quad x_1, \ldots, x_d \in \mathbb{R}.$$

In this case, the survival function of component X_j equals $\bar{F}_j$, $j = 1, \ldots, d$, and the correspondence between $\bar{F}$ and $\hat{C}$ is one-to-one if all survival functions $\bar{F}_1, \ldots, \bar{F}_d$ are continuous.

It is important to note at this point the fact that the function $\hat{C}$ in Corollary 1.2.7 is a proper copula, called a '*survival copula*', that is, a distribution function of some random vector on $[0,1]^d$, and not a survival function. In particular, if $(U_1, \ldots, U_d)$ is a random vector with copula C as joint distribution function, then its survival function $\bar{C}(u_1, \ldots, u_d) = \mathbb{P}(U_1 > u_1, \ldots, U_d > u_d)$ is not a copula, and in particular not equal to $\hat{C}$.

FAQ 1.2.8 (When do I need Sklar's Theorem for survival functions?)
Many copulas applied in practice are derived from well-understood stochastic models, for example from multivariate normal or multivariate exponential laws. For specific examples we refer to Chapter 4. It is also very important to know the survival analog of Sklar's Theorem, and not only the original result, because especially in the context of portfolio credit-risk modeling (and more generally reliability theory), it is very natural to consider survival functions rather than distribution functions. Why is this the case? The lifetime of a company is a random variable X taking only positive values, since future time points are conveniently interpreted as the values on the positive half-axis. The most popular parametric model for a probability distribution on the positive half-axis $[0, \infty)$ is the exponential distribution, that is $\bar{F}(x) := \mathbb{P}(X > x) = \exp(-\lambda x)$, $x \geq 0$, for a model parameter $\lambda > 0$. If nothing else, the exponential distribution is so popular because its survival function has many nice and useful analytical properties that can be exploited in applications, such as $\bar{F}(x)\bar{F}(y) = \bar{F}(x+y)$. In particular, the

distribution function $F(x) = 1 - \exp(-\lambda x)$ does not share the last property. Many popular stochastic models for lifetimes in credit risk can be viewed as extensions of the exponential distribution, which – implicitly or explicitly – exploit the nice structure of the exponential function for mathematical derivations. This algebraic structure of the exponential function is much more natural on the level of survival functions than it is on the level of distribution functions. In particular, multivariate concepts of the exponential distribution rely on a treatment of multivariate survival functions. In order to apply copula theory for these concepts, the survival analog of Sklar's Theorem is necessary.

1.2.3 How to Apply Sklar's Theorem?

We now discuss what Sklar's Theorem can be used for. Generally speaking, Sklar's Theorem can be applied in two directions:

(a) Analyzing distribution functions, see Section 1.2.3.1: $F \rightsquigarrow C \oplus (F_1, \ldots, F_d)$.
(b) Constructing distribution functions, see Section 1.2.3.2: $C \oplus (F_1, \ldots, F_d) \rightsquigarrow F$.

1.2.3.1 Analyzing Distribution Functions

Thinking about the example in Section 1.1.1, it might be reasonable to analyze data arising from realizations of a random vector in two subsequent steps: (i) analyze the univariate marginals $(F_1, \ldots, F_d)$, and (ii) analyze the remaining dependence C. Sklar's Theorem tells us precisely that this procedure is possible. Suppose we observe n iid realizations $(X_1^{(i)}, \ldots, X_d^{(i)})$, $i = 1, \ldots, n$, from a random vector $(X_1, \ldots, X_d)$. When analyzing the samples from component j, we might apply tools from either (i) parametric statistics, or (ii) non-parametric statistics.

(i) **Parametric approach:** It is assumed that the distribution function F_j of X_j stems from a certain parametric family of distribution functions, for example from the family of exponential distribution functions where $F_j(x) = 1 - \exp(-\lambda_j x)$, $x \geq 0$. Given this assumption, what is left to estimate is the unknown parameter, that is, the parameter $\lambda_j > 0$ in the case of the exponential law. For many popular parametric families of probability distributions there exist well-established estimation routines to obtain the parameters from the observed samples $X_j^{(1)}, \ldots, X_j^{(n)}$, for example in the exponential case a good estimator is given by $\hat{\lambda}_{j,n} = n / \sum_{i=1}^{n} X_j^{(i)}$. The parametric ansatz suffers from the drawback that the observed data might not really be explained very well by any member of the assumed parametric family, that is, we face model risk. However, if the fit is reasonable, it has the advantage that the fitted model can be used in all further investigations, for example the estimation of the dependence structure. For a good reference on parametric estimation, the interested reader is referred to [Shao (1999)].

(ii) **Non-parametric approach:** Only minimal, or even no, pre-knowledge on the distribution function F_j of X_j is assumed, and rather the whole function $x \mapsto F_j(x)$ is estimated from the data. A popular example of a non-parametric estimator for absolutely continuous distributions on the unit interval $[0, 1]$ is the Bernstein density estimator, see for example [Ghosal (2001)] for an analytical study. The most common non-parametric estimator for univariate distribution functions is the 'empirical distribution function', which is defined by

$$\hat{F}_{j,n}(x) := \frac{1}{n} \sum_{i=1}^{n} 1_{\{X_j^{(i)} \leq x\}}, \quad x \in \mathbb{R},$$

and which is well known to converge almost surely and uniformly in x to the true distribution function F_j of X_j, as $n \to \infty$.

Having estimated the univariate distribution functions $F_1, \ldots, F_d$ by estimators $\hat{F}_{1,n}, \ldots, \hat{F}_{d,n}$, what is left to estimate is the copula C. By virtue of Equation (1.2), and given the estimated marginals, the random vectors

$$(U_1^{(i)}, \ldots, U_d^{(i)}) := (\hat{F}_{1,n}(X_1^{(i)}), \ldots, \hat{F}_{d,n}(X_d^{(i)})), \quad i = 1, \ldots, n,$$

might approximately (depending on the goodness of the marginal estimators) be thought of as being realizations[4] of the random vector

$$(U_1, \ldots, U_d) := (F_1(X_1), \ldots, F_d(X_d)),$$

which has the copula C as joint distribution function – assuming the true marginals to be continuous. For estimating the copula C based on these samples, again one can either apply a parametric approach, that is, assume C is from a certain family and estimate the parameter(s), or a non-parametric approach.[5] One of the most intuitive, and simple-to-implement, parametric estimation strategies is to compute empirical counterparts to copula-based dependence measures. We refer to Section 6.1 for further details, but we'd like to remark at this point that this strategy is completely analogous to the correlation measurement introduced in the first example of Section 1.1.1, only the correlation coefficient is replaced by another – and from some viewpoints more robust – dependence measure.

1.2.3.2 Constructing Distribution Functions

Given an arbitrary copula C and univariate distribution functions $F_1, \ldots, F_d$, Sklar's Theorem shows us how to obtain a well-defined multivariate distribution function F. This is very convenient for modeling. For instance, thinking in particular about the example of modeling default times in Section 1.1.2, there are situations when there is good knowledge about the single components $(F_1, \ldots, F_d)$ but very limited knowledge about the dependence structure C between the components. Consequently, it might be necessary to simply choose C from some flexible, parametric family

---

[4] We speak of (pseudo-)observations to distinguish from the observations from the copula, see Chapter 6 for a deeper treatment.

[5] A multivariate extension of the univariate Bernstein density estimator is presented in [Bouezmarni, Rolin (2007)], for multivariate extensions of the empirical distribution function we refer to Chapter 6 for more information.

of copulas, and then fit the remaining parameter(s) to the limited observable data. The paradigm example for such a situation is portfolio credit-risk modeling, when only market prices for a few dependence-sensitive products are observed, and from this limited data set a high-dimensional dependence model must be inferred. Such a task cannot be accomplished without huge modeling efforts, that is, a battery of (hopefully realistic) assumptions on the underlying copula. Typically, one decides on one specific parametric family of copula models by criteria such as computational tractability, distributional properties that have been found in empirical data sets of similar companies, or even just plain knowledge, because not too many copula families are well studied and well developed enough to be known to many practitioners. One goal of this book is to provide a broad audience with such knowledge.

1.3 General Copula Properties

Before we discuss the most popular copula families in Chapter 4, we gather in this section some general thoughts about the classification of copulas with respect to stylized properties.

First of all, many popular copula families are 'exchangeable', meaning that the value of the copula is invariant under permutations of its arguments, that is,

$$C(u_1,\ldots,u_d) = C(u_{\pi(1)},\ldots,u_{\pi(d)}), \quad u_1,\ldots,u_d \in [0,1], \tag{1.4}$$

for arbitrary bijections $\pi : \{1,\ldots,d\} \rightarrow \{1,\ldots,d\}$. In the bivariate case $d = 2$, exchangeability boils down to the property $C(u_1,u_2) = C(u_2,u_1)$ for all $u_1,u_2 \in [0,1]$. In probabilistic terms exchangeability corresponds to a strong symmetry property. For instance, the conditional probability distribution of the first component given all the others equals the conditional probability distribution of the last component given all the others, that is, the dependence structure does not distinguish between components at all. When looking at a scatter plot from a bivariate exchangeable copula, one observes a great level of symmetry with respect to the diagonal $\{u_1 = u_2\}$, because exchangeability means that the distribution of the points in the graph is invariant under a switch of axes. For instance, when looking at the scatter plots in Figure 1.2, it appears to be reasonable to assume an exchangeable copula behind the returns of the BMW and the Daimler stock. There are several reasons why popular copula families are exchangeable:

(a) Exchangeability can be a natural, desirable property for a dependence model, as one can observe from the scatter plot in Figure 1.2 for the stock returns between BMW and Daimler.

(b) The stochastic motivation behind a certain copula might stem from a so-called one-factor model, which naturally implies an exchangeable copula. To be more precise, many popular families of copulas are derived from a stochastic model in which the components are given as $U_j := f(M,\epsilon_j)$ for an iid sequence of random variables $\{\epsilon_j\}_{j\in\mathbb{N}}$, interpreted as idiosyncratic risk, and a global stochastic factor M being responsible for the dependence between components. Such models always give rise to exchangeable copulas.

(c) The permutation invariance property (1.4) simplifies the algebraic access to the study of the function C in large dimensions. For instance, many high-dimensional copulas can be written down in quite compact form precisely due to the fact that they are exchangeable. Popular examples comprise the families of Archimedean copulas (see Section 4.2) and of Lévy-frailty copulas (see Section 4.3.1), which have the simple form

$$\varphi(\varphi^{-1}(u_1) + \cdots + \varphi^{-1}(u_d)), \text{ resp. } u_{[1]}^{a_0} u_{[2]}^{a_1} \cdots u_{[d]}^{a_{d-1}},$$

where $u_{[1]} \leq \cdots \leq u_{[d]}$ denotes the ordered list of $u_1, \ldots, u_d \in [0, 1]$.

For some applications, exchangeability is an undesired property, see FAQ 4.1.3. To this end, researchers recently put some considerable efforts into designing flexible, high-dimensional non-exchangeable dependence structures. Prominent examples are pair–copula constructions, see, for example, [Kurowicka, Joe (2010)], and hierarchical Archimedean copulas, see Section 4.2.2. Generally speaking, however, one may conclude that such structures are more difficult to work with.

FAQ 1.3.1 (Is there a test for exchangeability?)

If you have a given set of (bivariate) observations, you can actually test for exchangeability, see [Genest et al. (2012)]. Roughly speaking, the idea is to estimate the copula C from data and compare the distance between the estimated copula and the one with permuted arguments. If the distance so obtained is too big, then the hypothesis of exchangeability is rejected. This is available via the command exchTest() of the R-package copula.

Another symmetry property of copulas is '*radial symmetry*', which means that a copula is its own survival copula, that is, $\hat{C} = C$. Concerning a probabilistic interpretation, this means that the random vector $(U_1, \ldots, U_d) \sim C$ has the same distribution as the random vector $(1 - U_1, \ldots, 1 - U_d) \sim \hat{C}$. Regarding the interpretation in the bivariate case with respect to a scatter plot, it means that the points in the plot are scattered symmetrically around the counterdiagonal $\{u_2 = 1 - u_1\}$. The most prominent copulas equipped with this property are Gaussian copulas, and more generally elliptical copulas, see Section 4.1.2. Radial symmetry can be thought of as a multivariate extension of the concept of symmetric univariate distributions, of which the normal law is the most prominent representative (recall the symmetric around the mean, bell-shaped density of the normal law). Just like the lack of skewness can sometimes be an undesirable feature of a univariate law, radial symmetry is sometimes an undesired property of a multivariate law in applications, see FAQ 4.1.2.

Finally, another shortcoming of the univariate normal law (in some applications) is the lack of heavy tails (implying too little probability for extreme scenarios). A related concept for multivariate distributions is the concept of '*tail dependence*'. Loosely speaking, this concept aims at quantifying the properties of a multivariate distribution in its tails. On the level of copulas this boils down to investigating its behavior in the corners of its domain $[0, 1]^d$. There exist different mathematical notions of tail dependence, but by far the most prominent measures are the upper- and lower-tail dependence coefficients, which are defined for bivariate copulas. We refer the reader to Section 3.3 for a precise definition.

EXERCISES

1. Judge from looking at the bivariate scatter plots in Figure 1.4 whether the underlying copula might be (i) exchangeable, and (ii) radially symmetric.

2. Show that the generalized inverse F^{-1} of a distribution function F is always càglàd, that is, is left-continuous $(F^{-1}(y) = \lim_{u \uparrow y} F^{-1}(u)$ for all $y)$ and admits limits from the right $(\lim_{u \downarrow y} F^{-1}(u)$ exists for all $y)$.

3. Historical VaR-computation: Denote by $s_0, s_1, \ldots, s_n$ the historically observed time series of a portfolio value, and denote by $x_1, \ldots, x_n$ the corresponding return time series, where $x_i := (s_i - s_{i-1})/s_{i-1}$, $i = 1, \ldots, n$. The Value-at-Risk (VaR) of a portfolio (return) at a confidence level of $\alpha = 99\,\%$ is defined as the 1\,%-quantile of the random variable X_{n+1}, that is, of the next return. If X_{n+1} has distribution function F, the α-quantile is simply defined by $F^{-1}(\alpha)$ with the generalized inverse F^{-1}. The most basic historical VaR method assumes that X_{n+1} is a discrete random variable taking a value in $\{x_1, \ldots, x_n\}$ with $\mathbb{P}(X_{n+1} = x_i) = 1/n$ for all i. A usual choice in practice is $n = 250$, corresponding to one year (250 business days) of historical data. Show that the historical 99\,%-VaR in this case is given by the third smallest value of $x_1, \ldots, x_{250}$.

4. Assume that the random vector $(X_1, \ldots, X_d)$ has existing covariance matrix Σ, identical marginal laws, and an exchangeable copula as dependence structure. Show that $\mathrm{Cor}(X_j, X_k) = \mathrm{Cor}(X_1, X_2) \geq -1/(d-1)$ for all $j \neq k$.

5. Consider $\alpha \in [0,1]$ and define $C_\alpha : [0,1]^2 \to [0,1]$ by

$$C_\alpha(u_1, u_2) := \min\{u_1, u_2\} \max\{u_1, u_2\}^{1-\alpha}, \quad u_1, u_2 \in [0,1].$$

Show that C_α defines a copula, which is known as a Cuadras–Augé copula, see [Cuadras, Augé (1981)].

6. A copula C is not completely determined by all of its bivariate marginal copulas. To see this, consider U_1, U_2 independent and $\mathcal{U}[0,1]$-distributed. Define U_3 as

$$U_3 := (1 - U_2 + U_1)\mathbf{1}_{\{U_2 > U_1\}} + (U_1 - U_2)\mathbf{1}_{\{U_2 \leq U_1\}}. \tag{1.5}$$

Show that U_3 is also $\mathcal{U}[0,1]$-distributed, so (U_1, U_2, U_3) has a 3-variate copula C as joint distribution function. Show that the bivariate marginal copulas of C are given by the independence copula, that is, show that U_j, U_k, $j \neq k$, are independent. Finally, show that C is not the independence copula by showing that U_1, U_2, U_3 are not independent.

7. A Bernstein density estimator for densities on $[0,1]$:
   a. If $g : [0,1] \to [0,1]$ is continuous, we denote by

$$B_K[g](x) := \sum_{j=0}^{K} g\left(\frac{j}{K}\right) \binom{K}{j} x^j (1-x)^{K-j}, \quad x \in [0,1],$$

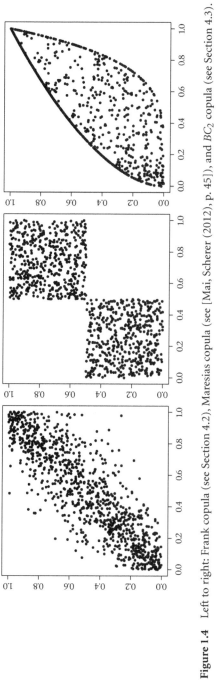

Figure 1.4 Left to right: Frank copula (see Section 4.2), Maresias copula (see [Mai, Scherer (2012), p. 45]), and BC_2 copula (see Section 4.3).

the K-th 'Bernstein polynomial' associated with g. Show that $B_K[g]$ converges uniformly to g as $K \to \infty$.

b. If $F : [0,1] \to [0,1]$ is an absolutely continuous distribution function on $[0,1]$, show that $B_K[F]$ is also an absolutely continuous distribution function on $[0,1]$ with density

$$
b_K[F](x) := \sum_{j=1}^{K} \left(F\left(\frac{j}{K}\right) - F\left(\frac{j-1}{K}\right) \right) \frac{K!}{(j-1)!(K-j)!} x^{j-1}(1-x)^{K-j}.
$$

This corresponds to a mixture of so-called Beta densities.

c. Given iid samples $X^{(1)}, \ldots, X^{(n)} \sim F$ with density f, a non-parametric Bernstein density estimator for f is given by

$$
\hat{f}_n[K](x) := \sum_{j=1}^{K} \left(\frac{1}{n} \sum_{i=1}^{n} 1_{\left\{ \frac{j-1}{K} \le X^{(i)} < \frac{j}{K} \right\}} \right) \frac{K!}{(j-1)!(K-j)!} x^{j-1}(1-x)^{K-j},
$$

where $K \in \mathbb{N}$ is a free 'smoothing parameter'. Justify why this might be a reasonable density estimator.

2 Which Rules for Handling Copulas Do I Need?

This chapter introduces several computation techniques that are fundamental in copula theory. Learning these rules is not only important for working with copulas, it also helps to improve one's capability of understanding dependence in general. In particular, it sharpens one's awareness that in the context of dependence modeling some issues that might on first glimpse look straightforward (because they are straightforward in the univariate case) implicitly bear a subtle difficulty.

2.1 The Fréchet–Hoeffding bounds

One of the most important properties of the correlation coefficient is the fact that it is bounded between -1 and $+1$. This means that the correlation coefficient, and in a similar way many other dependence measures that will be discussed in Chapter 3, measures dependence in terms of a single number on a finite scale. The value -1 at the left end of the scale intuitively corresponds to the most negative association, whereas the value $+1$ at the right end of the scale corresponds to the most positive association. The middle value 0 is typically thought of as corresponding to independence, although this is incorrect for the case of the correlation coefficient in general, see FAQ 3.1.4. Unlike such numeric dependence measures, a copula is a mathematical object that collects full information about the dependence structure without projecting it onto a single number. Analogous to numeric dependence measures, there exist lower and upper bounds on the family of all copulas that might be viewed as the extreme cases of most negative and most positive dependence – the so-called '*Fréchet–Hoeffding bounds*':

$$W_d(u_1,\ldots,u_d) := \max\{u_1 + \cdots + u_d - (d-1), 0\}$$

$$\text{('lower Fréchet–Hoeffding bound'),}$$

$$M_d(u_1,\ldots,u_d) := \min\{u_1,\ldots,u_d\}$$

$$\text{('upper Fréchet–Hoeffding bound').}$$

The following result, originally due to [Hoeffding (1940), Fréchet (1951)], states that all copulas lie between these two bounds. A deep treatment, including applications, is [Rüschendorf (1991)]. Refined bounds, given some measure of association, are presented in [Nelsen et al. (2011)].

Theorem 2.1.1 (Fréchet–Hoeffding bounds)
Let $C : [0,1]^d \to [0,1]$ be an arbitrary copula. Then C is bounded below (resp. above) by W_d (resp. M_d), that is,

$$W_d(u_1,\ldots,u_d) \leq C(u_1,\ldots,u_d) \leq M_d(u_1,\ldots,u_d), \quad u_1,\ldots,u_d \in [0,1].$$

These bounds are sharp in the sense that M_d is itself a copula, and for each point $\boldsymbol{u} := (u_1,\ldots,u_d) \in [0,1]^d$ one can find a copula $C_{\boldsymbol{u}}$ satisfying the equality $C_{\boldsymbol{u}}(u_1,\ldots,u_d) = W_d(u_1,\ldots,u_d)$.

Proof
Exercise 1 shows that M_d is indeed a copula. To see that it dominates an arbitrary copula C point-wise, we consider a random vector $(U_1,\ldots,U_d)$ on a probability space $(\Omega, \mathcal{F}, \mathbb{P})$ with joint distribution function

$$\mathbb{P}(U_1 \leq u_1,\ldots,U_d \leq u_d) = C(u_1,\ldots,u_d), \quad u_1,\ldots,u_d \in [0,1].$$

Fix $u_1,\ldots,u_d \in [0,1]$. For each component $j = 1,\ldots,d$ we observe that the event $\{U_j \leq u_j\}$ contains the event $\{U_1 \leq u_1,\ldots,U_d \leq u_d\}$, implying that

$$u_j = \mathbb{P}(U_j \leq u_j) \geq \mathbb{P}(U_1 \leq u_1,\ldots,U_d \leq u_d) = C(u_1,\ldots,u_d). \tag{2.1}$$

Since the left-hand side of (2.1) depends on j, while the right-hand side does not, we can consider the minimum over all components $j = 1,\ldots,d$ on both sides to observe that

$$M_d(u_1,\ldots,u_d) = \min_{j=1,\ldots,d} \{u_j\} \geq C(u_1,\ldots,u_d),$$

establishing the upper bound. Turning to the lower bound, we recall the following facts from probability calculus for measurable events $A, A_1,\ldots,A_n \in \mathcal{F}$:

$$\mathbb{P}(A_1 \cup A_2 \cup \cdots \cup A_n) \leq \mathbb{P}(A_1) + \mathbb{P}(A_2) + \cdots + \mathbb{P}(A_n), \tag{2.2}$$

$$\mathbb{P}(A^c) = 1 - \mathbb{P}(A), \text{ and } (A_1 \cap A_2 \cap \cdots \cap A_n)^c = A_1^c \cup A_2^c \cup \cdots \cup A_n^c. \tag{2.3}$$

These facts are applied to establish the lower bound as follows:

$$u_1 + \cdots + u_d - (d-1) = 1 - \sum_{j=1}^{d}(1 - u_j) = 1 - \sum_{j=1}^{d}\mathbb{P}(U_j > u_j)$$

$$\overset{(2.2)}{\leq} 1 - \mathbb{P}(\{U_1 > u_1\} \cup \cdots \cup \{U_d > u_d\}) \overset{(2.3)}{=} \mathbb{P}(\{U_1 \leq u_1\} \cap \cdots \cap \{U_d \leq u_d\})$$

$$= C(u_1,\ldots,u_d).$$

Since $C(u_1, \ldots, u_d) \geq 0$ is trivial, we conclude $C \geq W_d$ point-wise. The proof of the sharpness statement regarding the lower bound is more involved in general, the interested reader is referred to [Nelsen (2006), p. 48]. However, in the case $d = 2$, Exercise 2 shows that W_2 is indeed a proper copula itself, hence the bound is sharp. $\square$

Since the upper Fréchet–Hoeffding bound M_d is itself a copula, it is sometimes also called a '*comonotonicity copula*'. A random vector $(U_1, \ldots, U_d)$ with $U_j \sim \mathcal{U}[0,1]$ has M_d as joint distribution function if and only if $U_1 = \cdots = U_d$ holds with probability one, which is reasonably identified as the most positive dependence imaginable, see Exercise 1. On the other hand, the lower Fréchet–Hoeffding bound is itself a copula only in dimension $d = 2$, where it is also sometimes called a '*countermonotonicity copula*'. A random vector (U_1, U_2) with $U_j \sim \mathcal{U}[0,1]$ has W_2 as joint distribution function if and only if $U_1 = 1 - U_2$ holds with probability one, which is identified as the most negative dependence imaginable, see Exercise 2. A visualization is provided in Figure 2.1.

Furthermore, the 'middle case' of stochastic independence is reflected by the so-called '*independence copula*' $\Pi_d(u_1, \ldots, u_d) = u_1 \cdot u_2 \cdots u_d$, sometimes also called the '*product copula*'; Π is the Greek 'P', which in mathematics is also used as the product sign, hence the naming. Unlike in the case of the linear correlation coefficient, on the level of copulas independence can be nailed down exactly, as the following lemma states. Its proof is just a rewriting of the definition of stochastic independence.

Lemma 2.1.2 (Independence $\Leftrightarrow C = \Pi_d$)
A random vector $(X_1, \ldots, X_d)$ has stochastically independent components if and only if its distribution function can be split into its marginals and the independence copula Π_d, that is,

$$F(x_1, \ldots, x_d) = \mathbb{P}(X_1 \leq x_1, \ldots, X_d \leq x_d)$$
$$= \mathbb{P}(X_1 \leq x_1) \cdot \ldots \cdot \mathbb{P}(X_d \leq x_d) = \Pi_d(F_1(x_1), \ldots, F_d(x_d)).$$

The analogous lemmata in the cases M_d and W_d are the subject of Section 2.3.

2.2 Switching from Distribution to Survival Functions

From a given copula C and univariate marginals $F_1, \ldots, F_d$ we can either construct a multivariate distribution function via $F(x_1, \ldots, x_d) := C(F_1(x_1), \ldots, F_d(x_d))$, see Theorem 1.2.4, or alternatively a multivariate survival function via $\bar{G}(x_1, \ldots, x_d) := C(1 - F_1(x_1), \ldots, 1 - F_d(x_d))$, see Corollary 1.2.7. Both constructions might lead to completely different models, that is, $F \neq G$ in general. Whether the stochastic model implied by F or G fits better the scope of the respective application depends on the dependence properties of the copula C. For example, assume that the marginals satisfy $F_j(0) = 0$ and are strictly increasing and continuous on $[0, \infty)$, $j = 1, \ldots, d$. We interpret the component X_j of the resulting random vector as the default time of a credit-risky asset in a portfolio of size d. If C assigns a lot of probability mass close to the corner $\{0\}^d$, then F assigns a lot of probability mass close to the corner $\{0\}^d$, that is, there is a high likelihood of all default times being jointly small, which might

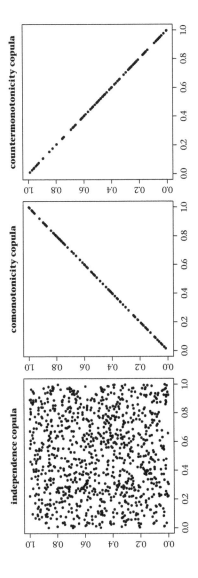

Figure 2.1 Left: bivariate scatter plot of samples drawn from the independence copula Π_2. Note that there are no systematic clusterings observable. Middle: scatter plot of the comonotonicity copula M_2, where in each sample both components take precisely the same value, so all samples fall on the diagonal. Right: countermonotonicity copula W_2, where all samples fall on the counter diagonal.

be a desirable property of the resulting credit-risk model. However, assume we have a copula C that does not assign a lot of mass close to the corner $\{0\}^d$, but instead assigns a lot of mass close to the opposite corner $\{1\}^d$. In this case, G, and not F, assigns a lot of probability mass to the corner $\{0\}^d$. In financial applications, the probability mass close to some corner is often quantified in terms of so-called 'tail dependence coefficients', see Chapter 3 for further details regarding this notion.

Generally speaking, assume we want to compare two different multivariate distributions, one constructed via the classical Sklar's Theorem for distribution functions and another one constructed via Sklar's Theorem for survival functions. Clearly, comparing a distribution function with a survival function is comparing apples with oranges. Instead, we have to convert the constructed survival function of the second model into its corresponding distribution function, which can then be compared to the distribution function of the first model. We now show how this task is accomplished.

Since it is educational, we provide the bivariate case as an illustrative example. Assume that (X_1, X_2) is a random vector on a probability space $(\Omega, \mathcal{F}, \mathbb{P})$ with distribution function $F(x_1, x_2) := \mathbb{P}(X_1 \leq x_1, X_2 \leq x_2)$, which admits the representation $F(x_1, x_2) = C(F_1(x_1), F_2(x_2))$, for $x_1, x_2 \in \mathbb{R}$, with a bivariate copula C and two univariate distribution functions F_1, F_2. We want to compute the survival function of (X_1, X_2) and the survival copula $\hat{C}$ of C. To this end, recall from probability calculus that for arbitrary $A, B \in \mathcal{F}$ we have $\mathbb{P}(A \cup B) = \mathbb{P}(A) + \mathbb{P}(B) - \mathbb{P}(A \cap B)$. Applying this rule in the third equality below, we find

$$
\begin{aligned}
\bar{F}(x_1, x_2) :&= \mathbb{P}(X_1 > x_1, X_2 > x_2) = 1 - \mathbb{P}(\{X_1 \leq x_1\} \cup \{X_2 \leq x_2\}) \\
&= 1 - \mathbb{P}(X_1 \leq x_1) - \mathbb{P}(X_2 \leq x_2) + \mathbb{P}(X_1 \leq x_1, X_2 \leq x_2) \\
&= 1 - F_1(x_1) - F_2(x_2) + F(x_1, x_2) \qquad (2.4) \\
&= 1 - (1 - \bar{F}_1(x_1)) - (1 - \bar{F}_2(x_2)) + C(1 - \bar{F}_1(x_1), 1 - \bar{F}_2(x_2)) \\
&= \bar{F}_1(x_1) + \bar{F}_2(x_2) - 1 + C(1 - \bar{F}_1(x_1), 1 - \bar{F}_2(x_2)). \qquad (2.5)
\end{aligned}
$$

Since the survival copula is a function $\hat{C}$ satisfying $\hat{C}(\bar{F}_1(x_1), \bar{F}_2(x_2)) = \bar{F}(x_1, x_2)$, we conclude from (2.5) that

$$
\hat{C}(u_1, u_2) = C(1 - u_1, 1 - u_2) + u_1 + u_2 - 1.
$$

Notice in particular that this function is not equal to the survival function $\bar{C}$ corresponding to the copula C. The latter is given by

$$
\bar{C}(u_1, u_2) = C(u_1, u_2) - u_1 - u_2 + 1,
$$

which can also be seen from the computation above with the special choice $F = C$ and $F_1 = F_2 = \mathrm{id}_{[0,1]}$ in (2.4).

To make the earlier argument more explicit, assume we construct two different stochastic models for dependent lifetimes (X_1, X_2) and (Y_1, Y_2). The marginal distribution of X_1 and Y_1 is denoted by F_1, and the marginal law of X_2 and Y_2 by F_2, so that both models have identical marginals. However, we opt for two different copulas, say C_X and C_Y. Applying Sklar's Theorem 1.2.4 and Sklar's Theorem for survival functions (Corollary 1.2.7), we model the joint distribution function F_X of (X_1, X_2) and the joint survival function $\bar{F}_Y$ of (Y_1, Y_2) via

$$F_X(x_1, x_2) := C_X(F_1(x_1), F_2(x_2)), \quad \bar{F}_Y(x_1, x_2) := C_Y(\bar{F}_1(x_1), \bar{F}_2(x_2)).$$

Since the marginal laws are identical in both models, comparing the multivariate laws may be done by comparing only the copulas. However, it is not appropriate to compare C_X with C_Y! Rather one must compare $\hat{C}_X$ with C_Y. This is a common pitfall in copula modeling. In particular, when one is only used to elliptical copulas (for example the Gaussian copula), this pitfall disappears because, in that particular case, $\hat{C} = C$ due to radial symmetry, see Section 1.3 for further details.

In the general case of dimension $d \geq 2$ the above computation relating a distribution function to its survival function, resp. a copula to its survival copula, relies on a generalization of the identity $\mathbb{P}(A \cup B) = \mathbb{P}(A) + \mathbb{P}(B) - \mathbb{P}(A \cap B)$. This so-called 'principle of inclusion and exclusion' states that the probability of a union of events $A_1, \ldots, A_d \in \mathcal{F}$ can be computed from probabilities involving only intersections of the same events as

$$\mathbb{P}\left(\bigcup_{j=1}^{d} A_j \right) = \sum_{j=1}^{d} (-1)^{j+1} \sum_{1 \leq i_1 < \cdots < i_j \leq d} \mathbb{P}\left(\bigcap_{k=1}^{j} A_{i_k} \right), \tag{2.6}$$

see, for example, [Billingsley (1995), p. 24]. The resulting conversion formula is given in the following useful lemma generalizing the bivariate computations presented above. The proof of Lemma 2.2.1 is similar to the bivariate case, using the principle of inclusion and exclusion (2.6).

Lemma 2.2.1 (Distribution function/copula $\rightsquigarrow$ survival function/copula)
The survival copula $\hat{C}$ of a copula C is given as

$$\hat{C}(u_1, \ldots, u_d) = 1 + \sum_{j=1}^{d} (-1)^j \sum_{1 \leq i_1 < \cdots < i_j \leq d} C_{i_1, \ldots, i_j}(1 - u_{i_1}, \ldots, 1 - u_{i_j}),$$

where $C_{i_1, \ldots, i_j}$ is the j-dimensional marginal copula of C, which is obtained from C by plugging the components $i_1, \ldots, i_j$ of $(u_1, \ldots, u_d) \in [0, 1]^d$ into the respective arguments of C, and setting all other arguments to one.

The survival function $\bar{F}$ of a distribution function F is given as

$$\bar{F}(x_1, \ldots, x_d) = 1 + \sum_{j=1}^{d} (-1)^j \sum_{1 \leq i_1 < \cdots < i_j \leq d} F_{i_1, \ldots, i_j}(x_{i_1}, \ldots, x_{i_j}),$$

where $F_{i_1,...,i_j}$ is the j-dimensional marginal distribution function of F, which is obtained from F by plugging the components $i_1,...,i_j$ of $(x_1,...,x_d) \in \mathbb{R}^d$ into the respective arguments of F, and setting all other arguments to infinity.

2.3   Invariance Under Strictly Monotone Transformations

When applying a strictly monotone transformation to the components of a random vector $(X_1,...,X_d)$, only the marginal laws change but its copula is unaltered.

Lemma 2.3.1 (Strictly monotone transformations)
Let $(X_1,...,X_d)$ be a random vector with continuous marginals and copula C.

(a)   For functions $g_1,...,g_d : \mathbb{R} \to \mathbb{R}$, which are strictly increasing on the range of the respective components, the copula of $(g_1(X_1),...,g_d(X_d))$ is again C.

(b)   For functions $g_1,...,g_d : \mathbb{R} \to \mathbb{R}$, which are strictly decreasing on the range of the respective components, the copula of $(g_1(X_1),...,g_d(X_d))$ is the survival copula $\hat{C}$ of C.

Proof

(a)   To simplify presentation, we assume that the g_j are strictly increasing everywhere, not only on the range of the X_j. Fix $j = 1,...,d$ and denote by F_j the distribution function of X_j. Then the distribution function of $g_j(X_j)$ is given by

$$G_j(x) := \mathbb{P}(g_j(X_j) \leq x) = \mathbb{P}(X_j \leq g_j^{-1}(x)) = F_j(g_j^{-1}(x)) = F_j \circ g_j^{-1}(x),$$

where the second equality follows from strict increasingness of g_j and g_j^{-1} is the regular inverse of g_j. Since g_j is strictly increasing, g_j^{-1} is continuous, hence G_j is also continuous as a concatenation of two continuous functions. Accordingly, the random vector $(g_1(X_1),...,g_d(X_d))$ has a unique copula which we denote by $\tilde{C}$. It is now easy to see that

$$\tilde{C}(G_1(x_1),...,G_d(x_d)) = \mathbb{P}(g_1(X_1) \leq x_1,...,g_d(X_d) \leq x_d)$$
$$= \mathbb{P}(X_1 \leq g_1^{-1}(x_1),...,X_d \leq g_d^{-1}(x_d))$$
$$= C(F_1 \circ g_1^{-1}(x_1),...,F_d \circ g_d^{-1}(x_d))$$
$$= C(G_1(x_1),...,G_d(x_d)),$$

where the second equality follows again from the strict increasingness of the g_j. By continuity of the G_j we find for each $u_j \in [0,1]$ a value $x_j \in \mathbb{R}$ such that $G_j(x_j) = u_j$, so that we may conclude $\tilde{C}(u_1,...,u_d) = C(u_1,...,u_d)$ for all $(u_1,...,u_d) \in [0,1]^d$ from the last equality.

(b)   This can be deduced from part (a) and the fact that $(1 - F_1(X_1),...,1 - F_d(X_d))$ has distribution function $\hat{C}$, cf. Exercise 9.   □

Assume F_1 and F_2 are two strictly increasing and continuous univariate distribution functions, for example, two normal distribution functions with different means and variances. If $X_1 \sim F_1$, it follows that $X_2 := F_2^{-1} \circ F_1(X_1) \sim F_2$, since for $x \in \mathbb{R}$ we have

$$\mathbb{P}(X_2 \leq x) = \mathbb{P}(F_2^{-1} \circ F_1(X_1) \leq x) = \mathbb{P}(X_1 \leq F_1^{-1} \circ F_2(x)) = F_1(F_1^{-1} \circ F_2(x)) = F_2(x).$$

Therefore, the strictly increasing transformation $F_2^{-1} \circ F_1$ applied to $X_1 \sim F_1$ results in a random variable X_2 with distribution function F_2. Applying such a transformation component-by-component to a given random vector allows us to change all marginals of the random vector to personal taste. Lemma 2.3.1 shows that the copula is not affected by such a transformation. This fact plays an important role both in data analysis applications and in modeling applications. Concerning the former, it was already noted in Chapter 1 that if $g_1 = F_1, \ldots, g_d = F_d$ are the continuous marginal distribution functions of the components $X_1, \ldots, X_d$, then the random vector $(U_1, \ldots, U_d) := (F_1(X_1), \ldots, F_d(X_d))$ has copula C as joint distribution function. Hence, this so-called 'probability integral transformation' standardizes the marginals to uniform distributions on $[0, 1]$. This data transformation is a helpful first step in many data analysis applications such as dependence estimation, see Figure 2.2 for a visualization in terms of histograms.

FAQ 2.3.2 (Where does this appear in Finance?)
For instance, if dependence between the values of two stock prices at some future time point is modeled in terms of a copula, their logarithmic values have the same copula. Also, the conversion into other currencies by multiplication with the respective FX rates, or scale changes of credit spreads from percent into basis points, have no effect on the dependence structure. This invariance of the copula under strictly increasing margin transformations is not shared by the popular concept of correlation coefficients!

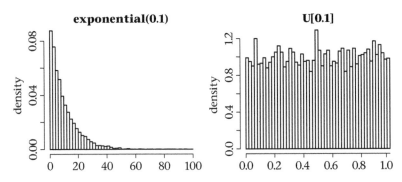

Figure 2.2 Left: histogram of $n = 5000$ iid realizations $X^{(1)}, \ldots, X^{(n)}$ from the exponential law with mean 10. Right: histogram of the transformed variates $U^{(1)} := 1 - \exp(-0.1 X^{(1)}), \ldots, U^{(n)} := 1 - \exp(-0.1 X^{(n)})$, which are $\mathcal{U}[0, 1]$-distributed. This plot is created using the R command hist().

Corollary 2.3.3 ($C = M_d \Leftrightarrow$ comonotonicity)
A random vector $(X_1, \ldots, X_d)$ with marginals $F_1, \ldots, F_d$ has copula M_d if and only if

$$(X_1, \ldots, X_d) \stackrel{d}{=} (F_1^{-1}(U), \ldots, F_d^{-1}(U)), \quad U \sim \mathcal{U}[0,1].$$

The symbol $\stackrel{d}{=}$ means equality in distribution.

Proof
The d-dimensional vector $(U, \ldots, U)$ has M_d as joint distribution function by Exercise 1. It can be shown, see [Mai, Scherer (2012), p. 17] for details, that $(F_1^{-1}(U), \ldots, F_d^{-1}(U))$ has copula M_d and marginals $F_1, \ldots, F_d$, hence the claim.
  In case the marginals $F_1, \ldots, F_d$ are continuous and strictly increasing, the claim can alternatively be seen immediately from Lemma 2.3.1: $F_1^{-1}, \ldots, F_d^{-1}$ are strictly increasing transformations in this case, hence the copula of $(U, \ldots, U)$ remains unchanged under this transformation, showing that the copula of $(F_1^{-1}(U), \ldots, F_d^{-1}(U))$ is M_d. Moreover, for each component $j = 1, \ldots, d$ it holds that

$$\mathbb{P}(F_j^{-1}(U) \leq x) = \mathbb{P}(U \leq F_j(x)) = F_j(x), \quad x \in \mathbb{R},$$

showing that the marginals of $(F_1^{-1}(U), \ldots, F_d^{-1}(U))$ are the desired ones. $\square$

Corollary 2.3.3 justifies the notion 'comonotonicity', since all components move coherently into the same direction as one common factor U. For instance, if $X_1, \ldots, X_d$ denote stock returns, then comonotonicity means that either all stocks move up, or all stocks move down, only the size of the up-/down-moves can differ between the stocks. Let us provide two further (quite popular) examples within a financial context which implicitly apply the concept of comonotonicity.

FAQ 2.3.4 (Where does this appear in Finance? (continued))
Firstly, in interest rate term structure modeling so-called LIBOR market models have become the market standard. These model the future evolution of an (infinite-dimensional) interest rate term structure by simply modeling only the future evolution of a finite set of forward LIBOR rates. In typical models the dependence between these single LIBOR rates is given in terms of a correlation matrix. The simplest special case, which is often applied in practice due to the availability of efficient tree-pricing algorithms, is the case of equicorrelation and corresponds precisely to comonotonicity between the LIBOR rates. The interested reader can find a good introduction into LIBOR market models in [Brigo, Mercurio (2001)]. Secondly, when trading a stock derivative and a fixed-income product referring to one and the same company at the same time, a joint model for the company's stock (in order to price the stock derivative in concern) and the company's default risk (in order to price the fixed-income product in concern) is required. Such models are called credit-equity models, and probably some of the most popular among them are called '1.5-factor credit-equity models'. Their underlying idea is to first model the stock-price process, and secondly define the company's credit spread as a decreasing function

of the stock price. This implies that the dependence between stock price and credit spread is given by the countermonotonicity copula W_2, see [Carr, Linetsky (2006), Linetsky (2006), Carr, Wu (2009), Carr, Madan (2010)] for popular examples of such models. Equivalently, the dependence between stock and the negative of the credit spread is given by the comonotonicity copula M_2.

One important special case of Lemma 2.3.1(b) is the case when $(X_1,\ldots,X_d) :=$ $(U_1,\ldots,U_d)$ has uniform marginals, that is, actually has the distribution function (and not only the copula) C. Applying the decreasing transformations $g_j(u) := 1 - u$, $u \in [0,1]$, $j = 1,\ldots,d$, yields the vector $(g_1(U_1),\ldots,g_d(U_d)) = (1 - U_1,\ldots,1 - U_d)$, which has $\hat{C}$ not only as a copula but also as a distribution function. Hence, this example shows how to generate random variates from the survival copula $\hat{C}$ when a simulation algorithm for the copula C is available, namely by simply applying the aforementioned transformation.

Finally, in the bivariate case it is possible to characterize the lower Fréchet–Hoeffding bound in terms of a stochastic model similarly to how the upper bound was characterized in Corollary 2.3.3. The logic of the proof is also similar to that of Corollary 2.3.3.

Corollary 2.3.5 ($C = W_2 \Leftrightarrow$ countermonotonicity)
A bivariate random vector (X_1, X_2) with marginals F_1, F_2 has copula W_2 if and only if

$$(X_1, X_2) \overset{d}{=} (F_1^{-1}(U), F_2^{-1}(1 - U)), \quad U \sim \mathcal{U}[0,1].$$

2.4 Computing Probabilities from a Distribution Function

Having at hand a stochastic model for a random vector $(X_1,\ldots,X_d)$, one would think that one of the most basic tasks is the computation of a probability such as

$$\mathbb{P}(a_1 < X_1 \leq b_1,\ldots,a_d < X_d \leq b_d), \quad -\infty < a_j < b_j < \infty, j = 1,\ldots,d.$$

It is obvious that such probabilities are of interest. For instance, think of $(X_1,\ldots,X_d)$ as a model for the d lifetimes of credit-risky assets. One might then be interested in the probability that all assets survive one more year, but then all of them default within the succeeding year. This corresponds to the case $a_1 = \ldots = a_d = 1$ and $b_1 = \ldots = b_d = 2$. However, if the dimension d of the model is large, the computation of this basic probability might already cause serious problems, even if we have an analytical formula for the distribution function F of $(X_1,\ldots,X_d)$. The reason is that we face a large sum with alternating signs, namely

$$\mathbb{P}(a_1 < X_1 \leq b_1,\ldots,a_d < X_d \leq b_d) = \sum_{(c_1,\ldots,c_d) \in \times_{j=1}^d \{a_j,b_j\}} (-1)^{|\{j : c_j = a_j\}|} F(c_1,\ldots,c_d)$$

$$= F(b_1,\ldots,b_d) - F(a_1, b_2,\ldots,b_d) - \cdots - F(b_1,\ldots,b_{d-1}, a_d)$$

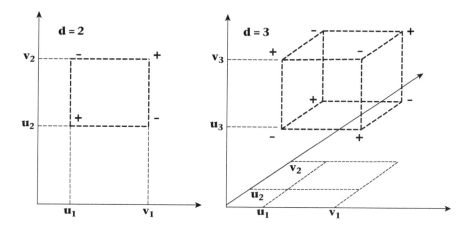

Figure 2.3 Computation of cube probabilities in low dimensions ($d = 2$ and $d = 3$).

$$+ F(a_1, a_2, b_3, \ldots, b_d) + \cdots + F(b_1, \ldots, b_{d-2}, a_{d-1}, a_d)$$
$$- F(a_1, a_2, a_3, b_4, \ldots, b_d) - \cdots\cdots + (-1)^d F(a_1, \ldots, a_d).$$

Observe that these are precisely 2^d summands, which implies that this computation becomes a numerically burdensome task for large d. In the low-dimensional cases $d = 2$ and $d = 3$, Figure 2.3 visualizes which corners of the square, resp. cube, enter the sum with a positive sign and which ones with a negative sign. The following numeric example makes explicit why the evaluation of such seemingly simple sums may be a numerical challenge.

Example 2.4.1 (A numeric example)
We know from Exercise 1 that M_d is a copula in arbitrary dimension d, hence we find a random vector $(U_1, \ldots, U_d) \sim M_d$. Moreover, it follows from Corollary 2.3.3 that

$$\mathbb{P}(0.25 < U_1 \leq 0.75, \ldots, 0.25 < U_d \leq 0.75) = \mathbb{P}(0.25 < U_1 \leq 0.75)$$
$$= 0.75 - 0.25 = 0.5.$$

However, the simplicity of this computation relies heavily on the fact that we have knowledge about the stochastic model behind the copula M_d, which we extract from Exercise 1 and use in the first equality above. Without this knowledge, and instead using the general formula stated above with brute force, we end up with

$$M_d(0.75, \ldots, 0.75) - M_d(0.25, 0.75, \ldots, 0.75) - \cdots - M_d(0.75, \ldots, 0.75, 0.25)$$
$$+ M_d(0.25, 0.25, 0.75, \ldots, 0.75) + \cdots + M_d(0.75, \ldots, 0.75, 0.25, 0.25)$$

$$- M(0.25, 0.25, 0.25, 0.75, \ldots, 0.75) - \cdots + (-1)^d M(0.25, \ldots, 0.25)$$

$$= 0.75 - \binom{d}{1} 0.25 + \binom{d}{2} 0.25 - \binom{d}{3} 0.25 + \cdots + (-1)^d \binom{d}{d} 0.25 = 0.5.$$

This computation shows that, even though the result 0.5 is a probability and hence between 0 and 1, the summands that have to be added and subtracted can become huge. For instance, if $d = 10$, the last line in the computation above reads

$$0.75 - 2.5 + 11.25 - 30 + 52.5 - 63 + 52.5 - 30 + 11.25 - 2.5 + 0.25 = 0.5.$$

2.5 Copula Derivatives

Many copulas that appear in applications are '*absolutely continuous*'. This means that they admit an integral representation of the form

$$C(u_1, \ldots, u_d) = \int_0^{u_1} \int_0^{u_2} \cdots \int_0^{u_d} c(v_1, \ldots, v_d) \, dv_d \, dv_{d-1} \ldots dv_1,$$

for a non-negative function $c : (0,1)^d \to [0, \infty)$, called the '*(copula) density*' of C. Compared to the copula, the copula density has the advantage that it visualizes nicely where the probability mass is located. If only the copula C is given, its density – if existent, which requires additional regularity on C like almost sure (a.s.) equality of mixed partial derivatives – can be computed from C via successive partial differentiation, that is,

$$c(u_1, \ldots, u_d) = \frac{\partial}{\partial u_1} \frac{\partial}{\partial u_2} \cdots \frac{\partial}{\partial u_d} C(u_1, \ldots, u_d). \tag{2.7}$$

Example 2.5.1 (The bivariate Gaussian copula)
In the following, $\Phi(x) := \int_{-\infty}^{x} \exp(-y^2/2) \, dy/\sqrt{2\pi}$ denotes the distribution function of a standard normally distributed random variable. The most prominent absolutely continuous copula is probably the bivariate '*Gaussian copula*', which is defined in integral form by:

$$C_\rho(u_1, u_2) = \int_0^{u_1} \int_0^{u_2} c_\rho(v_1, v_2) \, dv_2 \, dv_1,$$

$$c_\rho(u_1, u_2) = \frac{1}{\sqrt{1 - \rho^2}} \exp\left(\frac{2\rho \, \Phi^{-1}(u_1) \, \Phi^{-1}(u_2) - \rho^2 \left(\Phi^{-1}(u_1)^2 + \Phi^{-1}(u_2)^2 \right)}{2(1 - \rho^2)} \right),$$

for a dependence parameter $\rho \in (-1, 1)$. The copula density $c_\rho(u_1, u_2)$ is visualized in Figure 2.4 for increasing levels of dependence. In particular, the probability mass

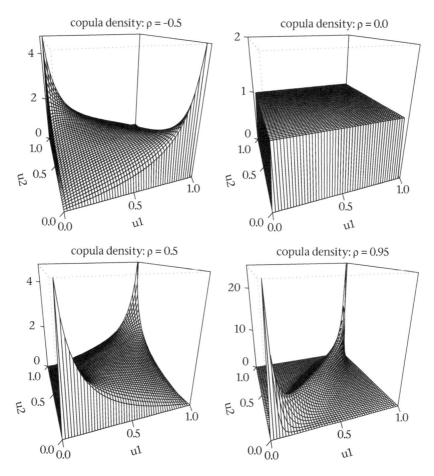

Figure 2.4 Bivariate Gaussian copula density c_ρ for increasing parameter ρ, visualized using persp() from the R-package graphics.

moves from the counterdiagonal $\{u_2 = 1 - u_1\}$ for $\rho \approx -1$ to the diagonal $\{u_1 = u_2\}$ for $\rho \approx 1$, with uniformly scattered probability mass for $\rho = 0$.

Another important fact one has to keep in mind about partial derivatives of a copula is that they have a probabilistic meaning. More precisely, if (U_1, U_2) has the copula C as joint distribution function, then the function

$$h_x : u_1 \mapsto \frac{\partial}{\partial x} C(u_1, x), \quad x \in (0,1),$$

can typically be computed for almost every $x \in (0,1)$, and thus has a right-continuous version (if the few points for which the partial derivative has a jump are defined by their limits from the right). It equals the distribution function of U_1 conditioned on the event $\{U_2 = x\}$. For some bivariate copulas, the function h_x can be computed, and even inverted, in closed form. In this case it follows that the random vector $(h_{V_2}^{-1}(V_1), V_2)$ for two independent $\mathcal{U}[0,1]$-distributed random variables V_1, V_2 has the copula C as joint distribution function. For many copulas which are given in algebraically closed form, for example Archimedean copulas, see Section 4.2 for details, this implies a very convenient and quick simulation algorithm, see Section 5.1.1.

2.6   Constructing New Copulas from Existing Ones

In some applications a given parametric family of copulas might not be flexible enough to fit the observed data or to model the stylized facts one seeks to incorporate. In such a case it might be interesting to combine several copulas in order to create a richer model.[1] Scattered in the literature there exist some approaches to combine/enrich parametric families of copulas, some of which are listed below.

(a)   **Convex mixture copulas:** Given a family $\{C_m(u_1,\ldots,u_d)\}_{m\in\mathcal{M}}$ of d-dimensional copulas and a probability measure μ on the parameterizing set $\mathcal{M}$, it follows that the mixture

$$C(u_1,\ldots,u_d) := \int_{\mathcal{M}} C_m(u_1,\ldots,u_d)\,\mu(dm)$$

is a copula itself. Why? Considering a probability space supporting a collection of independent random vectors $(X_1^{(m)},\ldots,X_d^{(m)}) \sim C_m$, $m \in \mathcal{M}$, and an independent random variable $M \sim \mu$, the random vector $(X_1,\ldots,X_d) := (X_1^{(M)},\ldots,X_d^{(M)})$ has joint distribution function C. An important special case is obtained when $\mathcal{M} = \{1,\ldots,n\}$, and $\mu(\{i\}) = w_i$ for probability weights $w_1,\ldots,w_n > 0$ with $w_1 + \cdots + w_n = 1$. In particular, this shows that the arithmetic average of n copulas is again a copula.

(b)   **Geometric mixture of extreme-value copulas:** Given n extreme-value copulas[2] $C_i(u_1,\ldots,u_d)$, $i = 1,\ldots,n$, and weights $w_1,\ldots,w_n > 0$ with $w_1 + \cdots + w_n = 1$, the geometric average

$$C(u_1,\ldots,u_d) := \prod_{i=1}^{n} C_i(u_1,\ldots,u_d)^{w_i}$$

is again an extreme-value copula. Why? Considering a probability space supporting independent random vectors $(X_1^{(i)},\ldots,X_d^{(i)}) \sim C_i$, the random

---

[1] To provide an example: the motivation behind Archimax copulas, see Section 4.4, is to combine two popular copula families (Archimedean and extreme-value copulas).

[2] Such copulas satisfy the extreme-value copula property $C(u_1^t,\ldots,u_d^t) = C(u_1,\ldots,u_d)^t$, for all $t > 0$, and are formally introduced in Section 4.3.

vector

$$(U_1,\ldots,U_d) := \left(\max\left\{ (U_1^{(1)})^{\frac{1}{w_1}},\ldots,(U_1^{(n)})^{\frac{1}{w_n}} \right\},\ldots,\right.$$
$$\left.\max\left\{ (U_d^{(1)})^{\frac{1}{w_1}},\ldots,(U_d^{(n)})^{\frac{1}{w_n}} \right\} \right)$$

has joint distribution function C. Moreover, C is a proper extreme-value copula (that is, has uniform marginals and satisfies the extreme-value property), cf. Exercise 5.

(c) **Khoudraji asymmetrization**: For two bivariate extreme-value copulas C_1, C_2 and numbers $a, b \in (0,1)$, we may construct a new bivariate extreme-value copula by defining

$$C(u_1,u_2) := C_1(u_1^a, u_2^b)\, C_2(u_1^{1-a}, u_2^{1-b}),$$

which is a construction principle dating back to [Khoudraji (1995)], see also [Genest et al. (1998), Durante, Salvadori (2010), Liebscher (2008), Liebscher (2011)]. Why? Considering two independent random vectors $(U_1^{(i)}, U_2^{(i)}) \sim C_i$, $i = 1,2$, the random vector

$$(U_1, U_2) := \left(\max\{(U_1^{(1)})^{1/a},(U_1^{(2)})^{1/(1-a)}\}, \max\{(U_2^{(1)})^{1/b},(U_2^{(2)})^{1/(1-b)}\} \right)$$

is easily shown to have C as joint distribution function. Furthermore, C is an extreme-value copula (that is, has uniform marginals and satisfies the extreme-value property), cf. Exercise 6.

(d) **Morillas transform**: [Morillas (2005)] studies the question whether for a given d-dimensional copula C and a function $f : [0,1] \to [0,1]$ in one variable the function

$$C_f(u_1,\ldots,u_d) := f\big(C(f^{-1}(u_1),\ldots,f^{-1}(u_d))\big)$$

is again a copula. It is found that this is the case when the function f is strictly increasing and continuous on $[0,1]$ with $f^{-1}(1) = 1$, and has non-negative derivatives of all orders. Examples for such functions are $f(x) = 2/\pi \arcsin(x)$, $f(x) = \tan(x)/\tan(1)$, and $f(x) = x^r$ with $r \geq 1$. Unfortunately, [Morillas (2005)] does not provide a stochastic model for such copulas but only provides a purely analytic proof.

EXERCISES

1. Let $U \sim \mathcal{U}[0,1]$ and show that the d-dimensional vector $(U,\ldots,U)$ has M_d as joint distribution function.

2. Let $U \sim \mathcal{U}[0,1]$ and show that the vector $(U, 1-U)$ has W_2 as joint distribution function. Hence, W_2 is a bivariate copula.

3. Show that the bivariate Frank copula $C(u_1, u_2) = \varphi(\varphi^{-1}(u_1) + \varphi^{-1}(u_2))$ is its own survival copula, but the trivariate Frank copula $C(u_1, u_2, u_3) = \varphi(\varphi^{-1}(u_1) + \varphi^{-1}(u_2) + \varphi^{-1}(u_3))$ is not, where $\varphi(x) = -1/\theta \log(e^{-x}(e^{-\theta} - 1) + 1)$ for $\theta > 0$, see [Frank (1979), Genest (1987)].

4. Compute the density of the bivariate Frank copula.

5. Show that the geometric average of n extreme-value copulas is again an extreme-value copula.

6. Show that the Khoudraji asymmetrization yields a proper extreme-value copula, and compute its parameterizing function A, see Section 4.3 for details.

7. Show that an application of the Khoudraji asymmetrization with $C_1 = C_2 = M_2$ yields a copula of class BC_2 (cf. Table 4.3).

8. Let the copula $C : [0,1]^d \to [0,1]$ be the distribution function of the random vector $(U_1, \ldots, U_d)$ and consider the vectors $\boldsymbol{u}, \boldsymbol{v} \in [0,1]^d$ with $u_j < v_j$ for all $j = 1, \ldots, d$. Use the principle of inclusion and exclusion to show that

$$\sum_{\boldsymbol{w} \in \times_{j=1}^d \{u_j, v_j\}} (-1)^{|\{j : w_j = u_j\}|} C(\boldsymbol{w}) = \mathbb{P}\left(\bigcap_{j=1}^d \{u_j < U_j \leq v_j\} \right).$$

9. Prove part (b) in Lemma 2.3.1, assuming the g_j are strictly decreasing everywhere (not only on the range of the marginals).

10. Prove Lemma 2.2.1.

11. Prove Corollary 2.3.5 under the assumption that F_1, F_2 are strictly increasing and continuous. Hint: Use Exercise 2 and Lemma 2.3.1.

3   How to Measure Dependence?

The notion of dependence between two (or more) random variables is not a simple mathematical concept. Consequently, it is quite challenging to communicate information like the 'degree', 'level', or 'type' of dependence. A significant simplification is achieved if the information about the dependence structure is compressed into a single number that quantifies the degree of dependence on some scale ranging from -1 to $+1$, say. Obviously, this comes at the price of losing information, since it corresponds to a mapping from the set of copulas to the real numbers. Moreover, there are several methods by which this aggregation of information is possible. It is very important to understand the philosophy behind those different methods, as each dependence measure quantifies only a certain aspect of the dependence structure. Obviously, our aim is to measure the respective aspect of dependence that is relevant for the application we have in mind. Taking the correlation between X_1 and X_2 as an example, this dependence measure quantifies the degree of linear dependence, see below. Apart from measuring various aspects of dependence, dependence measures can also be used to estimate the parameters of a parametric family of copulas. This application compares a theoretical dependence measure with the empirical counterpart and selects the parameters of the copula such that both (theoretical and empirical) measures agree. For several dependence measures we have empirical estimates with known finite sample (or asymptotic) distribution. This allows us, for example, to perform hypothesis tests.

3.1   Pearson's Correlation Coefficient

By far the most prominent dependence measure is Pearson's correlation coefficient; we recall its definition below.

Definition 3.1.1 (Pearson's correlation coefficient and its sample version)
Consider the random vector (X_1, X_2) and define '*Pearson's correlation coefficient*' as

$$\rho = \mathrm{Cor}(X_1, X_2) := \frac{\mathrm{Cov}(X_1, X_2)}{\sqrt{\mathrm{Var}(X_1)}\sqrt{\mathrm{Var}(X_2)}}$$

$$= \frac{\mathbb{E}[(X_1 - \mathbb{E}[X_1])(X_2 - \mathbb{E}[X_2])]}{\sqrt{\mathbb{E}[(X_1 - \mathbb{E}[X_1])^2]}\sqrt{\mathbb{E}[(X_2 - \mathbb{E}[X_2])^2]}}.$$

Clearly, this measure of dependence only exists if the random variables X_1 and X_2 are square integrable, which we assume in the following. Often, we have a given set of data and want to estimate this quantity. The most common procedure to do so

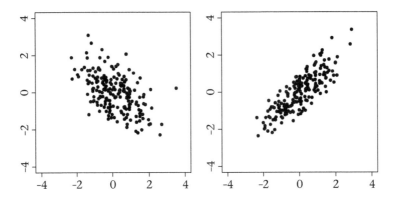

Figure 3.1 $n = 200$ samples of a bivariate standard normal distribution with true correlation $\rho = -0.5$ (left) and $\rho = 0.8$ (right). The empirical estimates are around $\hat{\rho}_n \approx -0.52$ (left) and $\hat{\rho}_n \approx 0.83$ (right).

is the following: given iid observations $(X_1^{(1)}, X_2^{(1)}), \ldots, (X_1^{(n)}, X_2^{(n)})$ from (X_1, X_2), the empirical (or sample) estimate for the correlation is

$$\hat{\rho}_n := \frac{\sum_{i=1}^{n}(X_1^{(i)} - \bar{X}_1)(X_2^{(i)} - \bar{X}_2)}{\sqrt{\sum_{i=1}^{n}(X_1^{(i)} - \bar{X}_1)^2}\sqrt{\sum_{i=1}^{n}(X_2^{(i)} - \bar{X}_2)^2}},$$

where[1] $\bar{X}_j := \frac{1}{n}\sum_{i=1}^{n}X_j^{(i)}, j = 1, 2$.

Figure 3.1 visualizes simulated values from bivariate normal distributions along with their theoretical and empirical Pearson's correlation coefficients. To gain a deeper understanding of Pearson's correlation coefficient, let us collect some of its important properties.

Lemma 3.1.2 (Properties of Pearson's correlation)
(a) The first observation is the range of the correlation, which is always within $[-1, 1]$, due to the Cauchy–Schwarz inequality. It is important to stress that, with fixed marginal laws $X_1 \sim F_1$ and $X_2 \sim F_2$, not all values in $[-1, 1]$ need to be attained. Hence, a seemingly small correlation of $\rho = 0.3$, say, might already be the maximal correlation possible given the choice of marginal laws. To make this more precise, one can show (see [Hoeffding (1940), Shih, Huang (1992), Embrechts et al. (2002)]) that the largest possible correlation between X_1 and X_2 with fixed marginal laws, denoted $\rho_\oplus$ (resp. smallest possible correlation $\rho_\ominus$), is achieved if X_1, X_2 are coupled by the comonotonicity (resp. countermonotonicity) copula M_2 (resp. W_2). For most choices of marginal laws, we have $-1 < \rho_\ominus < \rho_\oplus < 1$. This observation is illustrated in Example 3.1.3.
(b) Correlation between X_1 and X_2 is symmetric, that is, $\mathrm{Cor}(X_1, X_2) = \mathrm{Cor}(X_2, X_1)$. This property follows immediately from the definition of correlation.

---

[1] See [Bickel, Docksum (2006), Section 4.9.5] for details, further results, and examples under the hypothesis of a bivariate normal model.

(c) Correlation measures linear dependence: If (and only if) $X_2 = aX_1 + b$ almost surely, one has $\mathrm{Cor}(X_1, X_2) = \mathrm{sign}(a)\,1$, where $a \neq 0$ and the sign function returns $+1$ (resp. -1) when $a > 0$ (resp. $a < 0$). Moreover, one easily verifies the rule

$$\mathrm{Cor}(aX_1 + b, X_2) = \mathrm{sign}(a)\,\mathrm{Cor}(X_1, X_2), \quad a \neq 0,$$

which shows, for example, that the correlation is invariant under scalings. In a financial context this means, for example, that the correlation between two credit spreads is the same, irrespectively of if these are quoted in basis points or in percent. A non-linear transformation, however, like applying the logarithm, changes the correlation.

(d) The fact that the correlation changes when the marginal laws change also implies that the correlation is not a function of the copula between X_1 and X_2 alone. Hence, it mixes aspects of dependence and marginal laws.

(e) Another immediate observation is that when X_1 and X_2 are independent, their correlation is zero. This follows, since the expectation of the covariance factorizes given independent factors. Unfortunately, it is a common mis-belief that the opposite is also true. But uncorrelatedness does not imply independence in general,[2] as shown in FAQ 3.1.4.

(f) Estimating correlation with high precision requires a lot of data. To make this more precise, the distribution (and an asymptotic distribution) of the sample version of Pearson's correlation coefficient is known in the bivariate normal case, see [Fisher (1915)] or [Kenney, Keeping (1953), p. 220]. Plotting this distribution, which is done in Figure 3.2, shows that even with $n = 200$ samples we have quite some variance around the true value. As a rule of thumb to be concluded, estimating dependence typically requires more data than estimating marginal laws.

Example 3.1.3 (Bounds for the correlation)
Let us first consider two exponentially distributed random variables with rates one and λ, respectively, denoted $X_1 \sim \mathcal{E}(1)$ and $X_2 \sim \mathcal{E}(\lambda)$. The maximal correlation is obtained if these are connected via the comonotonicity copula M_2. Stochastically, this is achieved if we use the quantile transformation (with the same uniform variable $U \sim \mathcal{U}[0,1]$) and set $X_1 := F_1^{-1}(U) = -\log(1 - U)$ and $X_2 := F_2^{-1}(U) = -\log(1 - U)/\lambda$. One immediately observes that in this case X_2 is just a linear scaling of X_1, so their correlation is one and hence $\rho_\oplus = 1$. If we look at the lower bound $\rho_\ominus$, we use the stochastic model for the countermonotonic case $X_1 := F_1^{-1}(U) = -\log(1 - U)$ and $X_2 := F_2^{-1}(1 - U) = -\log(U)/\lambda$. To determine $\mathrm{Cor}(X_1, X_2)$ in this case, we need the variances (these are one for X_1 and λ^{-2} for X_2) and the covariance of X_1 and X_2. The covariance is

$$\mathrm{Cov}(X_1, X_2) = \int_0^1 (-\log(1 - u) - 1)\left(-\frac{1}{\lambda}\log(u) - \frac{1}{\lambda}\right) du \approx -\frac{0.6449}{\lambda},$$

---

[2] For the multivariate normal distribution it is indeed the case that independence and uncorrelatedness are synonyms.

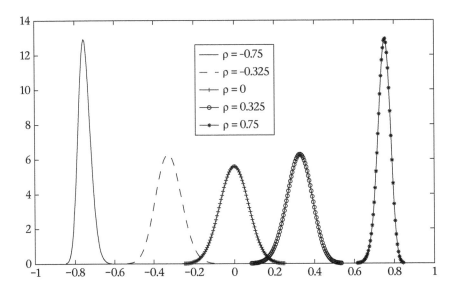

Figure 3.2   Densities of the Pearson's linear correlation estimator $\hat{\rho}_n$ for five different values of the true correlation parameter ρ, based on $n = 200$ iid samples, when the true distribution is bivariate normal.

and hence $\rho_{\ominus} \approx -0.6449$ which is strictly bigger than -1. Note that $\rho_{\ominus}$ is independent of λ. The next example is due to [Embrechts et al. (2002)], where they consider two lognormal variables $X_1 \sim \mathcal{LN}(0,1)$ and $X_2 \sim \mathcal{LN}(0,\sigma^2)$. In this case, they obtain the bounds

$$\rho_{\ominus} = \frac{e^{-\sigma} - 1}{\sqrt{e-1}\sqrt{e^{\sigma^2}-1}}, \qquad \rho_{\oplus} = \frac{e^{\sigma} - 1}{\sqrt{e-1}\sqrt{e^{\sigma^2}-1}}, \qquad (3.1)$$

that both shrink fast to zero as σ tends to infinity.

FAQ 3.1.4 (Does uncorrelated imply independent?)
No, this is a dangerous misunderstanding! The standard example to illustrate this fact is to take $X_1 \sim \mathcal{N}(0,1)$ and $X_2 := X_1^2$. It is then easy to verify that $\text{Cov}(X_1, X_2) = \text{Cor}(X_1, X_2) = 0$, but the two variables are functionally dependent. With a slight modification of this example one can even obtain both X_1 and X_2 being $\mathcal{N}(0,1)$ distributed, uncorrelated, but not independent: take as copula to connect them[3]

$$C(u_1, u_2) = \frac{1}{2}(M_2(u_1, u_2) + W_2(u_1, u_2)).$$

---

[3] Recall from Section 2.6 that the convex combination of copulas is again a copula. A simple stochastic model is to take $X_1 \sim \mathcal{N}(0,1)$, independent thereof $Z \sim \text{Bernoulli}(0.5)$, and to set $X_2 := (2Z-1)X_1$, see [Ash (2007)].

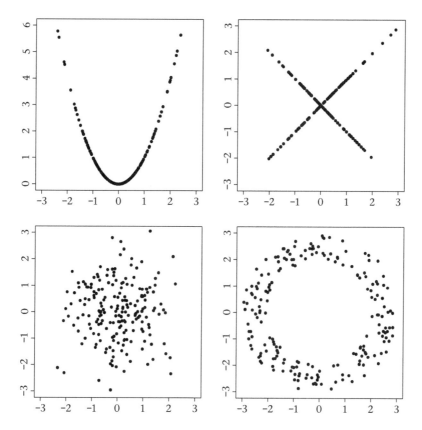

Figure 3.3 Scatter plots of four situations, where in each case the theoretical correlation is zero. The upper ones correspond to the two constructions in FAQ 3.1.4. In the bottom row, we have (left) independent $X_1, X_2 \sim \mathcal{N}(0,1)$ and (right) an example where we take as radius $r = 2 + Z$, where $Z \sim \mathcal{U}[0,1]$, and independently $\varphi \sim \mathcal{U}[0,2\pi]$ as angle and we set $X_1 := r\sin(\varphi), X_2 := r\cos(\varphi)$. The '2+' in the radius serves only to make the picture look nice.

Then $\mathrm{Cov}(X_1, X_2) = \mathrm{Cor}(X_1, X_2) = 0$. This shows that it truly requires a multivariate normal distribution to conclude that uncorrelated implies independent – normal marginal laws are not enough. See Figure 3.3 for a visualization and more examples.

Concluding, the classical correlation coefficient strongly depends on the choice of marginal laws and might not even be defined (if the marginals do not have existing second moments). These properties are sometimes not satisfying, which motivates the introduction of concordance measures.

3.2 Concordance Measures

The notion 'concordance measure' was introduced by [Scarsini (1984)], who aims at making the following intuition mathematically precise:[4] *'Two random variables X_1 and X_2 are concordant when large values of X_1 go with large values of X_2.'* A concordance

---

[4] This is quoted from [Scarsini (1984)], second sentence in the introduction. We replaced (X, Y) by (X_1, X_2) to remain consistent with our notation.

measure is formally defined as a mapping I from the set of bivariate distributions with continuous marginals to the interval $[-1,1]$ satisfying certain properties. These properties are:

(a) Symmetry: $I(X_1, X_2) = I(X_2, X_1)$, which resembles the symmetry of the correlation coefficient.

(b) Coherence: Consider two vectors (X_1, X_2) and (Y_1, Y_2) having copulas C_X and C_Y, respectively, and these are ordered as $C_X(u_1, u_2) \leq C_Y(u_1, u_2)$ for all $(u_1, u_2) \in [0,1]^2$. Then $I(X_1, X_2) \leq I(Y_1, Y_2)$. This intuitively means that the concordance ordering respects the ordering of copulas if these are ordered in the point-wise sense. This means that bigger values of $I(X_1, X_2)$ can be interpreted as 'stronger dependence'.

(c) Independence: If (X_1, X_2) are independent, their concordance measure is zero, that is, $I(X_1, X_2) = 0$. Note that the reverse direction does not need to hold.

(d) Change in sign: $I(-X_1, X_2) = -I(X_1, X_2)$. The motivation for this property is that a multiplication by -1 inverts the ordering of the affected components. Hence, the concordance measure 'flips' around zero.

(e) Convergence property: If $\{(X_1^{(n)}, X_2^{(n)})\}_{n \in \mathbb{N}}$ is a sequence of random vectors with associated sequence of joint distribution functions $\{F_n\}_{n \in \mathbb{N}}$ and F_n converges point-wise to F, the joint distribution of a random vector (X_1, X_2), then

$$\lim_{n \to \infty} I(X_1^{(n)}, X_2^{(n)}) = I(X_1, X_2).$$

To continue with specific examples of concordance measures, we first need to introduce the notion of 'concordant' and 'discordant' pairs. We say that (x_1, x_2) and (y_1, y_2) are concordant (resp. discordant) if $(x_1 - y_1)(x_2 - y_2) > 0$ (resp. $(x_1 - y_1)(x_2 - y_2) < 0$).

FAQ 3.2.1 (How to visualize concordance?)
It is easy to visualize this property, see Figure 3.4. Draw the points in consideration into a coordinate system and connect them with straight lines. Whenever the connecting line of a pair has positive slope we have concordance, and vice versa.

Definition 3.2.2 (Kendall's τ)
Consider the random vector (U_1, U_2) with copula C as joint distribution function. Then, 'Kendall's τ' is defined as

$$\tau = \tau_C := 4 \int_0^1 \int_0^1 C(u_1, u_2)\, dC(u_1, u_2) - 1 = 4\,\mathbb{E}[C(U_1, U_2)] - 1. \qquad (3.2)$$

Not clear at this stage, however, is the link to concordance and discordance, but this becomes clear when reformulating the expression of Kendall's τ. In fact, there exist a number of alternative expressions. These alternative expressions might be useful if Kendall's τ is to be computed for some specific family of copulas C. Kendall's τ is

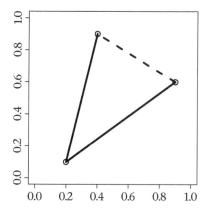

Figure 3.4   The points $(0.2, 0.1)$, $(0.4, 0.9)$, and $(0.9, 0.6)$. Each concordant (resp. discordant) pair is connected with a solid (resp. dashed) line.

furthermore defined for bivariate random vectors (X_1, X_2) with continuous marginals. In this case, the above definition applies to the unique copula of the random vector, irrespectively of the marginals. Obviously, this is a function of the copula alone, the marginal laws are not involved.

Lemma 3.2.3 (Properties of Kendall's τ and its empirical version)
(a)   Consider the independent random vectors (U_1, U_2) and (V_1, V_2), both having the copula C as joint distribution function. Then Kendall's τ equals

$$\tau = \mathbb{P}(\underbrace{(U_1 - V_1)(U_2 - V_2) > 0}_{\text{concordance}}) - \mathbb{P}(\underbrace{(U_1 - V_1)(U_2 - V_2) < 0}_{\text{discordance}}).$$

Hence, Kendall's τ can be interpreted as the difference of the probability of observing a concordant pair and the probability of a discordant pair. This immediately motivates the empirical version of Kendall's τ, see [Kruskal (1958)] for many details. For iid samples $(X_1^{(1)}, X_2^{(1)}), \ldots, (X_1^{(n)}, X_2^{(n)})$ it is given by

$$\hat{\tau}_n := \frac{\text{\# of concordant pairs} - \text{\# of discordant pairs}}{\text{\# of all pairs}}$$

$$= \frac{\sum_{1 \leq i < j \leq n} \text{sign}\left[(X_1^{(j)} - X_1^{(i)})(X_2^{(j)} - X_2^{(i)})\right]}{n(n-1)/2},$$

and $\text{sign}[x]$ returns $+1$, 0, or -1, if x is positive, zero, or negative. Note that if the sample comes from a distribution with continuous marginals, the probability for ties like $X_1^{(i)} = X_1^{(j)}$ is zero. In case the data set actually contains ties, there exist modified versions of Kendall's τ, see, for example, [Adler (1957)]. Another observation is that for examples with continuous marginals F_1 and F_2 we have

$(X_1 - Y_1)(X_2 - Y_2) > 0$ if and only if $(F_1(X_1) - F_1(Y_1))(F_2(X_2) - F_2(Y_2)) > 0$, which follows from F_1, F_2 being strictly increasing. This reflects the fact that Kendall's τ only depends on the underlying copula and not on the marginal laws. Example 3.2.4 illustrates the use of the empirical version of Kendall's τ.

(b) Kendall's τ is increasing in the point-wise ordering of copulas, that is, if $C(u_1, u_2) \leq \tilde{C}(u_1, u_2)$ for all $(u_1, u_2) \in [0,1]^2$ then $\tau_C \leq \tau_{\tilde{C}}$. Moreover, Kendall's τ of the independence copula is zero and $\tau_C = 1$ if and only if C is the comonotonicity copula. See [Scarsini (1984)] or [Nelsen (2006), Theorem 5.1.9] for a proof that Kendall's τ is a measure of concordance and hence satisfies these properties.

(c) There exist possible reformulations (see [Li et al. (2002)] for the first equality and [Nelsen (2006), Theorem 5.1.1] for the second equality) of the analytical expression, for example,

$$\tau_C = 1 - 4 \int_0^1 \int_0^1 \frac{\partial}{\partial u_1} C(u_1, u_2) \frac{\partial}{\partial u_2} C(u_1, u_2) du_1 \, du_2$$

$$= 4 \int_0^1 \int_0^1 C(u_1, u_2) \frac{\partial^2}{\partial u_1 \partial u_2} C(u_1, u_2) \, du_1 \, du_2 - 1,$$

where the last expression requires C to be absolutely continuous.

(d) Kendall's τ of the copula C is the same as Kendall's τ of the corresponding survival copula $\hat{C}$, see [Nelsen (2006), Corollary 5.1.2].

Example 3.2.4 (Stadium capacity compared to soccer results)
We consider the 2012/13 results of the first German soccer league 'Bundesliga' and compare these to the capacity of the respective teams' stadiums. The empirical Kendall's τ between final rank and stadium capacity is $\hat{\tau}_{18} = -0.386$, which supports our intuition that teams with a big stadium are more likely to be successful. Note that using Pearson's correlation coefficient instead of Kendall's τ is not meaningful in the present situation, since the relation between the two measurements 'rank' and 'capacity' should by no means be linear.

Another quite popular dependence measure is Speaman's ρ_S.

Definition 3.2.5 (Spearman's ρ_S)
Consider the random vector (X_1, X_2) with continuous marginal laws $X_j \sim F_j, j = 1, 2,$ and copula C. Consider the transformed vector $(U_1, U_2) := (F_1(X_1), F_2(X_2))$. Note that (U_1, U_2) has C as joint distribution function. Then, 'Spearman's ρ_S' is defined as Pearson's correlation coefficient of (U_1, U_2), that is,

$$\rho_S := \rho_{S,C} = \text{Cor}(U_1, U_2) = \text{Cor}(F_1(X_1), F_2(X_2)). \tag{3.3}$$

In this case, we do not have to worry about existence of the correlation coefficient, since $U_j \sim \mathcal{U}[0,1], j = 1, 2,$ are square integrable. Moreover, Spearman's ρ_S does

Table 3.1. *Final ranks of the Bundesliga season 2012/13 and the capacity of the respective teams' stadiums, as reported by* http://de.wikipedia.org/wiki/Liste_der_-größten_Fußballstadien_in_Deutschland

1	Bayern München	71,137	10	1. FC Nürnberg	50,000
2	Borussia Dortmund	80,645	11	VfL Wolfsburg	30,000
3	Bayer Leverkusen	30,210	12	VfB Stuttgart	60,441
4	Schalke 04	61,973	13	Mainz 05	34,034
5	SC Freiburg	25,000	14	Werder Bremen	42,358
6	Eintracht Frankfurt	51,500	15	FC Augsburg	30,660
7	Hamburger SV	57,000	16	TSG Hoffenheim	30,164
8	Borussia Mönchengladbach	54,067	17	Fortuna Düsseldorf	54,600
9	Hannover 96	49,000	18	Greuther Fürth	18,000

not depend on the marginal laws F_j, $j = 1,2$; their influence is removed by the transformation to uniform marginals.

Lemma 3.2.6 (Properties of Spearman's ρ_S and its empirical version)

(a) Many properties immediately follow from properties of Pearson's correlation ρ, such as symmetry and a zero Spearman's ρ_S of the independence copula. Moreover, one has $\rho_{S,C} = 1$ if and only if C is the comonotonicity copula. Again, we have ordering according to the point-wise ordering of copulas, that is, $C(u_1, u_2) \leq \tilde{C}(u_1, u_2)$ for all $(u_1, u_2) \in [0,1]^2$ implies $\rho_{S,C} \leq \rho_{S,\tilde{C}}$. Moreover, one obtains the same value for the corresponding survival copula, that is, $\rho_{S,C} = \rho_{S,\hat{C}}$, see [Nelsen (2006), Theorem 5.1.9] for the proofs.

(b) The empirical counterpart $\hat{\rho}_{S,n}$ is also related to the empirical version of the correlation, the difference being that absolute values are replaced by ranks in the sample. To formally define it, consider the sample $(X_1^{(1)}, X_2^{(1)}), \ldots, (X_1^{(n)}, X_2^{(n)})$ of iid observations from (X_1, X_2) (with continuous marginals, to avoid ties); the empirical (or sample) estimate of Spearman's ρ_S is

$$\hat{\rho}_{S,n} := \frac{\sum_{i=1}^n (\operatorname{rank}(X_1^{(i)}) - \frac{n+1}{2})(\operatorname{rank}(X_2^{(i)}) - \frac{n+1}{2})}{\sqrt{\sum_{i=1}^n (\operatorname{rank}(X_1^{(i)}) - \frac{n+1}{2})^2} \sqrt{\sum_{i=1}^n (\operatorname{rank}(X_2^{(i)}) - \frac{n+1}{2})^2}},$$

where $\operatorname{rank}(X_1^{(i)})$ denotes the rank statistic of $X_1^{(i)}$, see FAQ 3.2.7 for an example.[5] Again, this becomes more involved in the presence of ties, see [Iman, Conover (1978)], but we do not go into details here.

---

[5] Please be aware of the fact that this notation suppresses that ranks depend not only on the specific value of $X_1^{(i)}$ but on the full vector $(X_1^{(1)}, \ldots, X_1^{(n)})$.

Table 3.2. *Observations and their rank statistics*

i	1	2	3	4	5	i	1	2	3	4	5
$X_1^{(i)}$	1.1	2.3	4.9	0.5	5.5	$X_2^{(i)}$	0.9	1.2	5.2	3.3	6.0
$\text{rank}(X_1^{(i)})$	2	3	4	1	5	$\text{rank}(X_2^{(i)})$	1	2	4	3	5

(c) Besides the definition, there are some known equivalences (see [Nelsen (2006), Theorem 5.1.6] for proofs), for example

$$\rho_{S,C} = 12 \int_0^1 \int_0^1 (C(u_1, u_2) - u_1 u_2) du_1 du_2$$

$$= 12 \int_0^1 \int_0^1 C(u_1, u_2) du_1 du_2 - 3$$

$$= 3 \left(\mathbb{P}((U_1 - V_1)(U_2 - W_2) > 0) - \mathbb{P}((U_1 - V_1)(U_2 - W_2) < 0) \right),$$

for independent copies (U_1, U_2), (V_1, V_2), and (W_1, W_2) with distribution function C.

FAQ 3.2.7 (Can I have an example for 'ranks', please?)
Sure. Consider the observations in Table 3.2. The resulting empirical Spearman's ρ_S is $\hat{\rho}_{S,5} = 0.7$. If you are wondering where the term $(n+1)/2$ comes from in the definition of $\hat{\rho}_{S,n}$, this is simply the average of the rank statistics. If you add up the first n ranks, this is the same as adding up the natural numbers to n in a different order, yielding $n(n+1)/2$, which we divide by n to get the average.

3.2.1 Using Kendall's τ and Spearman's ρ_S

The most obvious application of Kendall's τ and Spearman's ρ_S is to use them to measure the strength of dependence implied by some copula or being empirically observed in some set of data. Besides this, there are at least the following two further applications:

(i) **Testing for independence:** Given a set $(X_1^{(1)}, X_2^{(1)}), \dots, (X_1^{(n)}, X_2^{(n)})$ of iid observations from (X_1, X_2), we can use the empirical versions of Kendall's τ and Spearman's ρ_S to test the hypothesis $\mathcal{H}_0$: X_1 and X_2 are independent. The intuition for such a test is pretty simple. If $\mathcal{H}_0$ is correct, then the empirical versions $\hat{\tau}_n$ and $\hat{\rho}_{S,n}$ must be 'close to' zero, which is the theoretical value under $\mathcal{H}_0$. To decide what 'close to' statistically means and to compute p-values, the exact (or asymptotic for big n) distribution of $\hat{\tau}_n$ and $\hat{\rho}_{S,n}$ is needed, which we have available, see, for example, [Schmid, Schmidt (2007), Dengler (2010), Genest et al. (2011)]. This allows us to test if $\hat{\tau}_n$ and $\hat{\rho}_{S,n}$ are significantly different from zero, in which case we can reject $\mathcal{H}_0$.

(ii) **Parameter estimation**: Many families of bivariate copulas are parameterized by a single parameter, θ say. In such a case one can typically express the above concordance measures as functions of this parameter, $\tau = f(\theta)$ and $\rho_S = g(\theta)$, say. Typically, the parameters of a copula have an intuitive meaning with respect to the strength of dependence and so $f(\theta)$ and $g(\theta)$ are in most cases increasing functions that have inverses f^{-1} and g^{-1}. This suggests the following estimation strategy: use some given sample and compute its empirical Kendall's τ, say. Then, obtain the estimate $\hat{\theta}_n := f^{-1}(\hat{\tau}_n)$. Similarly,[6] we can use $\hat{\theta}_n := g^{-1}(\hat{\rho}_{S,n})$. This estimation methodology will be explained in more detail in Chapter 6.

Let us close this section with the remark that there are, of course, other concordance measures studied in the literature, for example Blomqvist's β or Gini's γ. Moreover, there exist axiomatic approaches and many specific examples that generalize the idea of bivariate concordance measures to the d-variate case; a nice summary is provided in [Schmid et al. (2011)]. Such extensions allow us to measure the amount of dependence in a d-variate random vector.

FAQ 3.2.8 (What is implemented in R?)
The empirical versions of Person's correlation ρ, Kendall's τ, and Spearman's ρ_S can all be computed using the command `cor()`, with respective method specified. The functions `cor.test()` from the package `stats` and `Kendall()` from the package `Kendall` additionally return p-values for a test of independence.

3.3 Tail Dependence

Especially in financial applications we often face situations where we are concerned with extreme events. Examples are credit portfolios where default events have small probability and we want to model the probability of joint default events. An example from asset management is the joint drop of two (or more) stocks. In both cases, loosely speaking, it is not the 'center of the joint distribution' that matters to us but the 'tails'. In several real world situations it is reasonable to argue that dependence increases in the face of adverse events, due to, for example, herd behavior effects (panic selling) or technical reasons (broken limits automatically trigger further sales). In terms of asset management this means that diversification breaks down just when it is needed the most. To acknowledge joint extreme events a joint distribution is needed that puts probability mass on such events. The notion of tail dependence relates to questions like 'given X_1 is extreme, what is the conditional probability of X_2 also being extreme?' and formulates these precise mathematically. Consider the random vector (X_1, X_2) with copula C and marginal distribution functions F_1 and F_2. To quantify the event 'X_2 is extremely small' we say that X_2 is smaller than its α-quantile $F_2^{-1}(\alpha)$ for some α close to zero.[7] Given that event we can now compute the conditional probability of X_1 to be smaller than its α-quantile $F_1^{-1}(\alpha)$. The notion of (lower-) tail dependence is achieved when we let α tend to zero, as done in Definition 3.3.1. A graphical illustration is given in Figure 3.5.

---

[6] An extensive comparison is provided in [Kojadinovic, Yan (2010)].
[7] Note that the comparison of X_1, X_2 by their respective quantiles makes it independent of the marginal laws and allows us to express all involved probabilities in terms of the underlying copula C.

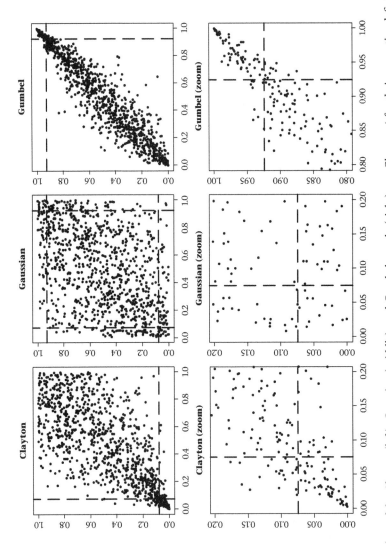

Figure 3.5 Scatter plots of the Clayton (left), Gaussian (middle), and Gumbel copula (right), see Chapter 4 for their respective definitions. In the second row we zoom into the corners for a better visualization. The Clayton copula has positive lower-tail dependence but zero upper-tail dependence, the Gaussian copula has zero tail dependence for both quantities, and the Gumbel copula has positive upper-tail dependence but no lower-tail dependence. This is visualized using vertical and horizontal bars that reflect $\alpha = 0.075$ and $\alpha = 0.925$, respectively; imagine these bars moving to zero or one. Note the increased number of points close to the corners in all cases where the copula has the respective tail dependence property. Loosely speaking, tail dependence is visualized in scatter plots by accumulations of observations in the respective corner.

Definition 3.3.1 (Tail dependence)

The lower- and upper-tail dependence coefficients of (X_1, X_2) with copula C are defined as

$$LTD_C := \lim_{\alpha \searrow 0} \mathbb{P}(X_1 \leq F_1^{-1}(\alpha)|X_2 \leq F_2^{-1}(\alpha)) = \lim_{u \searrow 0} \frac{C(u,u)}{u}, \tag{3.4}$$

$$UTD_C := \lim_{\alpha \nearrow 1} \mathbb{P}(X_1 > F_1^{-1}(\alpha)|X_2 > F_2^{-1}(\alpha)) = \lim_{u \nearrow 1} \frac{C(u,u) - 2u + 1}{1 - u}, \tag{3.5}$$

provided that these limits exist. Moreover, it is worth mentioning that the idea of tail dependence has also been generalized to dimensions beyond two, see [Frahm (2006), Li (2009)].

FAQ 3.3.2 (Can I estimate tail dependence coefficients from data?)

Estimating tail dependence coefficients from data is challenging, since this corresponds to estimating a property in the limit from finitely many points of data. If one knows the parametric family that is behind the given data, then one typically estimates the parameters and computes the tail dependence coefficients from the functional form of the copula. There also exist, however, proposals for non-parametric estimates, see [Schmidt, Stadtmüller (2006)].

EXERCISES

1. Show that in the four stochastic models of Figure 3.3, the random variables X_1 and X_2 are indeed uncorrelated.

2. In the exponential case of Example 3.1.3, explicitly compute the bound $\rho_\oplus = 1$ analytically via the formula for the correlation. Note that this is more involved than exploiting the stochastic representation of the comonotonicity copula.

3. The formulas in Equation (3.1) can efficiently be computed from the stochastic representations $X_1 := \exp(Z)$ and $X_2 := \exp(\pm \sigma Z)$, where $Z \sim \mathcal{N}(0,1)$, and the moment generating function of the standard normal distribution. Use this ansatz to verify the stated results.

4. Consider the Farlie–Gumbel–Morgenstern family $C_\theta(u_1, u_2) = u_1 u_2 + \theta u_1 u_2 (1 - u_1)(1 - u_2)$, see [Morgenstern (1956), Farlie (1960), Gumbel (1960)], and compute the theoretical values of Kendall's τ and Spearman's ρ_S as functions of the parameter θ. Observe that these do not fill the full range $[-1, 1]$.

5. Blomqvist's β: [Blomqvist (1950)] introduced the following measure of association for a random vector (X_1, X_2) with continuous marginals and medians $\tilde{x}_i = F_i^{-1}(0.5)$, $i = 1, 2$:

$$\beta(X_1, X_2) := \mathbb{P}((X_1 - \tilde{x}_1)(X_2 - \tilde{x}_2) > 0) - \mathbb{P}((X_1 - \tilde{x}_1)(X_2 - \tilde{x}_2) < 0),$$

called '*Blomqvist's β*'.

   a. Show that $\beta(X_1, X_2) = \beta_C$ depends solely on the copula of (X_1, X_2).

   b. Show that

$$\beta_C = 4\,C(0.5, 0.5) - 1$$

$$= \frac{C(0.5, 0.5) - \Pi_2(0.5, 0.5) + \bar{C}(0.5, 0.5) - \bar{\Pi}_2(0.5, 0.5)}{M_2(0.5, 0.5) - \Pi_2(0.5, 0.5) + \bar{M}_2(0.5, 0.5) - \bar{\Pi}_2(0.5, 0.5)}.$$

   Notice that the last formula implies an immediate extension to the multivariate case.

6. Show that Kendall's τ and Spearman's ρ_S for the comonotonicity (countermonotonicity) copula are one (minus one).

7. Consider the Cuadras–Augé copula $C_\alpha(u_1, u_2) = \min\{u_1, u_2\} \max\{u_1, u_2\}^{1-\alpha}$, where $\alpha \in [0, 1]$. Compute the tail dependence coefficients as functions of α.

8. Suppose the lower-tail dependence coefficient LTD_C for some copula exists. Show that $UTD_{\hat{C}} = LTD_C$. What does that mean if C is radially symmetric?

4 What Are Popular Families of Copulas?

This chapter reviews basic facts about the most commonly applied copula families. These comprise Gaussian copulas, t-copulas, and Archimedean copulas, as well as extreme-value copulas.

4.1 Gaussian Copulas

If $Y_1, \ldots, Y_d$ are independent, standard normally distributed random variables, $\mu_1, \ldots, \mu_d \in \mathbb{R}$, and $A = (a_{i,j}) \in \mathbb{R}^{d \times d}$ a matrix with full rank, the random vector

$$X := \begin{pmatrix} X_1 \\ \vdots \\ X_d \end{pmatrix} = \begin{pmatrix} \mu_1 \\ \vdots \\ \mu_d \end{pmatrix} + A \cdot \begin{pmatrix} Y_1 \\ \vdots \\ Y_d \end{pmatrix} = \begin{pmatrix} \mu_1 + a_{1,1} Y_1 + \cdots + a_{1,d} Y_d \\ \vdots \\ \mu_d + a_{d,1} Y_1 + \cdots + a_{d,d} Y_d \end{pmatrix} \in \mathbb{R}^d \quad (4.1)$$

is said to have a multivariate normal distribution. For each $j = 1, \ldots, d$, the j-th component X_j has a normal distribution with mean μ_j and variance $\sigma_j^2 := \sum_{l=1}^{d} a_{j,l}^2$. We furthermore denote by Σ the correlation matrix of $(X_1, \ldots, X_d)$, that is, the entry $\rho_{j,k}$ in row j and column k of Σ is defined by Pearson's correlation coefficient $\rho_{j,k} = \mathrm{Cor}(X_j, X_k), j, k = 1, \ldots, d$, see Chapter 3. Since the marginal laws are continuous (they are all univariate normal distributions), the copula of $(X_1, \ldots, X_d)$ is unique by virtue of Sklar's Theorem 1.2.4, and the corresponding copulas are called 'Gaussian copulas'. It can be shown that a Gaussian copula is independent of $\mu_1, \ldots, \mu_d$ and $\sigma_1^2, \ldots, \sigma_d^2$, see Exercise 1. Consequently, it is parameterized solely by Σ and we denote it by C_Σ. This is a remarkable fact, since thus the bivariate pairs, respectively pair correlations, already fully specify the multivariate distribution.

For $d = 2$ the Gaussian copula only depends on a single parameter $\rho := \rho_{1,2} = \rho_{2,1}$ (due to symmetry of the correlation coefficient), since

$$\Sigma = \begin{pmatrix} 1 & \rho \\ \rho & 1 \end{pmatrix}$$

in this case. We therefore denote the one-parametric bivariate Gaussian copula by C_ρ instead of C_Σ. It is given by

$$C_\rho(u_1, u_2) = \int_0^{u_1} \int_0^{u_2} \frac{\exp\left(\frac{2\rho\, \Phi^{-1}(v_1)\,\Phi^{-1}(v_2) - \rho^2\left(\Phi^{-1}(v_1)^2 + \Phi^{-1}(v_2)^2 \right)}{2(1-\rho^2)} \right)}{\sqrt{1-\rho^2}} \, dv_2 \, dv_1, \quad (4.2)$$

where $\Phi(x) := \int_{-\infty}^{x} \exp(-y^2/2)\,dy/\sqrt{2\pi}$ denotes the distribution function of a standard normally distributed random variable. From this algebraic expression for the Gaussian copula we can make two immediate, but important, observations. (i) The Gaussian copula is absolutely continuous, that is, it admits a copula density, which is precisely the function under the (double) integral in Equation (4.2). This density has already been visualized in Figure 2.4. (ii) Both the numerical evaluation and the analytical study of the Gaussian copula are burdensome because of the appearing double integral. Further important properties of the Gaussian copula are summarized in the subsequent paragraph.

FAQ 4.1.1 (The normal law is omnipresent in applications. Why so?)
There are a few reasons, of which we list a couple in the sequel.

(a) **Natural appearance**: Consider a random vector $\mathbf{X}$ with existing mean vector $\boldsymbol{\mu}$ and existing covariance matrix Σ. The (multivariate) central limit theorem states that when the same random experiment $\mathbf{X}$ is repeated in n independent trials, say $\mathbf{X}^{(1)}, \ldots, \mathbf{X}^{(n)}$, then the $\sqrt{n}$-scaled deviation from the mean $\frac{1}{\sqrt{n}} \sum_{i=1}^{n} (\mathbf{X}^{(i)} - \boldsymbol{\mu})$ has approximately a multivariate normal law with zero mean vector and covariance matrix Σ. Since probability theory is often used to model the random dispersion of some unknown future quantities around their expected values in applications, the central limit theorem provides a solid justification for the use of a normal distribution in such a model.

(b) **Mathematical tractability**: The multivariate normal distribution has an intrinsic, close connection to the theory of linear algebra. For instance, vectors of linear combinations of components of a multivariate normal random vector are again multivariate normal: if $\mathbf{X}$ is multivariate normal with mean vector $\boldsymbol{\mu} \in \mathbb{R}^d$ and covariance matrix $\Sigma \in \mathbb{R}^{d \times d}$, and $A \in \mathbb{R}^{m \times d}$, then $A\mathbf{X}$ is multivariate normal with mean vector $A\boldsymbol{\mu} \in \mathbb{R}^m$ and covariance matrix $A\Sigma A' \in \mathbb{R}^{m \times m}$. Many applications, for example the construction of factor models, the derivation of confidence intervals for hypothesis testing and estimation, and so on, can be deduced by resorting to the well-established apparatus of linear algebra.

(c) **Convenient parameterization**: The mean vector and covariance matrix specify the distribution completely. A finite number of parameters is a very convenient assumption for applications, in particular in large dimensions. Even better, resorting to the aforementioned toolbox of linear algebra, it is not too difficult to construct low-parametric families of multivariate normal distributions even for very large dimensions, for example by specifying only a small number of driving factors (for example 'principal component analysis') and linearly combining them to build a high-dimensional covariance matrix from the bottom up.

(d) **Intuitive stochastic model**: Along with the previous bullet point goes a quick-to-grasp intuitive understanding of the stochastic nature behind the multivariate normal law. The covariance matrix Σ specifies a certain 'dispersion area' around the expected mean $\boldsymbol{\mu}$. As mentioned earlier, many applications rely on the idea of modeling an expected outcome and certain dispersion around it, for which the normal distribution is a natural candidate.

(e) **Common ground**: Everyone knows the multivariate normal distribution, because it is already taught at universities worldwide in basic lectures. Its popularity in applications also stems from the fact that people from the applied sciences often do not know other multivariate distributions at all, so they naturally resort to the normal law simply because of a lack of alternatives.

As a consequence of these reasons, the multivariate normal distribution is by far the most popular distribution in financial (and other) applications. Unfortunately, in the past it has also been applied in situations when the real phenomenon to be modeled did not fit the interpretation of a dispersion around a mean so well, that is, when the normal distribution was not a lucky choice.

4.1.1 Important Stylized Facts of the (Bivariate) Gaussian Copula

A reader-friendly and comprehensive overview of properties of the bivariate Gaussian copula C_ρ can be found in [Meyer (2013)]. We collect the key features in the following.

(a) **Dependence range:** With ρ ranging in $[-1,1]$, the Gaussian copula C_ρ interpolates between the lower Fréchet–Hoeffding bound $C_{-1} = W_2$ and the upper Fréchet–Hoeffding bound $C_1 = M_2$. Moreover, the case of independence is included for $\rho = 0$, that is, $C_0 = \Pi$. This interpolation property allows us to model the full spectrum of dependence and is a very desirable feature of the model. In particular, it provides the parameter ρ with an intuitive meaning: dependence increases with ρ.

(b) **Concordance measures:** The following formulas for bivariate concordance measures are known for the Gaussian copula (see [Meyer (2013)] for references regarding their derivations):

$$\tau_\rho = \frac{2}{\pi} \arcsin(\rho), \qquad \text{(Kendall's } \tau\text{)}$$

$$\rho_S = \frac{6}{\pi} \arcsin(\rho/2), \qquad \text{(Spearman's } \rho_S\text{)}$$

$$\beta_\rho = \tau_\rho = \frac{2}{\pi} \arcsin(\rho). \qquad \text{(Blomqvist's } \beta\text{)}$$

(c) **Symmetries:** The Gaussian copula exhibits two very strong symmetries. (i) It is radially symmetric (even in all dimensions d), that is, it is equal to its own survival copula $C_\rho = \hat{C}_\rho$. When looking at scatter plots from the Gaussian copula (see Figure 4.1) this means intuitively that the points are scattered symmetrically around the counterdiagonal $\{(u_1, u_2) \in [0,1]^2 : u_2 = 1 - u_1\}$. (ii) The bivariate Gaussian copula is exchangeable, that is, it is invariant under permutations of its arguments $C_\rho(u_1, u_2) = C_\rho(u_2, u_1)$. When looking at scatter plots from the Gaussian copula (see Figure 4.1) this means intuitively that the points are scattered symmetrically around the diagonal $\{(u_1, u_2) \in [0,1]^2 : u_2 = u_1\}$. Both symmetry properties can lead to serious problems when it comes to financial modeling, which is pointed out in FAQ 4.1.2 and FAQ 4.1.3.

(d) **Tail independence:** The lower-tail dependence coefficient of the bivariate Gaussian copula with $\rho \in (-1, 1)$, that is, the limit of the expression $C_\rho(u, u)/u$

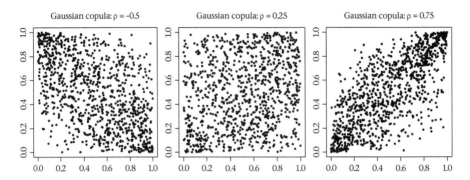

Figure 4.1   Scatter plots of the bivariate Gaussian copula with correlations $\rho = -0.5$ (left), $\rho = 0.25$ (middle), and $\rho = 0.75$ (right). Observe the great level of symmetry.

as u tends to zero, equals zero. By radial symmetry it immediately follows that the upper-tail dependence coefficient, that is, the limit of the expression $(C_\rho(u,u) - 2u + 1)/(1 - u)$ as u tends to one, equals zero as well. Thus, one says the Gaussian copula exhibits tail independence, which might not be desirable in the context of financial modeling, see FAQ 4.1.4.

Due to the popularity of the multivariate normal distribution and the lack of knowledge about other multivariate distributions in the pre-copula days, Gaussian copulas were naturally the first candidates to be applied by financial engineers when copula modeling became popular. With increasing research activity in the field of financial dependence modeling, people became aware of the fact that this first choice was not really appropriate for many applications and required a revision. That is why researchers explored other copulas, and some of these achievements are presented in this book. The following three questions aim to explain some critical aspects regarding Gaussian copulas.

FAQ 4.1.2 (What might be a problem with radial symmetry?)

Two of the most common financial modeling tasks, for which copulas are applied frequently, are (i) modeling the dependence between asset returns, and (ii) modeling the dependence between companies' default times. Unfortunately, for both tasks radial asymmetry is typically a desired property, and hence the Gaussian copula is inadequate. Regarding the dependence between two stock returns, some empirical studies, see, for example, [Ang, Chen (2002)], find that, on the one hand, joint negative returns can be observed quite frequently, for example because they are triggered by the same macro-event affecting both stock prices. On the other hand, joint positive returns are observed much less frequently, because positive stock returns are mostly of idiosyncratic nature and not triggered by macro-events. Regarding the dependence between two companies' default times, it is crucial for applications in risk management not to underestimate the effects that are caused by a joint early default of both companies, because such an event is typically the most severe scenario to consider. In the language of copulas, the most common way to quantify this effect is by applying a copula with positive lower-tail dependence for the default times.[1] However, if a radially symmetric copula is applied, this means intuitively that the dependence in the event of a joint long survival of both companies is the same as the dependence in the event of a joint early default. Similarly to the case of stock-return modeling, the event of a long survival of a company is intuitively rather expected to be driven by idiosyncratic factors and the long survival of the other company has only a secondary effect, if at all.

FAQ 4.1.3 (When is exchangeability critical?)
When combining an exchangeable copula with inhomogeneous marginals to a multivariate distribution, one must be very careful. To demonstrate this fact we construct a vector of two companies' default times X_1 and X_2. We firstly choose two marginal distributions, say X_1 and X_2 are both exponentially distributed with parameters $\lambda_1 > 0$ and $\lambda_2 > 0$, respectively. Secondly, we model the dependence between both default times by the Gaussian copula C_ρ. How can we understand the constructed dependence model between the two default times X_1 and X_2? It is intuitive (but wrong!) to think that under perfect dependence ($\rho = 1$) both default times coincide, because a joint default is commonly thought of as being the result of extreme dependence. In the same spirit, one might think that with increasing dependence, measured in terms of ρ, it becomes more likely that the two default times are close to each other. However, this intuition is only true if $\lambda_1 = \lambda_2$. If the marginals are different, we say inhomogeneous, we have modeled something that might not at all agree with this intuition. The problem is the incompatibility (in terms of a meaningful model for the present situation) of the copula and the marginals. Due to exchangeability, the density of the bivariate Gaussian copula is symmetric about the diagonal $\{u_1 = u_2\}$. Increasing the dependence via ρ squeezes the probability mass closer to the diagonal $\{u_1 = u_2\}$, eventually pushing it completely onto the diagonal for $\rho = 1$. This effect can be observed from Figure 2.4 in terms of the density. For homogeneous marginals, the diagonal corresponds to the event $\{X_1 = X_2\}$, which means that both default times coincide. This interpretation is lost with inhomogeneous marginals. When ρ tends to the boundary case, in the limit $\rho = 1$ we obtain the equality $X_2 = (\lambda_1/\lambda_2) X_1$. If $\lambda_1 = \lambda_2$, then both defaults happen at precisely the same time and our intuition holds true. In the case of inhomogeneous marginals $\lambda_1 \neq \lambda_2$, however, the default of one entity triggers the certain default of the other entity at a later point in time, which depends on the choice of the marginal distributions. So the choice of the marginal distributions has a strong influence on the time span between the two default times, even though this time span is a quantity that is intuitively rather viewed as being governed solely by the dependence between default times. When $\rho < 1$ the same effect is present, only in alleviated form, so this example is not academic. To make our point more concrete, consider a numeric example (visualized in Figure 4.2): assume that $\lambda_1 = 0.1$ and $\lambda_2 = 0.2$, meaning that the expected lifetime of X_1 is 10 years and the expected lifetime of X_2 is 5 years. Then with ρ approaching one, the probability that X_1 is roughly twice as big as X_2 is increasing, and in fact the probability that X_1 is close to X_2 decreases. If one wants to stick with inhomogeneous marginals, but desires a dependence parameter which increases the probability for a joint default, then one has

---

[1] Equivalently, positive upper-tail dependence coefficients for the survival copula of the default times.

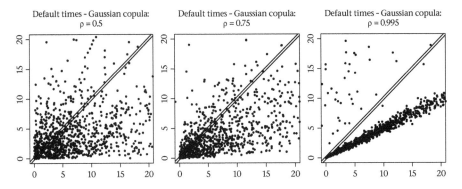

Figure 4.2   Simulated default times (X_1, X_2). The dependence is modeled via a Gaussian copula with varying parameter $\rho \in \{0.5, 0.75, 0.995\}$, the marginal laws are exponential with rates $\lambda_1 = 0.1$ and $\lambda_2 = 0.2$. The emphasized area around the diagonal illustrates the region $|X_1 - X_2| \leq 1/4$, that is, all scenarios where both defaults take place within one quarter of a year. On the right where ρ is close to the limiting case $\rho = 1$, X_1 is almost precisely twice as big as X_2.

to use an appropriate non-exchangeable copula, which depends on the marginals. For more on this topic, the reader is referred to Section 7.2.

The model for two default times constructed in FAQ 4.1.3 from a Gaussian copula and exponential marginal distributions is not uncommon in counterparty credit-risk modeling. For instance, the default time X_1 might be associated with a CDS protection seller[2] and the default time X_2 with the respective CDS's underlying reference entity in order to compute a so-called credit valuation adjustment (CVA). The CVA is an adjustment the CDS protection buyer has to make in order to take into account her counterparty risk with respect to the protection seller. This is the risk that the CDS protection becomes worthless in case the CDS protection seller herself defaults earlier than, or at the same time as, the underlying reference entity. With increasing dependence between the reference entity and the CDS protection seller one expects the CVA to increase, because intuitively one expects the probability for a joint default to increase. However, as FAQ 4.1.3 shows, this need not be the case if dependence is modeled poorly. For precise mathematical treatments of CVA in the context of credit default swaps, [Brigo, Chourdakis(2009), Brigo et al. (2013), Brigo et al. (2014)].

FAQ 4.1.4 (What is the problem with tail independence?)
The notion of tail dependence has gained increasing popularity in the field of credit-risk modeling, because it aims to quantify something that is not easy to measure in general, but important to risk-management departments: dependence in extremely distressed situations. Therefore, both researchers and practitioners have gratefully picked up the notion of tail dependence and use it frequently as a common ground to discuss a model's capability to deal with this challenging task, and also to compare different models. Estimates for the tail-dependence coefficient might be used as a basis for the quantification of capital requirements due to the possibility of an extreme scenario. Clearly, a model with zero tail dependence cannot be used for

---

[2] CDS is the abbreviation for credit default swap, see FAQ 7.2.1 for details.

such applications. In fact, the popularity of t-copulas, see Section 4.1.2 below, as an alternative to the Gaussian copula can be explained precisely by the fact that it has positive tail dependence coefficients.

4.1.2 Generalization to Elliptical Copulas

When copula modeling became popular, Gaussian copulas were the first to be applied because the multivariate normal law is the best known multivariate distribution. When looking for alternatives, academic researchers quickly realized that there already existed quite a convenient concept for generalizing the multivariate normal law: so-called elliptical distributions. The latter are a superclass of normal distributions sharing the feature that the popular concept of correlation coefficients is involved. Like in the case of the multivariate normal distributions, one can extract the implicit copula behind an elliptical distribution, leading to so-called elliptical copulas. For detailed background on the latter, we refer the interested reader to the textbooks [Fang et al. (1990), McNeil et al. (2005), Mai, Scherer (2012)]. Since the so-called t-copula is really the only elliptical copula (besides the Gaussian copula) whose popularity in financial applications is worth mentioning in an introductory outlet such as the present book, we only discuss t-copulas in some more detail.

Loosely speaking, t-copulas are like Gaussian copulas with the most obvious difference of exhibiting positive tail dependence coefficients. However, they are also radially symmetric and the bivariate t-copula is also exchangeable. Its definition and key features are listed in the following. Like Gaussian copulas are derived from multivariate normal laws, t-copulas are the (unique) copulas associated with multivariate t-distributions. In order to define the latter, we require the notion of an 'inverse Gamma distribution'. A random variable W is said to have an inverse Gamma distribution if it has the same probability law as the reciprocal of a Gamma-distributed random variable. Defining it formally in terms of its density, we say that W has an inverse Gamma distribution with parameters $\beta, \eta > 0$, and write $W \sim Inv\Gamma(\beta, \eta)$, if W has probability density function

$$f_W(x) = \mathbf{1}_{\{x>0\}} \frac{\eta^\beta \, e^{-\eta/x}}{x^{\beta+1} \Gamma(\beta)}.$$

Observe that this equals the density of $1/Z$ if Z has a Gamma distribution with parameters $\beta, \eta > 0$, which might be defined via its Laplace transform

$$\mathbb{E}\left[e^{-xZ}\right] = \left(1 + \frac{x}{\eta}\right)^{-\beta}, \quad x \geq 0. \tag{4.3}$$

With $Y_1, \ldots, Y_d$ independent and identically distributed according to a standard normal law, an independent random variable $W \sim Inv\Gamma(\nu/2, \nu/2)$ for some $\nu > 0$,

$\mu_1,\ldots,\mu_d \in \mathbb{R}$, and a matrix $A = (a_{i,j}) \in \mathbb{R}^{d\times d}$ with full rank, the random vector

$$
\begin{pmatrix} X_1 \\ \vdots \\ X_d \end{pmatrix} = \begin{pmatrix} \mu_1 \\ \vdots \\ \mu_d \end{pmatrix} + A \cdot \sqrt{W} \begin{pmatrix} Y_1 \\ \vdots \\ Y_d \end{pmatrix} = \begin{pmatrix} \mu_1 + a_{1,1}\sqrt{W}\,Y_1 + \cdots + a_{1,d}\sqrt{W}\,Y_d \\ \vdots \\ \mu_d + a_{d,1}\sqrt{W}\,Y_1 + \cdots + a_{d,d}\sqrt{W}\,Y_d \end{pmatrix} \in \mathbb{R}^d
$$

$$(4.4)$$

is said to have a '*multivariate t-distribution*' with ν degrees of freedom. Comparing (4.4) with (4.1), the sole difference is the appearance of the inverse Gamma random variable W. Since we observe from (4.3) that the Laplace transform of a Gamma-distributed random variable with parameters $\eta = \beta = \nu/2$ tends to the Laplace transform $x \mapsto \exp(-x)$ of the constant one as $\nu \to \infty$, it follows that the multivariate t-distribution converges (in law) to the multivariate normal distribution as the degrees of freedom ν tend to infinity. In this sense, the t-distribution can be viewed as a generalization of the normal distribution. A copula is said to be a '*t-copula*' if it is derived from a multivariate t-distribution via Sklar's Theorem by standardizing the univariate marginals. Similarly to the case of the Gaussian copula, it is independent of the means $\mu_1,\ldots,\mu_d$ and only depends on the degrees of freedom ν and a correlation matrix $\Sigma \in \mathbb{R}^{d\times d}$, which is defined by

$$
\Sigma_{i,j} := \frac{\sum_{k=1}^{d} a_{i,k}\, a_{j,k}}{\sqrt{\sum_{k=1}^{d} a_{i,k}^2 \sum_{k=1}^{d} a_{j,k}^2}}, \quad i,j = 1,\ldots,d,
$$

and we denote it by $C_{\nu,\Sigma}$. Please be aware that Σ is not the correlation matrix of $(X_1,\ldots,X_d)$. It is only a parameter that has to be a correlation matrix. The degrees of freedom ν also affect the final correlation matrix of $(X_1,\ldots,X_d)$.

In two dimensions, Σ is given by a single parameter ρ like in the Gaussian case and we denote the bivariate t-copula by $C_{\nu,\rho}$, which results in a two-parametric family of copulas. It is given by the following expression:

$$
C_{\nu,\rho}(u_1, u_2)
$$
$$
= \int_0^{u_1}\!\!\int_0^{u_2} \frac{\frac{\nu}{2}\Gamma\left(\frac{\nu}{2}\right)^2 \left(1 + \frac{t_\nu^{-1}(\nu_1)^2 + t_\nu^{-1}(\nu_2)^2 - 2\rho\, t_\nu^{-1}(\nu_1)\, t_\nu^{-1}(\nu_2)}{\nu(1-\rho^2)}\right)^{-\frac{\nu+2}{2}}}{\sqrt{1-\rho^2}\,\Gamma\left(\frac{\nu+1}{2}\right)^2 \left(\left(1 + \frac{t_\nu^{-1}(\nu_1)^2}{\nu}\right)\left(1 + \frac{t_\nu^{-1}(\nu_2)^2}{\nu}\right)\right)^{-\frac{\nu+1}{2}}}\, d\nu_2\, d\nu_1,
$$

where $t_\nu(x) := \int_{-\infty}^{x}(1 + y^2/\nu)^{-(\nu+1)/2}\, dy\, \Gamma((\nu+1)/2)/\sqrt{\nu\pi}\,/\Gamma(\nu/2)$ denotes the distribution function of a random variable which has a univariate t-distribution with ν degrees of freedom. Thus, we observe that it is an absolutely continuous copula. Figure 4.3 shows a scatter plot and the density of a bivariate t-copula, as well as the bivariate t-copula itself. Further key features of the bivariate t-copula are collected in the following.

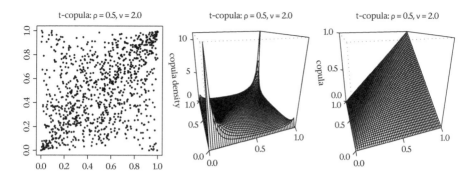

Figure 4.3 Scatter plot (left) and density (middle) of a bivariate t-copula, as well as the copula itself (right).

(a) **Symmetries:** Like the bivariate Gaussian copula, the bivariate t-copula is both radially symmetric and exchangeable. For many applications this causes the same problems that are described in FAQs 4.1.2 and 4.1.3 for the bivariate Gaussian copula.

(b) **Concordance measures:** Kendall's τ and Spearman's ρ_S for the bivariate t-copula are the same as for the bivariate Gaussian copula.[3] In particular, they do not depend on the degrees of freedom ν. More clearly, we have

$$\tau = \frac{2}{\pi} \arcsin(\rho), \qquad \text{(Kendall's } \tau)$$

$$\rho_S = \frac{6}{\pi} \arcsin(\rho/2). \qquad \text{(Spearman's } \rho_S)$$

(c) **Tail dependence:** Due to radial symmetry, the lower- and upper-tail dependence coefficients are identical. However, unlike in the case of the Gaussian copula, they are not zero. They are given by

$$UTD_{\nu,\rho} = LTD_{\nu,\rho} = 2 \cdot t_{\nu+1}\left(-\sqrt{\frac{(\nu+1)(1-\rho)}{1+\rho}}\right).$$

4.2 Archimedean Copulas

Elliptical copulas have, for some applications, two drawbacks: (i) their algebraic expression is complicated,[4] and (ii) their great level of symmetry. These facts triggered

---

[3] This follows, intuitively, because a multiplication with the inverse-Gamma variable does not change the ranks.

[4] For elliptical distributions and copulas it is much more natural to work with (copula) densities or characteristic functions than with distribution functions.

the search for multivariate distribution functions and copulas with convenient algebraic expression (sometimes termed explicit copulas, as opposed to implicit copulas) that can also account for asymmetries. One of the most popular families of copulas which can accomplish both is the class of '*Archimedean copulas*'. A copula $C_\varphi = \Pi_d$, is an Archimedean copula if it has the functional form[5]

$$C_\varphi(u_1,\ldots,u_d) = \varphi(\varphi^{-1}(u_1) + \cdots + \varphi^{-1}(u_d)), \qquad (4.5)$$

for a suitable, non-increasing function $\varphi : [0,\infty) \to [0,1]$ with $\varphi(0) = 1$ and $\lim_{x \to \infty} \varphi(x) = 0$, called the '*(Archimedean) generator*'. A result of [Malov (2001)] shows that a necessary and sufficient condition on the generator φ for C_φ to be a proper distribution function is '*d-monotonicity*', see also [McNeil, Nešlehová (2009)] who provide a probabilistic interpretation for this notion and derive a stochastic model for Archimedean copulas. For the precise definition of d-monotonicity we refer the interested reader to [Williamson (1956), Malov (2001), McNeil, Nešlehová (2009)]. We denote by Φ_d the set of all d-monotone Archimedean generators. It is known that $\Phi_2 \supsetneq \Phi_3 \supsetneq \ldots \supsetneq \Phi_\infty$, where Φ_∞ denotes the set of all '*completely monotone*' generators, that is, all φ with $\varphi(0) = 1$, which are infinitely often differentiable on the interior of their domain $(0,\infty)$, continuous at zero, and the derivatives satisfy $(-1)^k \varphi^{(k)}(x) \geq 0$ for all $x > 0, k \in \mathbb{N}_0$, where $\varphi^{(k)}$ denotes the k-th derivative of φ and $\varphi^{(0)} := \varphi$. In the present book we focus on completely monotone generators, because proper d-monotone generators are mainly of academic interest and appear only rarely in financial applications.[6] Each function $\varphi \in \Phi_\infty$ can be applied to define a copula in arbitrary dimension $d \geq 2$. By the seminal Bernstein Theorem, the set Φ_∞ coincides with the set of Laplace transforms of probability measures on $(0,\infty)$. The original reference is [Bernstein (1929)], see also [Schilling et al. (2010), Theorem 1.4, p. 3]. More clearly, for $\varphi \in \Phi_\infty$ there exists a positive random variable M, which is unique in distribution, such that φ can be written as $\varphi(u) = \mathbb{E}[\exp(-uM)], u \geq 0$. To provide an example, the function $\varphi(x) = \exp(-x)$ is completely monotone, since

$$\varphi^{(k)}(x) = (-1)^k \varphi(x), \quad k \geq 0, x \geq 0,$$

so that the derivatives have alternating signs as desired. Indeed, the random variable M is constantly one in this case. Interestingly, when putting this particular function $\varphi(x) = \exp(-x)$ into Definition (4.5) for an Archimedean copula, we observe that $\varphi^{-1}(y) = -\log(y)$ and $C_\varphi = \Pi_d$, showing that the independence copula is included in the Archimedean family. Since Laplace transforms of positive random variables are well-studied objects in probability theory, there exist quite a few example of Laplace transforms with nice algebraic expressions, which imply nice algebraic expressions for Archimedean copulas. Table 4.1 gathers the most popular Archimedean copulas and

---

[5] Some textbooks and papers interchange the roles of φ and φ^{-1}. Hence, some caution is required when working with different sources.

[6] The interested reader is referred to the reference [McNeil, Nešlehová (2009)] for background knowledge on d-monotone generators and their associated Archimedean copulas.

Table 4.1. *Popular completely monotone generators of Archimedean copulas.*

$\varphi_\theta(x)$	$\varphi_\theta^{-1}(y)$	$\theta \in$	name of copula	Kendall's τ
$(1+x)^{-1/\theta}$	$y^{-\theta} - 1$	$(0,\infty)$	Clayton	$\theta/(2+\theta)$
$e^{-x^{1/\theta}}$	$(-\log(y))^\theta$	$[1,\infty)$	Gumbel	$(\theta-1)/\theta$
$\dfrac{1-\theta}{e^x-\theta}$	$\log\left(\dfrac{1-\theta}{y}+\theta\right)$	$[0,1)$	Ali–Mikhail–Haq	$1-2\left(\theta+(1-\theta)^2\log(1-\theta)\right)/(3\theta^2)$

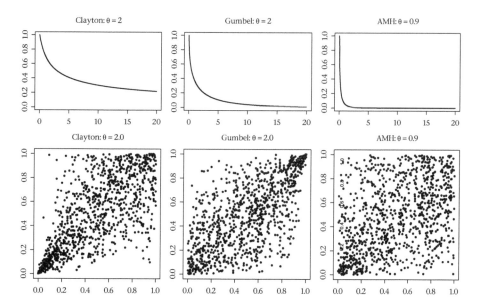

Figure 4.4   Scatter plots from different Archimedean copulas, and their respective generators.

their respective generators. Scatter plots from the three presented families are provided in Figure 4.4.

Regarding a stochastic representation for Archimedean copulas, the following (conveniently simple) model is originally due to [Marshall, Olkin (1988)]: if $\epsilon_1,\ldots,\epsilon_d$ are iid random variables with exponential distribution and mean one, that is, $\epsilon_j \sim \mathcal{E}(1)$ for $j = 1,\ldots,d$, and M is an independent positive random variable with Laplace transform φ, then the random vector

$$(U_1,\ldots,U_d) := \left(\varphi\left(\frac{\epsilon_1}{M}\right),\ldots,\varphi\left(\frac{\epsilon_d}{M}\right)\right) \tag{4.6}$$

has the copula C_φ as joint distribution function. This stochastic model provides a convenient recipe on how to simulate from Archimedean copulas and can be used to derive several important properties, of which we collect a few in the subsequent paragraph.

FAQ 4.2.1 (Where does the name 'Archimedean' come from?)
The *'Archimedean property'* traditionally refers to some set having an infinitely small or infinitely large element. For instance, the positive real numbers $(0, \infty)$ have the property that for any given number $\epsilon > 0$ we can find a smaller, positive number $\delta < \epsilon$. [Ling (1965)] studied so-called associative *'triangular norms'*, which are associative functions $T : [0, 1]^2 \to [0, 1]$ subject to certain properties. In particular, he was interested in their serial iterates $T^n : [0, 1]^{n+1} \to [0, 1]$, defined iteratively via $T^n(u_1, \ldots, u_{n+1}) := T(T^{n-1}(u_1, \ldots, u_n), u_{n+1})$ for $n \geq 3$. An Archimedean property for these serial iterates is constituted by demanding for arbitrary $u \in (0, 1)$ that the non-increasing sequence $\{T^n(u, \ldots, u)\}_{n \in \mathbb{N}}$ eventually falls below any arbitrary small level $\epsilon > 0$. [Ling (1965)] showed that associative triangular norms satisfying this property have the representation $T(u_1, u_2) = \varphi(\varphi^{-1}(u_1) + \varphi^{-1}(u_2))$ for some φ, which is precisely the analytic form of an Archimedean copula. In particular, Archimedean copulas share the Archimedean property of associative triangular norms, that is, for arbitrary $\epsilon > 0$ and $u \in (0, 1)$ we find an $n \in \mathbb{N}$ such that

$$C_\varphi(\underbrace{u, \ldots, u}_{n \text{ times}}) = \varphi(n\varphi^{-1}(u)) < \epsilon,$$

which simply follows from the fact that $\varphi(x)$ tends to zero as $x \to \infty$.

4.2.1   Stylized Facts of Archimedean Copulas

Compared to Gaussian copulas, the major differences of Archimedean copulas are their algebraically closed-form expression and their possibility to allow for radial asymmetry as well as positive tail dependence coefficients. However, like the bivariate Gaussian copula, they are also exchangeable, that is, invariant under permutations of their arguments, even in the multivariate case $d \geq 3$, where Gaussian copulas offer the flexibility of being asymmetric. For the reader's convenience we collect the key features in the following.

(a)   **Dependence range:** In theory, Archimedean copulas form an infinite-dimensional space of functions, because they are parameterized in terms of a function φ rather than finitely many parameters such as is the case for Gaussian copulas. In practice, however, one usually chooses a parametric family of Laplace transforms, that is, $\varphi = \varphi_\theta$ for a real parameter θ. Typical examples can be found in Table 4.1, further examples might be looked up in [Nelsen (2006), Charpentier, Segers (2009)]. In this case, the Archimedean copula is governed by a single parameter θ, that is, we may write $C_{\varphi_\theta} = C_\theta$, and the range of θ provides the range of different dependence structures. One can show that for every Laplace transform φ, it holds true that $C_\varphi \geq \Pi_d$ point-wise, see, for example [Mai, Scherer (2012), p. 67]. Intuitively, this means that negative dependence cannot be modeled by Archimedean copulas with completely monotone generators, which also implies that concordance measures are non-negative, see the next bullet point. However, typical Archimedean families, such as the first two in Table 4.1, are such that the independence copula Π_d and the upper Fréchet–Hoeffding bound are included as boundary cases, which is sufficient for most practical tasks.

(b) **Concordance measures**: Providing general useful formulas for concordance measures of an arbitrary Archimedean copula is only possible in terms of an integral involving the function φ, but whether this integral can be computed in convenient algebraically closed form depends highly on the generator. For instance, we have that (see [Genest, MacKay (1986)])

$$\tau = 1 - 4 \int_0^\infty x \cdot (\varphi^{(1)}(x))^2 \, dx, \qquad \text{(Kendall's } \tau) \qquad (4.7)$$

$$\rho_S = 12 \int_0^1 \int_0^1 C_\varphi(u_1, u_2) \, du_2 \, du_1 - 3, \qquad \text{(Spearman's } \rho_S) \qquad (4.8)$$

where the second formula for Spearman's ρ_S is actually valid for an arbitrary (not necessarily Archimedean) copula, see Chapter 3. In Table 4.1 we can see that for all presented families of Archimedean copulas, the concordance measure Kendall's τ is available in closed form. For the Gumbel and the Clayton copula, Kendall's τ ranges from zero to one as the copula parameter ranges within its domain, whereas for the Ali–Mikhail–Haq family one can show that Kendall's τ ranges only between zero and $1/3$, showing that the latter cannot be used to model very strong dependence.

(c) **Tail dependence coefficients**: One of the most striking facts about Archimedean copulas is that they are flexible enough to allow for asymmetric tail dependence coefficients, that is, the upper- and lower-tail dependence coefficients might be different. Moreover, these are given by the following formulas, provided the respective limits exist:[7]

$$LTD_{C_\varphi} = 2 \cdot \lim_{x \nearrow \infty} \frac{\varphi^{(1)}(2x)}{\varphi^{(1)}(x)} = \lim_{x \nearrow \infty} \frac{\varphi(2x)}{\varphi(x)},$$

$$UTD_{C_\varphi} = 2 - 2 \cdot \lim_{x \downarrow 0} \frac{\varphi^{(1)}(2x)}{\varphi^{(1)}(x)}.$$

Revisiting the examples in Table 4.1, we observe the following tail dependencies

$$\text{Clayton:} \quad LTD_\theta = 2^{-1/\theta}, \quad UTD_{C_\theta} = 0,$$

$$\text{Gumbel:} \quad LTD_\theta = 0, \quad UTD_\theta = 2 - 2^{1/\theta},$$

$$\text{Ali–Mikhail–Haq:} \quad LTD_\theta = 0, \quad UTD_\theta = 0,$$

showing that different types of asymmetry patterns can be achieved with Archimedean copulas. An example for an Archimedean copula with both positive upper- and lower-tail dependence is provided by the two-parametric, completely monotone generator $\varphi_{\theta_1,\theta_2}(x) = (1 + x^{\theta_1})^{-1/\theta_2}$ with parameters $\theta_1 \in (0,1]$ and

---

[7] See [Larsson, Nešlehová (2011)] for an example where these limits do not exist.

$\theta_2 \in (0, \infty)$ (so-called '*inner-power Clayton copula*'[8]). We observe that the tail dependence coefficients are given by $UTD_{\theta_1, \theta_2} = 2 - 2^{\theta_1}$ and $LTD_{\theta_1, \theta_2} = 2^{-\theta_1/\theta_2}$. Note that the Clayton copula arises as a special case for $\theta_1 = 1$.

(d) **Density**: Archimedean copulas with completely monotone generator are absolutely continuous and their density is obtained by taking iteratively the partial derivatives of $C_\varphi(u_1, \ldots, u_d)$ with respect to all components $u_1, \ldots, u_d$. In dimension $d = 2$ this yields the density

$$c_\varphi(u_1, u_2) = \frac{\partial^2}{\partial u_1 \, \partial u_2} C_\varphi(u_1, u_2) = \frac{\varphi^{(2)}(\varphi^{-1}(u_1) + \varphi^{-1}(u_2))}{\varphi^{(1)}(\varphi^{-1}(u_1)) \, \varphi^{(1)}(\varphi^{-1}(u_2))}, \quad u_1, u_2 \in (0, 1).$$

Computing the density in larger dimensions $d \geq 2$ becomes burdensome due to the involved d-fold derivative $\varphi^{(d)}$. This problem is addressed (and solved for many Archimedean families) in [Hofert et al. (2012)].

FAQ 4.2.2 (Can I test if my data comes from an Archimedean copula?)
In the bivariate case, there is a test for Archimedeanity, proposed by [Bücher et al. (2012)].

4.2.2 Hierarchical Archimedean Copulas

It was already mentioned in FAQ 4.1.3 that the exchangeability of the bivariate Gaussian copula can be an undesired property in applications. Archimedean copulas are even exchangeable in every dimension $d \geq 2$, hence they also have this undesired property. This fact has led researchers to explore generalizations of Archimedean copulas to non-exchangeable structures, which have become very popular, especially in financial applications, see [Savu, Trede (2010), Hofert, Scherer (2011)] and Figure 8.2 for a visualization. The idea of hierarchical Archimedean copulas is a priori purely algebraic and was introduced and further developed in [Joe (1993), Joe, Hu (1996), McNeil (2008), Hofert (2008), Hering et al. (2010)]. To provide an example, assume we are given numbers $J, d_1, \ldots, d_J \in \mathbb{N}$ and let us introduce the notation $d := d_1 + \cdots + d_J$, as well as $(u_1, \ldots, u_d) =: (\boldsymbol{u}_1, \ldots, \boldsymbol{u}_J)$, meaning that we group the first d_1 indices into group 1, the next d_2 indices into group 2, and so on. Given a d_1-dimensional Archimedean copula C_{φ_1}, a d_2-dimensional Archimedean copula C_{φ_2}, ..., a d_J-dimensional Archimedean copula C_{φ_J}, and a J-dimensional Archimedean copula C_{φ_0}, wouldn't it be nice if we could work with the 'patchwork copula'

$$C(u_1, \ldots, u_d) = C_{\varphi_0}(C_{\varphi_1}(\boldsymbol{u}_1), \ldots, C_{\varphi_J}(\boldsymbol{u}_J))? \tag{4.9}$$

Yes, it would, because this would imply that a random vector $(\boldsymbol{U}_1, \ldots, \boldsymbol{U}_J) \sim C$ has the following desirable properties:

(i) $\boldsymbol{U}_j \sim C_{\varphi_j}$ for $j = 1, \ldots, J$, so inside group j the components are connected with 'inner copula' C_{φ_j}, and

---

[8] This copula has been applied to the pricing of loan credit default swaps (LCDX) in [Hieber, Scherer (2013)].

(ii)   if $i_1,\ldots,i_k$ are indices picked from k different groups, then $(U_{i_1},\ldots,U_{i_k}) \sim C_{\varphi_0}$, so the copula joining components from different groups is the 'outer copula' C_{φ_0}.

This means that an understanding of the quite complex dependence structure between the components of $(U_1,\ldots,U_J)$ can be retrieved from the easier to grasp dependence structures of the Archimedean building components. Unfortunately, there is one problem with this approach: the involved Archimedean generators $\varphi_0,\ldots,\varphi_J$ must satisfy non-trivial compatibility conditions in order for (4.9) to define a proper copula. These conditions are stated in the following theorem, see [Joe (1997), McNeil (2008)] for part (a) and [Hering et al. (2010)] for part (b).

Theorem 4.2.3 (Hierarchical Archimedean copulas)
Let $\varphi_0,\ldots,\varphi_J \in \Phi_\infty$ be completely monotone Archimedean generators (that is, Laplace transforms of positive random variables).

(a)   If the first derivative of $\varphi_0^{-1} \circ \varphi_j$ is completely monotone for all $j = 1,\ldots,J$, then (4.9) is a copula.
(b)   The condition in part (a) is satisfied if and only if the functions $\varphi_1,\ldots,\varphi_J$ are of the form $\varphi_j(x) = \varphi_0 \circ \Psi_j$, $j = 1,\ldots,J$, for functions $\Psi_j : [0,\infty) \to [0,\infty)$ which are infinitely often differentiable on $(0,\infty)$, continuous at zero, and satisfy $\Psi(0) = 0$, $\lim_{x \to \infty} \Psi_j(x) = \infty$, as well as $(-1)^{k+1} \Psi_j^{(k)}(x) \geq 0$, $k \geq 1$.

Functions $\Psi : [0,\infty) \to [0,\infty)$ that are infinitely often differentiable on $(0,\infty)$, which satisfy $\Psi(0) = 0$ as well as $(-1)^{k+1} \Psi_j^{(k)}(x) \geq 0$, $k \geq 1$, such as in part (b) of Theorem 4.2.3, are called 'Bernstein functions'. In other words, part (b) of Theorem 4.2.3 might be restated as 'φ_j must be of the form $\varphi_0 \circ \Psi_j$ with an unbounded, continuous Bernstein function Ψ_j for all j'. Table 4.2 provides a list of the most popular parametric families of Bernstein functions, which can be applied in Theorem 4.2.3. For further examples of Bernstein functions and more theoretical background on them we refer the interested reader to the excellent textbook [Schilling et al. (2010)].

FAQ 4.2.4 (Why is the reformulation in terms of Bernstein functions useful?)
Part (b) of Theorem 4.2.3 is basically a reformulation of part (a) involving the additional notion of Bernstein functions. It is a valid question to ask to what extent

Table 4.2. *Some one-parametric families of Bernstein functions that can be applied in Theorem 4.2.3 and allow for a simple algebraic expression for themselves and their inverses (so that the resulting hierarchical Archimedean copula has a closed-form expression).*

$\Psi_\theta(x)$	$\Psi_\theta^{-1}(y)$	$\theta \in$
x^θ	$y^{1/\theta}$	$(0,1]$
$\log(1+x/\theta)$	$\theta(e^y - 1)$	$(0,\infty)$
$\theta x + \frac{(1+\theta)x}{\theta+x}$	$\frac{1}{2\theta}\left(y-1-\theta-\theta^2 + \sqrt{(\theta^2+\theta+1-y)^2 + 4\theta^2 y}\right)$	$(0,\infty)$

the introduction of this new notion is of any use. The usefulness actually consists of two advantages: firstly, there exist numerous examples of parametric families of Bernstein functions that might be plugged in, for example [Schilling et al. (2010), p. 218–277] list more than one hundred such families. Secondly, when using part (a) with a given outer generator φ_0 it is very difficult to find suitable φ_j that are compatible with it. Part (b) tells us precisely which φ_j are admissible. In particular, the involved Bernstein functions need not satisfy any compatibility conditions. This second advantage becomes especially appealing when further subgroupings are desired, which corresponds to defining 'inner-inner' generators by further concatenations of Bernstein functions without having to take care about further compatibility conditions.

4.3 Extreme-value Copulas

A copula C is said to be an '*extreme-value copula*' if it satisfies the extreme-value property $C(u_1,\ldots,u_d)^t = C(u_1^t,\ldots,u_d^t)$ for all $t \geq 0$, $u_1,\ldots,u_d \in [0,1]$. As the nomenclature suggests, these copulas play a dominant role in extreme-value theory, see [Gudendorf, Segers (2010)] for an introduction to this topic. However, extreme-value copulas are not only interesting because of their interpretation as being the dependence structure between certain rare events. Already from a purely algebraic viewpoint, the extreme-value property allows us to derive useful structural results on extreme-value copulas. In particular, similarly to the case of Archimedean copulas and contrary to the case of elliptical copulas, this allows us to construct many parametric families of extreme-value copulas with an algebraically closed expression. Moreover, we have already encountered some nice algebraic properties of extreme-value copulas in Section 2.6.

For an extreme-value copula C it is standard to introduce its so-called '*stable tail dependence function*'

$$\ell(x_1,\ldots,x_d) := -\log\big(C(e^{-x_1},\ldots,e^{-x_d})\big), \quad x_1,\ldots,x_d \geq 0,$$

which allows us to write C in terms of ℓ as

$$C(u_1,\ldots,u_d) = \exp\big(-\ell(-\log(u_1),\ldots,-\log(u_d))\big), \quad u_1,\ldots,u_d \in [0,1].$$

Of course, this rewriting is possible for an arbitrary copula, but the extreme-value property implies that ℓ is homogeneous of order one, that is, ℓ satisfies

$$\ell(\gamma\,x_1,\ldots,\gamma\,x_d) = \gamma\,\ell(x_1,\ldots,x_d), \quad \text{for all } \gamma > 0 \text{ and } x_1,\ldots,x_d \geq 0. \qquad (4.10)$$

This homogeneity property can be used in order to derive integral representations for ℓ, and hence C, so that extreme-value copulas can be parameterized conveniently in terms of certain measures, see, for example, [Ressel (2013)]. Moreover, translating the analytical characterization of FAQ 1.2.2 for arbitrary copulas into similar conditions on the function ℓ, one obtains the following theorem. For a proof see [Ressel (2013)] and, in a slightly different form, [Molchanov (2008)].

Theorem 4.3.1 (Extreme-value copulas)
A function $C \colon [0,1]^d \to [0,1]$ is an extreme-value copula if and only if the function

$$\ell(x_1,\ldots,x_d) := -\log\left(C(e^{-x_1},\ldots,e^{-x_d})\right), \quad x_1,\ldots,x_d \geq 0,$$

satisfies the following properties:

(i) ℓ is homogeneous of order one, that is, (4.10) holds;

(ii) ℓ is normalized, that is, $\ell(1,0,\ldots,0) = \ell(0,1,0,\ldots,0) = \ldots = \ell(0,\ldots,0,1) = 1$;

(iii) ℓ is fully d-max-decreasing, that is, for each d-dimensional rectangle[9] $\times_{j=1}^d [b_j, a_j]$, being a subset of $(0,\infty)^d$, one has:

$$0 \leq \sum_{(c_1,\ldots,c_d)\in\times_{j=1}^d\{a_j,b_j\}} (-1)^{|\{j:c_j=a_j\}|}\ell(c_1,\ldots,c_d).$$

There exist a couple of closed-form examples for stable tail dependence functions, and hence for extreme-value copulas. In Section 4.3.1 we provide a very important example and below we outline that in the bivariate case $d = 2$ stable tail dependence functions are quite a convenient object to study. Another example is given here.

Example 4.3.2 (The Galambos copula)
For $\theta \in (0,\infty)$, the function

$$\ell_\theta(x_1,\ldots,x_d) = \sum_{\emptyset\neq I\subset\{1,\ldots,d\}} (-1)^{|I|+1} \left(\sum_{j\in I} x_j^{-\theta}\right)^{-1/\theta}$$

satisfies the conditions (i)–(iii) of Theorem 4.3.1 and, hence, the function

$$C_\theta(u_1,\ldots,u_d) = \exp\left(-\ell_\theta(-\log(u_1),\ldots,-\log(u_d))\right), \quad u_1,\ldots,u_d \in (0,1],$$

is an extreme-value copula, called a 'Galambos copula', the nomenclature dating back to [Galambos (1975)].

In the bivariate case, an extreme-value copula can (more conveniently) be parameterized by

$$C(u_1,u_2) = (u_1\,u_2)^{A\left(\frac{\log(u_2)}{\log(u_1\,u_2)}\right)}, \quad u_1, u_2 \in [0,1], \tag{4.11}$$

---

[9] Notice that $b_j \leq a_j$ is assumed here, as opposed to the d-increasingness condition in FAQ 1.2.2.

where the function A is retrieved from the stable tail dependence function ℓ via $A(x) := \ell(1 - x, x)$ for $x \in [0, 1]$. Translating conditions (i)–(iii) in the bivariate case to conditions on the function A, we obtain the following corollary.

Corollary 4.3.3 (Bivariate extreme-value copulas)
The bivariate function (4.11) is an (extreme-value) copula if and only if the parameterizing function $A : [0, 1] \to [1/2, 1]$ is convex, continuous at the boundaries 0 and 1 with $A(0) = A(1) = 1$, and satisfies $\max\{x, 1 - x\} \leq A(x) \leq 1$ for all $x \in [0, 1]$.

The analytical characterization of bivariate extreme-value copulas in terms of the function A in Corollary 4.3.3 turns out to be very useful for constructing closed-form extreme–value copulas, for studying dependence properties of extreme–value copulas, and for deriving parameter estimation techniques for extreme-value copulas.[10] Reconsidering Example 4.3.2, the bivariate Galambos copula is associated with the function

$$A_\theta(x) = 1 - (x^{-\theta} + (1 - x)^{-\theta})^{-1/\theta}, \quad x \in [0, 1], \tag{4.12}$$

which is visualized in Figure 4.5 for different levels of the dependence parameter θ. Notice that the function A_θ is a priori only defined on the interior $(0, 1)$, but the boundary values are defined as the respective limits $A_\theta(0) := \lim_{x \downarrow 0} A_\theta(x) = 1$ and $A_\theta(1) := \lim_{x \uparrow 1} A_\theta(x) = 1$.

A few further examples for parametric families of functions A, and hence bivariate extreme-value copulas, are provided in Table 4.3. In particular, the Gumbel copula is the only copula which is both an extreme-value copula and an Archimedean copula, see [Genest, Rivest (1989)]. Cuadras–Augé copulas are introduced in and named after [Cuadras, Augé (1981)], Hüsler–Reiss copulas date back to [Hüsler, Reiss (1989)], t–EV copulas are introduced in [Demarta, McNeil (2005)], and BC_2–copulas are discussed by [Mai, Scherer (2011b)].

4.3.1 Marshall–Olkin copulas

One very popular subfamily of extreme-value copulas is the family of 'Marshall–Olkin copulas'. They are obtained when the stable tail dependence function is given by

$$\ell(x_1, \ldots, x_d) = \sum_{\emptyset \neq I \subset \{1, \ldots, d\}} \lambda_I \max\left\{ \frac{x_j}{\sum_{J : j \in J} \lambda_J} : j \in I \right\}, \quad x_1, \ldots, x_d \geq 0, \tag{4.13}$$

with parameters $\lambda_I \geq 0$, $\emptyset \neq I \subset \{1, \ldots, d\}$, satisfying $\sum_{I : j \in I} \lambda_I > 0$ for each $j = 1, \ldots, d$. One immediately recognizes that in the bivariate case this gives rise to the parameterizing function

$$A(x) = \frac{\lambda_{\{1\}}(1 - x)}{\lambda_{\{1\}} + \lambda_{\{1,2\}}} + \frac{\lambda_{\{2\}} x}{\lambda_{\{2\}} + \lambda_{\{1,2\}}} + \lambda_{\{1,2\}} \max\left\{ \frac{1 - x}{\lambda_{\{1\}} + \lambda_{\{1,2\}}}, \frac{x}{\lambda_{\{2\}} + \lambda_{\{1,2\}}} \right\},$$

---

[10] See Section 6.4.1 and [Gudendorf, Segers (2010)] for an overview of references dealing with this topic.

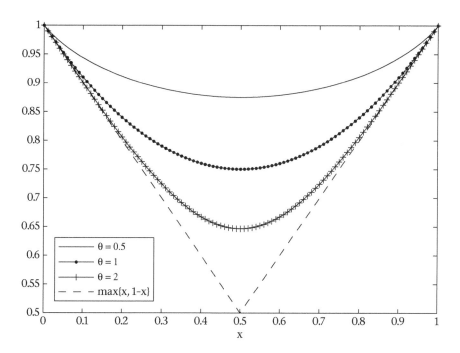

Figure 4.5 The parameterizing function A_θ, see (4.12), of the Galambos copula for different levels of the dependence parameter θ. In terms of interpretation, the closer the function A is to the constant 1 (corresponding to the independence case), the lower the dependence. If A is symmetric around $x = 1/2$ (which is the case in the present example), then the copula is exchangeable.

for $x \in [0,1]$, with parameters $\lambda_{\{1\}}, \lambda_{\{2\}}, \lambda_{\{1,2\}} \geq 0$ satisfying $\lambda_{\{1\}} + \lambda_{\{1,2\}} > 0$ and $\lambda_{\{2\}} + \lambda_{\{1,2\}} > 0$. Marshall–Olkin copulas are derived from the so-called '*Marshall–Olkin distribution*', which is a prominent concept of a multivariate exponential distribution, introduced in and named after [Marshall, Olkin (1967)]. Since exponential distributions are quite natural candidates for companies' default times, the Marshall–Olkin distribution has been applied to the modeling of insurance claims and portfolio-credit risk in [Frees et al. (1996), Giesecke (2003), Lindskog, McNeil (2003), Mai, Scherer (2009a), Sun et al. (2012)].

FAQ 4.3.4 (What's the motivation behind the Marshall–Olkin distribution?)
A random variable X has a univariate exponential distribution if its survival function is given by $\bar{F}(x) := \mathbb{P}(X > x) = \exp(-\lambda x)$ for some parameter $\lambda > 0$ and arguments $x \geq 0$, that is, by the exponential function. Since the exponential function is essentially the only function f satisfying the so-called '*Cauchy equation*' $f(x)f(y) = f(x+y)$, see [Billingsley (1995), Appendix A20, p. 540], it follows that the univariate exponential law is characterized by the so-called '*lack-of-memory property*', stating that the residual lifetime of X is independent of its age, that is,

$$\mathbb{P}(X > x+y \mid X > y) = \mathbb{P}(X > x), \quad \text{for all } x, y \geq 0.$$

Table 4.3. *Some parametric families of bivariate extreme-value copulas, given by their parameterizing function A. Recall that Φ denotes the distribution function of a standard normally distributed random variable, and t_ν denotes the distribution function of a random variable with t-distribution and ν degrees of freedom.*

$A_\theta(x)$	$\theta \in$	name of copula
$(x^\theta + (1-x)^\theta)^{1/\theta}$	$[1,\infty)$	Gumbel
$(1-x)\,\Phi\left(\theta + \frac{1}{2\theta}\log\left(\frac{1-x}{x}\right)\right) + x\,\Phi\left(\theta + \frac{1}{2\theta}\log\left(\frac{x}{1-x}\right)\right)$	$(0,\infty)$	Hüsler–Reiss
$\max\{x, 1-x\} + (1-\theta)\min\{x, 1-x\}$	$[0,1]$	Cuadras–Augé

$A_{\theta_1,\theta_2}(x)$	$(\theta_1,\theta_2) \in$	
$\max\{\theta_1\,x, \theta_2\,(1-x)\} + \max\{(1-\theta_1)\,x, (1-\theta_2)(1-x)\}$	$[0,1] \times [0,1]$	BC_2
$x\,t_{\theta_1+1}\left(\sqrt{\frac{1+\theta_1}{1-\theta_2^2}}\left(\left(\frac{x}{1-x}\right)^{\frac{1}{\theta_1}} - \theta_2\right)\right)$		
$\quad + (1-x)\,t_{\theta_1+1}\left(\sqrt{\frac{1+\theta_1}{1-\theta_2^2}}\left(\left(\frac{1-x}{x}\right)^{\frac{1}{\theta_1}} - \theta_2\right)\right)$	$(0,\infty) \times (-1,1)$	t-EV

In their seminal work, [Marshall, Olkin (1967)] introduce the multivariate lack-of-memory-property for a random vector $(X_1, \dots, X_d)$ and show that the Marshall–Olkin distribution is characterized by it. From this perspective, it is justified to call the Marshall–Olkin distribution a multivariate exponential distribution. Marshall–Olkin copulas arise as the survival copulas of Marshall–Olkin distributions. We would like to mention at this point that there also exist other concepts of multivariate exponential distributions in the literature, which are not characterized by the multivariate lack-of-memory property but instead by the so-called min-stability property.

A second important motivation behind Marshall–Olkin distributions is an interesting stochastic interpretation. Given its $2^d - 1$ parameters $\{\lambda_I\}$, $\emptyset \neq I \subset \{1, \dots, d\}$, consider a collection of $2^d - 1$ independent exponential random variables $E_I \sim \mathcal{E}(\lambda_I)$. If some parameters are zero, that is, $\lambda_I = 0$ for some I, then the associated E_I are conveniently assumed to equal infinity. It can be shown that the random vector $(X_1, \dots, X_d)$ defined via

$$X_j := \min\{E_I : j \in I\}, \quad j = 1, \dots, d, \tag{4.14}$$

follows a Marshall–Olkin distribution with marginals $X_j \sim \mathcal{E}(\sum_{I:j\in I}\lambda_I)$ and the extreme-value survival copula associated with the stable tail dependence function (4.13). Applications in reliability theory, insurance, and financial mathematics use this stochastic model with X_j being interpreted as the failure (resp. default) time of component j in a system (resp. portfolio) of d components. The random variable E_I is interpreted as the arrival time of an exogenous shock that affects all components indexed by the subset I, so that component j fails as soon as the first shock arrives

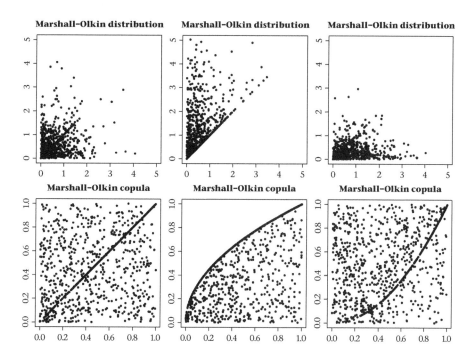

Figure 4.6 Scatter plots of the bivariate Marshall–Olkin distribution (top row) and its associated Marshall–Olkin survival copulas (bottom row). In the example to the left, the parameters are $\lambda = (\lambda_{\{1\}}, \lambda_{\{2\}}, \lambda_{\{12\}}) = (1,1,1)$, implying an exchangeable model. This corresponds to the singular component of the survival copula on the diagonal. The parameters in the middle are $\lambda = (1,0,1)$, implying that the second component cannot trigger prior to the first one. The parameters in the right are $\lambda = (0.5,2,1)$, an example for a non-exchangeable case, where again the singular component is bent. Notice that the survival copula of the Marshall–Olkin vector (X_1, X_2) is the distribution function of the random vector $(U_1, U_2) = (\exp(-(\lambda_{\{1\}} + \lambda_{\{1,2\}})X_1), \exp(-(\lambda_{\{2\}} + \lambda_{\{1,2\}})X_2))$, so $\mathbb{P}(X_1 \leq X_2) = 1$ implies $\mathbb{P}\big(U_2 \leq U_1^{\frac{\lambda_{\{2\}} + \lambda_{\{1,2\}}}{\lambda_{\{1\}} + \lambda_{\{1,2\}}}}\big) = 1$.

which affects it, explaining the definition of X_j in (4.14). The Marshall–Olkin distribution and its associated survival copula is visualized in Figure 4.6.

Furthermore, Marshall–Olkin copulas give rise to the quite tractable subfamily of so-called 'Lévy-frailty copulas', which are introduced in [Mai, Scherer (2009b)] and applied to collateralized debt obligation (CDO) pricing in Section 8.3. More precisely, if X is a random variable taking values in $[0,1]$ and we denote its moments by $a_k := \mathbb{E}[X^k]$, $k \in \mathbb{N}_0$, it can be shown that the function

$$C(u_1, \ldots, u_d) = u_{[1]}^{a_0} u_{[2]}^{a_1} \cdots u_{[d]}^{a_{d-1}}, \quad u_1, \ldots, u_d \in [0,1], \qquad (4.15)$$

Table 4.4. *Some one-parametric families of random variables on $[0,1]$, which give rise to parametric families of Lévy-frailty copulas via (4.15). Notice that Γ denotes the Gamma function.*

$a_k(\theta)$	$\theta \in$	law of X
$(k+1)^\theta - k^\theta$	$(0,1]$	$f_X(x) = \frac{\theta(1-x)}{\Gamma(1-\theta)x}(-\log(x))^{-\theta-1}$
$\theta + (1-\theta)\mathbf{1}_{\{k=0\}}$	$(0,1)$	Bernoulli(θ)
$\Gamma(\theta+k)/(\Gamma(\theta)\,k!)$	$(0,1)$	Beta$(\theta, 1-\theta)$
$(1+k)^{-\theta}$	$(0,\infty)$	$X \stackrel{d}{=} \exp(-\mathrm{Gamma}(1,\theta))$

with $u_{[1]} \leq \cdots \leq u_{[d]}$ denoting the ordered list of $u_1, \ldots, u_d$, is a Marshall–Olkin copula with parameters given by

$$\lambda_I = \sum_{k=0}^{|I|-1} (-1)^k \binom{|I|-1}{k} a_{d-|I|+k} = \mathbb{E}[X^{d-|I|}(1-X)^{|I|-1}], \quad \emptyset \neq I \subset \{1,\ldots,d\},$$

see [Mai, Scherer (2011a)] for a derivation. This implies that one can construct numerous examples of low-parametric Marshall–Olkin copulas from parametric families of random variables on $[0,1]$. In particular, for the bivariate case $d = 2$ one obtains the Cuadras–Augé copula from Table 4.3. Table 4.4 gathers a few one-parametric examples[11] for potential choices of the parameters a_k in (4.15).

4.3.2 Stylized Facts of Extreme-value Copulas

In the following, we collect some stylized facts about (primarily bivariate) extreme-value copulas. Summarizing them briefly, extreme-value copulas allow for asymmetries, might or might not have a density, and often have a closed-form expression.

(a) **Dependence range:** Similarly to the case of Archimedean copulas with completely monotone generators, a d-dimensional extreme-value copula C always satisfies $\Pi_d \leq C \leq M_d$ point-wise, meaning that only non-negative association between components can be achieved, which can be deduced directly from property (iii) in Theorem 4.3.1, cf. Exercise 9. Typical parametric families, such as the ones presented in this section, include Π_d and M_d as boundary cases and their parameter(s) interpolate between these two extremes, which is sufficient for most practical applications.

(b) **Concordance measures:** In the bivariate case, the most prominent concordance measures have a representation in terms of the parameterizing function A, see

---

[11] *Bernoulli(θ) denotes the Bernoulli distribution with success probability θ, Beta(a,b) denotes the Beta distribution as defined in [Mai, Scherer (2012), p. 4], Gamma(β,η) denotes the two-parametric Gamma distribution, which may be defined via its Laplace transform in (4.3).*

[Hürlimann (2003), Ghoudi et al. (1998)] for a derivation:

$$\tau = \int_0^1 \frac{x(1-x)}{A(x)} \, dA'(x), \qquad \text{(Kendall's } \tau) \qquad (4.16)$$

$$\rho_S = 12 \int_0^1 \frac{1}{(1+A(x))^2} \, dx - 3, \qquad \text{(Spearman's } \rho_S) \qquad (4.17)$$

where $dA'(x) = A'(x) \, dx$ in case A is twice differentiable. For non-twice differentiable functions A, the integration operator $dA'(x)$ is also defined because of the convexity of A. For example, for the Cuadras–Augé copula, see Table 4.3, we obtain

$$dA'(x) = \begin{cases} -\theta \, dx, & \text{if } t < \frac{1}{2} \\ +\theta \, dx, & \text{if } t > \frac{1}{2} \end{cases},$$

so that Kendall's τ results in $\tau_A = \theta/(2-\theta)$, cf. Exercise 7.

(c) **Tail dependence**: Extreme-value copulas are naturally asymmetric, which is also reflected in the tail dependence coefficients. In the bivariate case these are given in terms of the function A, and it is observed that the lower-tail dependence parameter is dichotomous, see [Gudendorf, Segers (2010)]:

$$UTD_A = 2\,(1 - A(1/2)), \quad LTD_A = \begin{cases} 0, & \text{if } A(1/2) > 1/2 \\ 1, & \text{if } A(1/2) = 1/2 \end{cases}.$$

For extreme-value copulas, there also exists a fair amount of literature about tail-dependence properties in the multivariate case $d \geq 3$, and the interested reader is referred to the article [Li (2009)] for further details.

(d) **Density**: Extreme-value copulas might have a density but need not. For instance, Marshall–Olkin copulas and BC_2 copulas are not absolutely continuous, while the Gumbel copula, the Galambos copula, the t-EV copula, and the Hüsler–Reiss copula have densities. These densities can be computed using Formula (2.7), that is, by iteratively taking the partial derivatives with respect to each component.

4.4 Archimax Copulas

In earlier sections we have learned about Archimedean copulas and extreme-value copulas. In particular, we have seen that, contrary to Gaussian and elliptical copulas, these copula families often allow for closed-form algebraic expressions. The idea of Archimax copulas is to combine Archimedean copulas and extreme-value copulas in order to obtain a superclass of both, and thus more flexible dependence models. It dates back to [Capéraà et al. (2000)] and was further developed by [Charpentier et al. (2014)], where a proof of the following theorem can be found.

Theorem 4.4.1 (Archimax copulas)
If ℓ is a stable tail dependence function and φ is a completely monotone Archimedean generator, then the function

$$C_{\ell,\varphi}(u_1,\ldots,u_d) = \varphi\big(\ell(\varphi^{-1}(u_1),\ldots,\varphi^{-1}(u_d))\big), \quad u_1,\ldots,u_d \in [0,1],$$

is a copula.

If the stable tail dependence function $\ell(x_1,\ldots,x_d) = x_1 + \ldots + x_d$ is chosen, then $C_{\ell,\varphi} = C_\varphi$ is simply the Archimedean copula with generator φ. Conversely, for the Archimedean generator $\varphi(x) = \exp(-x)$, the Archimax copula $C_{\ell,\varphi}$ boils down to the extreme-value copula with associated stable tail dependence function ℓ. All parametric families for ℓ and φ discussed in the previous sections can be combined in order to define an Archimax copula. In particular, if ℓ is chosen as in (4.13) one obtains the subfamily of 'scale mixtures of Marshall–Olkin copulas' that is studied in [Li (2009), Bernhart et al. (2013)]. Moreover, in the bivariate case it is again possible to replace the bivariate function $\ell(x_1,x_2)$ by the univariate function $A(x) = \ell(1-x,x)$ to write bivariate Archimax copulas in the following simplified form:

$$C_{A,\varphi}(u_1,u_2) = \varphi\left((\varphi^{-1}(u_1) + \varphi^{-1}(u_2)) A\left(\frac{\varphi^{-1}(u_2)}{\varphi^{-1}(u_1) + \varphi^{-1}(u_2)}\right)\right).$$

It is shown in [Capéraà et al. (2000)] that the value of Kendall's τ for $C_{A,\varphi}$ is given by

$$\tau_{A,\varphi} = \tau_A + (1 - \tau_A)\,\tau_\varphi,$$

where τ_A is Kendall's τ of the extreme–value copula associated with A, given by (4.16), and τ_φ is Kendall's τ of the Archimedean copula C_φ, given by (4.7). It follows that Kendall's τ of an Archimax copula is necessarily always greater than or equal to Kendall's τ of its underlying extreme-value copula. In a similar spirit, one can derive coefficients of tail dependence, even generalizations to the multivariate case, and the interested reader is referred to [Capéraà et al. (2000), Bernhart et al. (2013)] for details.

EXERCISES

1. Show that the copula of the random vector (4.1) is independent of the means $\mu_1,\ldots,\mu_d$ and the variances $\sigma_1^2,\ldots,\sigma_d^2$.
2. Compare the densities of a bivariate standard Gaussian and a bivariate standard t-distribution with a contour plot. Plot (in the same figure) the levels $(0.15, 0.10, 0.05, 0.01, 0.001)$ for a mean vector $\boldsymbol{\mu} = (0,0)$, covariance matrix Σ with unit variances on the diagonal and off-diagonal entries $\rho = 0.5$, and $\nu = 2$ degrees

of freedom. To implement this in R, use the function `contour` with input vectors `x=y=seq(-5, 5, by=0.1)`. To evaluate the multivariate Gaussian and t densities, use the package `mnormt`.

3. Show that the following functions are completely monotone:

$$f(x) = e^{-\lambda x}, \qquad \lambda > 0, \quad x \geq 0,$$

$$g(x) = \frac{\lambda}{x+\lambda}, \qquad \lambda > 0, \quad x \geq 0,$$

$$h(x) = \mathbb{E}[e^{-xM}], \qquad x \geq 0, \qquad M \text{ a non-negative random variable.}$$

More examples and computation rules are given in [Miller, Samko (2001)].

4. Show that if φ_1 and φ_2 are both completely monotone with $\varphi_1(0) = \varphi_2(0) = 1$, then the same applies to their product $\varphi_1 \varphi_2$. Does the same also hold for their concatenation $\varphi_1 \circ \varphi_2$?

5. Prove that $\Psi(x) = x^\theta$ is a Bernstein function if $\theta \in (0,1]$. Is it also a Bernstein function if $\theta > 1$?

6. Prove that if φ is in Φ_∞ and Ψ is a Bernstein function, then $\varphi \circ \Psi$ is in Φ_∞.

7. Compute Kendall's τ and Spearman's ρ_S for the Cuadras–Augé copula, see Table 4.3.

8. Consider the survival copula of $(\epsilon_1/M,\ldots,\epsilon_d/M)$, where M is a Gamma $(1/\theta,1)$-distributed random variable independent of the iid unit exponentially distributed ϵ_k, $k = 1,\ldots,d$. This Archimedean copula is called a Clayton copula. Show that the corresponding generator is $\varphi(x) = (1+x)^{-1/\theta}$ and calculate Kendall's τ and the tail dependence coefficients of the Clayton copula.

9. Prove that $C \geq \Pi_d$ point-wise for a d-dimensional extreme-value copula C.

10. Following the interpretation of FAQ 4.3.4, consider two default times (X_1,X_2) with two-dimensional Marshall–Olkin distribution and exponentially distributed marginals with parameters $\lambda_1,\lambda_2 > 0$. Show that the probability of a joint default event, that is, $\mathbb{P}(X_1 = X_2)$, is maximized if the parameters $\lambda_{\{1\}},\lambda_{\{2\}},\lambda_{\{1,2\}}$ fulfill $\lambda_{\{1,2\}} = \min\{\lambda_1,\lambda_2\}$, $\lambda_{\{1\}} = \max\{0,\lambda_1 - \lambda_2\}$ and $\lambda_{\{2\}} = \max\{0,\lambda_2 - \lambda_1\}$. What is $\mathbb{P}(X_1 \leq X_2)$ in this case?

11. Let $(X_1^{(i)},\ldots,X_d^{(i)})$, $i \in \mathbb{N}$, be iid random vectors with positive, absolutely continuous components and joint survival function $\bar{F}$.

   a. Compute the multivariate survival function $\bar{F}_n$ of the following random vector with componentwise minima:

   $$n\left(\min_{i=1,\ldots,n} \{X_1^{(i)}\},\ldots, \min_{i=1,\ldots,n} \{X_d^{(i)}\}\right), \qquad n \in \mathbb{N}.$$

   b. Assume there exists a multivariate survival function $\bar{F}_0$ such that $\bar{F}_n \to \bar{F}_0$ point-wise, as $n \to \infty$. Show that the marginals of $\bar{F}_0$ are exponential and the survival copula is of extreme-value kind.

12. Show that ℓ_θ of Example 4.3.2 satisfies (i)–(iii) of Theorem 4.3.1.

13. Prove Corollary 4.3.3.

5 How to Simulate Multivariate Distributions?

Before we start, let us note that we use 'to simulate' and 'to sample' as synonyms throughout. The present chapter (i) provides a motivation for the simulation of random vectors, and (ii) shows how this can be achieved. A probability law is a priori a purely analytical object, that is, a function which gets sets as input and returns numbers in $[0, 1]$. We interpret the input sets as events that might happen or not, and the output as probabilities corresponding to the likelihood of occurrence of the input events. For example, the uniform distribution $\mathcal{U}[a, b]$ assigns the value $(y - x)/(b - a)$ to the interval $[x, y]$ for $a \leq x < y \leq b$. In most applications, we work with a parametric family of probability laws, that is, the likelihood of some event can be altered by changing the parameters of the probability law. For instance, the two-parametric family $\mathcal{U}[a, b]$ of uniform distributions assigns the value 0.5 to the set $[0, 1]$ if $a = 0$ and $b = 2$; and it assigns the value 0.25 to the same set $[0, 1]$ if the parameters are changed to $a = -1$ and $b = 3$.

FAQ 5.0.1 (What is stochastic simulation?)

The term '*stochastic simulation*' refers to the availability of a computer program which gets as input (the parameters of) a probability law and produces a number of independent samples from it, that is, the output of the program is a list of realizations from the input probability law. In particular, this means that the output is typically different when the same program, with the same input parameters, is run repeatedly, because the output is random.[1] However, the randomness of the output follows the desired probability law. For example, a computer program which simulates the law $\mathcal{U}[a, b]$ gets as input the parameters $a < b$ and produces as output a random list of numbers in the interval $[a, b]$. The generated numbers should be scattered evenly within the interval $[a, b]$, which is the characterizing feature of the uniform distribution. Since the present book is particularly focused on multivariate probability distributions on (subsets of) $\mathbb{R}^d$, the output of the respective simulation algorithms will be a list of vectors in $\mathbb{R}^d$.

In the context of dependence modeling we are concerned with the development and analysis of multivariate stochastic models (for example the description of several default times). Such a multivariate treatment is in most cases much more involved than working with related univariate problems (for example the description of a single default time). Hence, in many cases one cannot derive analytical expressions for the target object one has in mind (for example the price of some portfolio-credit

---

[1] If one wants to reproduce the output of a simulation study, one has to set a so-called seed. Then the random number generator produces the same sequence of numbers each time the program is run. In R, this is done with the command `set.seed()`.

derivative). Stochastic simulation is a very flexible technique to overcome such problems, as explained in FAQ 5.0.2.

FAQ 5.0.2 (What do we need stochastic simulation algorithms for?)
First of all, if we study a multivariate distribution, for example if we derive estimation strategies for its parameters or if we compute certain dependence measures, the availability of a simulation algorithm of the distribution in question can be of great help in order to verify our theoretical considerations empirically. Secondly, as practitioners we study multivariate probability distributions because we apply these as models for real world phenomena that can only be described reasonably by stochastic objects. For instance, we might be investors in two stocks and, consequently, the respective future stock returns are of great interest to us. Clearly, we do not know these numbers but we have some opinion about their stochastic nature. For example, we believe that they will be positive rather than negative (that's why we invested in these two stocks), but we also know that they both might be negative (but hope this happens with small probability). As mathematicians we can transform this opinion into a stochastic model for the two stock returns, which results in a bivariate probability distribution on $\mathbb{R}^2$. Because we believe that the future stock returns can become negative, it makes no sense to assume that the marginal laws of this probability distribution are exponential, rather a bivariate normal distribution might be appropriate. Thinking further, we might not like the symmetry features of the normal distribution and, consequently, opt for a model with asymmetric copula and, for example, some marginal distributions with significant skewness. Given such a model, we are interested in its properties, for example how big is the probability that my portfolio return is smaller than a certain barrier? Depending on how difficult the question is, and depending on how specialized the model is, we might face the problem that we cannot answer our question analytically. For instance, denoting the random vector of our two stock returns by (X_1, X_2), we might be interested in the expected value $\mathbb{E}[f(X_1, X_2)]$ or the variance of $f(X_1, X_2)$, where the function f depends on our question. For instance, if

$$f(X_1, X_2) = \begin{cases} 1, & \text{if } \left(\log \left(\frac{w_1 S_1 \exp(X_1) + w_2 S_2 \exp(X_2)}{w_1 S_1 + w_2 S_2} \right) \right) > B \\ 0, & \text{else} \end{cases},$$

with a barrier B, current stock prices S_1, S_2, and portfolio weights $w_1, w_2 > 0$, then the expected value $\mathbb{E}[f(X_1, X_2)]$ yields the probability that our future portfolio return remains above the barrier B. Depending on our model and the nature of the function f, we might be able to compute this value. In many cases, however, we simply cannot achieve this analytically. In such a situation, the so-called 'Monte-Carlo method' might be a feasible solution, see Algorithm 5.0.3 below.

Another example in mathematical finance, where difficult-to-compute expectation values of the form $\mathbb{E}[f(X_1, \ldots, X_d)]$ occur frequently, is derivative pricing. By classical arbitrage pricing theory the price of an attainable European derivative depending on d underlying securities can be written in terms of such an expected value. The underlying securities' price processes must satisfy certain no-arbitrage conditions, which implies that their joint probability distribution is called 'risk-neutral'. For a reader-friendly introduction into this general theory, the interested reader is referred to [Bingham, Kiesel (2003)]. Again, if the derivative-pricing model, which is basically a stochastic model for the underlying securities under the risk-neutral measure, is too complex, the derivative's price $\mathbb{E}[f(X_1,\ldots,X_d)]$ might not allow for a closed formula and must be solved via Monte-Carlo algorithms.

Algorithm 5.0.3 (Generic Monte-Carlo simulation)
Our aim is to estimate the expected value $\mathbb{E}[f(X_1,\ldots,X_d)]$. We have as given a sampling algorithm for the random vector $(X_1,\ldots,X_d)$, that is, a computer program that returns independent realizations of $(X_1,\ldots,X_d)$. We proceed as follows:

(1) Simulate n independent (and identically distributed) samples of the random vector $(X_1,\ldots,X_d)$, which we denote as $(X_1^{(i)},\ldots,X_d^{(i)})$, $i=1,\ldots,n$.
(2) Return the arithmetic average of the desired function of the samples, that is, the value

$$\frac{1}{n}\sum_{i=1}^{n}f(X_1^{(i)},\ldots,X_d^{(i)}) \approx \mathbb{E}[f(X_1,\ldots,X_d)].$$

The justification of Algorithm 5.0.3 stems from the strong law of large numbers, which states that for a sequence of independent and identically distributed random variables $Z_1, Z_2,\ldots$ with finite mean it follows almost surely that

$$\frac{1}{n}\sum_{i=1}^{n}Z_i \to \mathbb{E}[Z_1], \quad n \to \infty.$$

Applying this statement to the random variables $Z_i := f(X_1^{(i)},\ldots,X_d^{(i)})$ verifies why Algorithm 5.0.3 makes sense.

FAQ 5.0.4 (What are the pros and cons of the Monte-Carlo method?)
On the one hand, the most obvious drawback of the Monte-Carlo method is that it requires quite a lot of runtime, because one needs to simulate a huge number n of scenarios to create a sufficiently accurate estimate for the desired expectation value. In particular, if one wishes to calibrate the model's parameters to observed data, then one needs to re-evaluate the expected value in question multiple times for different parameter sets. Another disadvantage is that, depending on the specific problem, the variance of the random variable $f(X_1,\ldots,X_d)$ in question might be huge. In order to obtain a reasonable confidence interval in such a case, we might require a very high number of samples n. For this reason, it is always important to provide a confidence interval together with a Monte-Carlo estimator, because otherwise one cannot judge its accuracy.

On the other hand, the most striking advantage of the Monte-Carlo method is its applicability to very complex models. It is often the only method feasible, in particular if the dimension d is large. Moreover, provided the variance σ^2 of $f(X_1,\ldots,X_d)$

is finite, the standard deviation of the Monte-Carlo estimate equals $1/\sqrt{n}$ times σ, implying that the convergence rate of the Monte-Carlo estimator is known and problem-invariant. Furthermore, applying the central limit theorem, an asymptotic $(1-\alpha)$-confidence interval can be computed quite easily by adding and subtracting the value $\sigma/\sqrt{n}\,\Phi^{-1}(1-\alpha/2)$ from the Monte-Carlo estimate for the mean, for example for $\alpha = 0.05$ or $\alpha = 0.01$. If σ is unknown, which is typically the case, it may simply be replaced with its canonical estimator

$$
\hat{\sigma}_n^2 = \frac{1}{n-1} \sum_{i=1}^{n} \left(f(X_1^{(i)}, \ldots, X_d^{(i)}) - \frac{1}{n} \sum_{j=1}^{n} f(X_1^{(j)}, \ldots, X_d^{(j)}) \right)^2 ,
$$

and asymptotically the confidence interval is still valid by the continuous mapping theorem. Regarding the accuracy of the Monte-Carlo estimator, in order to reduce the length of the confidence interval resulting from the Monte-Carlo method with n samples by a factor of 0.1, a new run of the Monte-Carlo method is required, with $100\,n$ simulations. For more background on the Monte-Carlo method, the interested reader is referred to [Korn et al. (2010)].

FAQ 5.0.5 (What do we need for a stochastic simulation algorithm?)
As mentioned earlier, a simulation algorithm is a computer program which returns realizations of a random vector with given probability distribution. Such a program typically consists of two building components: (i) a random number generator for the involved standard univariate probability laws, and (ii) an analytical part of code which combines and transforms the generated univariate samples to a vector with the desired distribution. Concerning (i), we notice that most statistical software packages contain simulation algorithms for standard, univariate probability laws, so they need not be programmed by the practitioner himself, see Section 5.1.3 for further details. Concerning (ii), we review some basic techniques in Section 5.1 to follow. However, we'd like to note at this point that Sklar's Theorem 1.2.4 can sometimes also be a useful tool to split the simulation of a random vector $(X_1,\ldots,X_d)$ into two, possibly simpler, steps. If $(X_1,\ldots,X_d)$ has copula C and marginal distribution functions $F_1,\ldots,F_d$, then we may simulate from $(X_1,\ldots,X_d)$ in the following way:

(1) Simulate a random vector $(U_1,\ldots,U_d)$ with distribution function C.
(2) Return the random vector $(X_1,\ldots,X_d) := (F_1^{-1}(U_1),\ldots,F_d^{-1}(U_d))$, where F_j^{-1} denotes the generalized inverse, see Definition 1.2.6, of the marginal distribution function $F_j, j = 1,\ldots,d$.

Clearly, this technique suffers from the drawback that one needs to be able to evaluate the (generalized) inverse of the marginal laws efficiently. However, this is often possible and therefore a simulation algorithm for the random vector $(U_1,\ldots,U_d)$ associated with a copula C can be applied to numerous multivariate distribution functions, that is, is invariant of the marginals to some degree. In particular for practical applications this is an important observation, because one can find statistical software packages which have simulation algorithms for different copula classes pre-implemented, see

Section 5.1.3 below. This might make it unnecessary to implement a complicated simulation algorithm oneself.

5.1 How to Simulate from a Copula?

This section is organized as follows. Section 5.1.1 presents a general simulation technique that is feasible for many bivariate copulas, but which does not work (as easily) in larger dimensions. Section 5.1.2 presents simulation algorithms for dedicated, in particular high-dimensional, copula families, where the simulation algorithm is derived from an underlying stochastic model. Finally, Section 5.1.3 gives some advice on how to find and implement simulation algorithms beyond this introduction.

FAQ 5.1.1 (How to sample the survival copula $\hat{C}$?)
If you have some simulation algorithm available that produces samples $(U_1,\ldots,U_d)$ from the copula C, then simply return $(1 - U_1,\ldots,1 - U_d)$ as a sample from the survival copula $\hat{C}$.

5.1.1 Simulation based on Analytical Techniques

If a bivariate copula $C(u_1,u_2)$ has a sufficiently simple (and smooth) algebraic expression, then there exists a very efficient, analytical simulation algorithm which can often be applied. It has already been noted in Section 2.5 that for typical copula families the partial derivative

$$h_{u_2}(u_1) := \frac{\partial}{\partial u_2} C(u_1, u_2), \quad u_1 \in (0,1), \tag{5.1}$$

exists for almost every $u_2 \in (0,1)$. The notion 'almost every' stems from measure theory and is nothing to worry about in a practical situation. Except for some pathological examples, for typical bivariate copulas, especially absolutely continuous copulas, h_{u_2} exists for every $u_2 \in (0,1)$. For some prominent copulas it may occur that h_{u_2} is not defined for finitely many (typically only for one) $u_2 \in (0,1)$, an example is provided by the Cuadras–Augé copula $C_\alpha(u_1,u_2) := \min\{u_1,u_2\} \max\{u_1,u_2\}^{1-\alpha}$, see Table 4.3, for which $h_{0.5}$ is not well defined. However, for the few exceptions where the partial derivative does not exist, we simply define it as the point-wise limit $h_{u_2} := \lim_{x\downarrow u_2} h_x$, which is well defined. The partial derivative h_{u_2} is sometimes called an '*h-function*' in the context of so-called '*pair copula constructions*', where it plays a dominant role, see [Aas et al. (2009)] for an introduction.

   The importance of the h-function h_{u_2} stems from the fact that it has a probabilistic meaning. More precisely, it equals the distribution function of U_1 conditioned on the event that $U_2 = u_2$. In particular, denoting by $h_{u_2}^{-1}$ its (generalized) inverse and by V some $\mathcal{U}[0,1]$-distributed random variable, the random variable $h_{u_2}^{-1}(V)$ has distribution function h_{u_2}. This implies that a random vector $(U_1, U_2) \sim C$ can be simulated according to the following extremely fast and simple simulation algorithm.

Algorithm 5.1.2 (Conditional sampling method)
Required as input for the algorithm is a bivariate copula $C : [0,1]^2 \to [0,1]$ with h-functions h_{u_2}, $u_2 \in (0,1)$, as computed in (5.1).

(1) Simulate independent random variables U_2, V with $\mathcal{U}[0,1]$-distribution.
(2) Return the vector (U_1, U_2), where $U_1 := h_{U_2}^{-1}(V)$.

To provide an example, if φ is the completely monotone generator of an Archimedean copula $C_\varphi(u_1, u_2) = \varphi(\varphi^{-1}(u_1) + \varphi^{-1}(u_2))$, then the h-functions are given by

$$h_{u_2}(u_1) = \frac{\varphi^{(1)}(\varphi^{-1}(u_1) + \varphi^{-1}(u_2))}{\varphi^{(1)}(\varphi^{-1}(u_2))}, \quad u_1, u_2 \in (0,1).$$

In many cases, see, for example, [Aas et al. (2009)], it is possible to compute the required inverses of this function in closed form as well. For instance, if $\varphi(x) = (1+x)^{-1/\theta}$, which corresponds to the Clayton copula, we observe that

$$h_{u_2}(u_1) = \left(\frac{u_2^{-\theta}}{u_1^{-\theta} + u_2^{-\theta} - 1} \right)^{\frac{1}{\theta}+1}, \quad h_{u_2}^{-1}(v) = \left(1 - u_2^{-\theta} + u_2^{-\theta} v^{-\theta/(1+\theta)} \right)^{-\frac{1}{\theta}}.$$

Besides the fact that, depending on the considered copula, it might be tedious to compute the partial derivative of a copula and its (generalized) inverse, the major shortcoming of the conditional sampling method is that it is very difficult to extend it to larger dimensions $d \geq 3$. Even though this is possible in theory, see [O'Brien (1975), Rüschendorf (1981), Rüschendorf (2009)], the order of the involved partial derivatives and the number of required (generalized) inverses grows with the dimension, making the approach practically infeasible. In practice, the simulation of random vectors in large dimensions is typically only possible along a sufficiently easy stochastic model, see Section 5.1.2.

5.1.2 Simulation Along a Stochastic Model

Most copulas, especially those in dimensions $d \geq 3$, stem from an intuitive stochastic model, which can be exploited in order to derive a simulation algorithm. As opposed to the conditional sampling method, there is no need to work with the functional form of the copula analytically, for example by computing partial derivatives. However, the stochastic models for two different copula families, and hence the resulting simulation algorithms, might be completely different, and there is no panacea like the conditional sampling method in the bivariate case. Nevertheless, some of the most popular copula families allow for efficient simulation algorithms, and we briefly review them for the families introduced in Chapter 4.

5.1.2.1 Gaussian Copulas and t-Copulas

As Equation (4.1) shows, a random vector $(X_1, \ldots, X_d)$ with multivariate normal distribution can be constructed by linearly combining independent and identically distributed standard normally distributed random variables. In order to simulate a multivariate normal law with pre-determined correlation matrix Σ, we require the computation of a matrix A satisfying $A A' = \Sigma$. The so-called 'Cholesky decomposition' provides a feasible algorithm accomplishing this task and is pre-implemented in many software packages.[2] The interested reader is referred to [Golub, van Loan (1989), p. 97] for details. The precise simulation algorithm for a d-dimensional Gaussian copula C_Σ is the following.

Algorithm 5.1.3 (Simulating the Gaussian copula)
Input for the algorithm is a positive definite correlation matrix $\Sigma \in \mathbb{R}^{d \times d}$.

(1) Compute the Cholesky decomposition of Σ, providing a lower triangular matrix A, satisfying $A A' = \Sigma$.
(2) Simulate a list of d independent random variables $Y_1, \ldots, Y_d$ with standard normal distribution function.
(3) Compute the random vector

$$\begin{pmatrix} X_1 \\ \vdots \\ X_d \end{pmatrix} = A \cdot \begin{pmatrix} Y_1 \\ \vdots \\ Y_d \end{pmatrix},$$

which has a multivariate normal law with zero mean vector, unit variances, and correlation matrix Σ.
(4) Return $(U_1, \ldots, U_d)$, where $U_j := \Phi(X_j)$, $j = 1, \ldots, d$. Recall that Φ was the cumulative distribution function of the standard normal law.

Revisiting the derivation (4.4) of the multivariate t-distribution, we obtain a similar algorithm for the t-copula.

Algorithm 5.1.4 (Simulating the t-copula)
Input for the algorithm is a positive definite correlation[3] matrix $\Sigma \in \mathbb{R}^{d \times d}$ and the degrees of freedom $\nu > 0$.

(1) Compute the Cholesky decomposition of Σ, providing a lower triangular matrix A satisfying $A A' = \Sigma$.
(2) Simulate a list of d independent random variables $Y_1, \ldots, Y_d$ with standard normal distribution function. Independently, simulate a random variable W with an $Inv\Gamma(\nu/2, \nu/2)$-distribution.

---

[2] In the language R, the command $\texttt{chol}(\Sigma)$ returns the upper triangular part B of the Cholesky decomposition of Σ, so $B' B = \Sigma$ and one may choose $A = B'$.

[3] Let us again stress the fact that for the t-distribution the matrix Σ must be read as a parameterizing matrix and is not the actual correlation matrix of the resulting t-distribution. This also depends on the degrees of freedom ν and is given by $\nu/(\nu - 2)\, \Sigma$ whenever $\nu > 2$.

(3)   Compute the random vector

$$\begin{pmatrix} X_1 \\ \vdots \\ X_d \end{pmatrix} = \sqrt{W}\, A \cdot \begin{pmatrix} Y_1 \\ \vdots \\ Y_d \end{pmatrix}.$$

(4)   Return $(U_1, \ldots, U_d)$, where $U_j := t_\nu(X_j)$, $j = 1, \ldots, d$.

The simulation of the inverse Gamma random variable W may be accomplished by computing the reciprocal of a Gamma-distributed random variable. The simulation of the latter is typically pre-implemented in most statistical software packages, for example via `rgamma()` in R.

5.1.2.2   Archimedean Copulas with Completely Monotone Generator

In Equation (4.6) of Section 4.2 we have already presented a simple stochastic model for Archimedean copulas, which leads to the following simulation algorithm.

Algorithm 5.1.5 (Simulating an Archimedean copula)
Input for the algorithm is a completely monotone generator φ of an Archimedean copula. Recall that φ equals the Laplace transform of a positive random variable M.

(1)   Simulate a list of d independent random variables $\epsilon_1, \ldots, \epsilon_d$ with unit exponential distribution. Independently, simulate a random variable M whose Laplace transform equals φ.
(2)   Return $(U_1, \ldots, U_d)$, where $U_j := \varphi(\epsilon_j / M)$, $j = 1, \ldots, d$.

Many completely monotone generators of Archimedean copulas correspond to Laplace transforms of random variables, for which a simulation algorithm is pre-implemented in most statistical software packages. If not, we refer to Section 5.1.3 for details. Revisiting the three parametric examples of Table 4.1 in Section 4.2, the Clayton copula corresponds to M being Gamma-distributed, the Gumbel copula corresponds to M having a positive stable distribution, and the Ali–Mikhail–Haq family corresponds to M having a geometric distribution. For the simulation of hierarchical Archimedean copulas, the interested reader is referred to [Hofert (2008), McNeil (2008), Hering et al. (2010)] or [Mai, Scherer (2012), Chapter 2.4].

5.1.2.3   Extreme-value Copulas

In theory, extreme-value copulas arise as the asymptotic copulas for $n \to \infty$ when the componentwise minima over n iid random vectors is taken and scaled appropriately, cf. Exercise 11 in Chapter 4. Even though this directly yields an approximate sampling strategy whenever the involved iid random vectors can be simulated efficiently, such a procedure is clearly inefficient. Unfortunately, for many extreme-value copulas, for example such as the Galambos copula, the authors are not aware of a simpler simulation algorithm. However, for some families of extreme-value copulas, alternative models are known. For instance, the Gumbel copula is an Archimedean copula, hence Algorithm 5.1.5 applies. Another big class of extreme-value copulas for which efficient simulation algorithms are known comprise the family of Marshall–Olkin copulas, and the subclass of Lévy-frailty copulas. Since the derivation of the respective algorithms goes beyond the scope of this introductory book, the interested reader is referred to [Mai, Scherer (2012), Chapter 3]. In order to provide at least one simulation algorithm for a multivariate extreme-value copula other than the Gumbel copula, we exemplarily provide a simulation algorithm for the one-parametric Lévy-frailty copula

$$C_\alpha(u_1,\dots,u_d) = (u_1 u_2 \cdots u_d)^\alpha \min\{u_1,\dots,u_d\}^{1-\alpha}, \tag{5.2}$$

for a parameter $\alpha \in [0,1]$, cf. the second family in Table 4.4, see also [Durante et al. (2007)]. For this, a pretty simple simulation algorithm can be given. See Figure 5.1 for a visualization.

Algorithm 5.1.6 (Simulating the copula C_α from (5.2))
Input is the parameter $\alpha \in [0,1]$.

(1) Simulate d iid exponential random variables $\epsilon_1,\dots,\epsilon_d$ with mean 1.
(2) Simulate one exponential random variable S with parameter $1-\alpha$.
(3) Compute the random vector $(X_1,\dots,X_d)$ via

$$X_j := \begin{cases} \epsilon_j/\alpha, & \text{if } (\alpha S \geq \epsilon_j) \\ S, & \text{if } (\alpha S < \epsilon_j) \end{cases}, \quad j=1,\dots,d.$$

(4) Return $(U_1,\dots,U_d)$, where $U_j := \exp(-X_j), j=1,\dots,d$.

5.1.2.4 Archimax copulas

Since Archimax copulas are motivated by an 'analytical joint venture' of the Archimedean and the extreme-value classes, it is not surprising that their simulation is

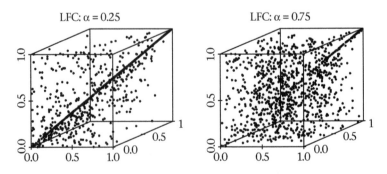

Figure 5.1   Scatter plot of the 3-dimensional Lévy-frailty copula as described in Algorithm 5.1.6. Note how with decreasing α the singular component becomes more pronounced. The plot was created using the R-command `scatterplot3d()` from the equally named package.

also a concatenation of the simulation of an extreme-value copula and an Archimedean copula. The following algorithm can be found in [Charpentier et al. (2014)].

Algorithm 5.1.7 (Simulating an Archimax copula)
Input for the algorithm is a completely monotone generator φ of an Archimedean copula, and an extreme-value copula with stable tail dependence function ℓ.

(1) Simulate a random vector $(V_1, \ldots, V_d)$ whose distribution function is the extreme-value copula with stable tail dependence function ℓ.
(2) Simulate a random variable M with Laplace transform φ.
(3) Return $(U_1, \ldots, U_d)$, where $U_j := \varphi(-\log(V_j)/M)$, $j = 1, \ldots, d$.

5.1.3 Practical Guide for the Implementation

As one can see from the presented simulation algorithms above, we typically require simulation algorithms for standard univariate distributions. Most statistical software packages contain pre-implemented simulation algorithms for basic univariate laws such as the uniform distribution on $[0,1]$, the standard normal distribution, the exponential distribution, and the Gamma distribution.[4] If this is not the case or a more special law is required, for example the positive stable law for the Gumbel copula, we refer the reader to [Mai, Scherer (2012), Chapter 6], or the more elaborate textbook [Devroye (1986)]. Concerning a more comprehensive overview on simulation algorithms for multivariate distributions, we refer to [Mai, Scherer (2012)]. Special attention on numerical aspects when simulating the involved univariate laws associated with some Archimedean copulas can be found in [Hofert (2008)].

FAQ 5.1.8 (What dimensions d are doable in practice?)
This is an important question for concrete implementations. The answer, however, strongly depends on the copula family in question. Most convenient is a situation where the effort (in terms of computation time but also memory requirements) only increases about linearly in d. This situation appears, for example, in the case of Archimedean copulas with completely monotone generator, as one immediately observes from Algorithm 5.1.5. The same is true for other so-called one-factor models, explaining their popularity. For other parametric families like the Gaussian and the t-copula, the required effort increases polynomially in d, as we need a matrix multiplication within their stochastic model. The least favorable situation is when the effort increases exponentially in d, an example being the general Marshall–Olkin distribution. In order to apply such distributions to high-dimensional situations, one needs to consider (more efficient to implement) subfamilies, whose constructions require careful computations.

---

[4] In the language R, the respective function calls are `runif()`, `rnorm()`, `rexp()`, and `rgamma()`.

EXERCISES

1. Derive F^{-1} for the exponential law with parameter λ. Use this to simulate from the exponential distribution via the quantile method $F^{-1}(U)$, where $U \sim \mathcal{U}[0,1]$.

2. Assume that $\mathbb{P}(U_1 \leq u_1 | U_2 = u_2) = \lim_{\delta \to 0} \mathbb{P}(U_1 \leq u_1 | u_2 - \delta < U_2 \leq u_2 + \delta)$ and show that

$$\mathbb{P}(U_1 \leq u_1 | U_2 = u_2) = \frac{\partial}{\partial u_2} C(u_1, u_2).$$

3. Simulate random vectors (X_1, X_2) that have exponential $\lambda_1 = 0.1$ (resp. $\lambda_2 = 0.05$) marginal laws and different survival copulas. Estimate $\mathbb{P}(X_1 > 10, X_2 > 10)$ via a Monte-Carlo simulation and compare it to the theoretical values. Understand the role of dependence by varying the copula behind the model and the copula parameters.

4. Show that the inverse of the h-function of the bivariate Gaussian copula is given by

$$h_{u_2}^{-1}(v) = \Phi\big(\Phi^{-1}(v)(1 - \rho^2)^{1/2} + \rho \, \Phi^{-1}(u_2)\big).$$

5. Verify that $\Sigma = A A'$, where

$$\Sigma = \begin{pmatrix} 1 & 1/2 & 1/2 \\ 1/2 & 1 & 3/4 \\ 1/2 & 3/4 & 1 \end{pmatrix}, \quad A = \begin{pmatrix} 1 & 0 & 0 \\ 1/2 & \sqrt{3/4} & 0 \\ 1/2 & \sqrt{1/3} & \sqrt{5/12} \end{pmatrix}.$$

If you do this with R, note that `matrix()` creates a matrix, `t()` is the transpose of a matrix, and the matrix multiplication is called via `A%*%t(A)`.

6. Implement a function `SampleMO(n,λ)` that returns n samples of a d-dimensional Marshall–Olkin copula with parameter set $\lambda = \{\lambda_I\}_{\emptyset \neq I \subset \{1,\dots,d\}}$ as described in FAQ 4.3.4. Use this function to create scatter plots for the bivariate case where $\lambda = \{\lambda_{\{1\}}, \lambda_{\{2\}}, \lambda_{\{1,2\}}\}$. Run the program with $\lambda_{\{1\}} > \lambda_{\{2\}}, \lambda_{\{1\}} < \lambda_{\{2\}}$ and $\lambda_{\{1\}} = \lambda_{\{2\}}$. Explain the different shapes of the obtained scatter plots. For dimension $d \in \{2,\dots,7\}$ and arbitrary parameter sets λ, create 1000 samples of the Marshall–Olkin copula and plot the necessary runtime with respect to the dimension d.

7. Simulate $n = 1000$ samples from the copula constructed in Equation (1.5). Use the `pairs()` command to create bivariate scatter plots and observe that these all look like the independence copula. Use the command `scatterplot3d()`, from the R-package with identical name, to plot the three-dimensional scatter plot. Observe that this does not look like the three-variate independence copula.

6 How to Estimate Parameters of a Multivariate Model?

We are now concerned with the estimation and (very briefly) calibration of multivariate stochastic models. This task is crucial for applications, but quite challenging for various reasons that we illustrate in the following. As a general problem one could say that the amount of data needed to estimate the parameters of a multi-dimensional model is often larger than it is for the univariate marginal laws. In reality, one often has the situation that data is incomplete for some dimension during some periods of time, or that, say, returns of different stocks are known for different time periods. For instance, if some index constitutions change, this problem arises naturally. So only rarely does one have a long set of data with the same data quality in all dimensions.

Starting from Sklar's paradigm, that is, considering for the joint distribution F the separation into copula and marginal laws, it is reasonable to also try to separate the estimation into two steps: (i) the estimation of the marginal laws in a first step, followed by (ii) the estimation of the dependence structure thereafter. This is possible, but some technical problems have to be overcome.

By carrying out an estimation we try to select the stochastic model (or the parameters of some parametric family) in a way that the statistical properties of the model are in best possible agreement with collected observations. A categorization of the different estimation approaches proposed in the literature might be achieved along the available information (resp. assumptions) about the distribution function F. For instance, we might assume no specific family for F and, hence, work completely non-parametrically. In this case, one usually relies on empirical distribution functions and empirical copulas. Going further, we might know the parametric family of the marginal laws and/or the parametric family of the copula. Depending on the assumption one is willing to make, this allows us to use different estimation philosophies like maximum-likelihood methods.

In finance, a calibration (of the pricing measure) is sometimes preferred over an estimation (of the historical measure). The philosophy here is that derivative prices, that is, today's market values of financial positions with a maturity in the future, are observed and these derivative prices are seen as an aggregated opinion of all market participants about the future development of the modeled outcomes. Carrying out a calibration means selecting the parameters of the pricing model such that model prices replicate the observed derivative prices as accurately as possible. In this regard, the selected probability measure is forward looking and need not agree with historical data.

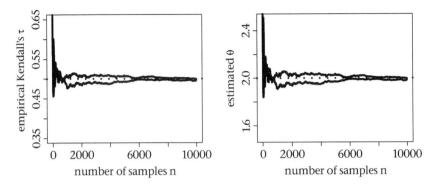

Figure 6.1   The empirical Kendall's τ (two processes of $\hat{\tau}_n$) given different sample sizes n and the resulting moment estimates for θ. The true values are $\tau = 0.5$ and $\theta = 2$, respectively. One observes that considerable sample sizes n are needed for satisfying estimation results. The setup is described in Example 6.1.1.

6.1 The Method of Moments

We consider a parametric copula C, say an Archimedean copula with one-parametric generator function $\varphi = \varphi_\theta$, and continuous marginal laws $F_1, \ldots, F_d$. The estimation idea behind the '*method of moments*' is strikingly simple: we compute some rank-based dependence measure like Kendall's τ or Spearman's ρ_S for the copula family C in consideration. Recall that such rank-based measures do not depend on the (continuous) marginal laws and they will be functions of the parameter of the copula model, say $\theta \mapsto f(\theta) = \tau$. Then, we estimate the empirical version of this dependence measure from our set of data.[1] This yields the estimate $\hat{\tau}_n$. For many copula families we observe that $\theta \mapsto f(\theta)$ is strictly increasing and maps onto $[-1, 1]$ or onto a subset of $[-1, 1]$, depending on the flexibility of the chosen parametric family of copulas. Then, we can identify the inverse f^{-1} and use as estimate $\hat{\theta}_n := f^{-1}(\hat{\tau}_n)$. This method has been analyzed for Archimedean copulas by [Genest, Rivest (1993)]. See also [Tsukahara (2005)] and the references therein. Let us now illustrate this method with Example 6.1.1.

Example 6.1.1 (Estimating the Gumbel copula)
Assume our copula is of Gumbel type, that is, the Archimedean generator is given by $\varphi_\theta(x) = \exp(-x^{1/\theta})$, where $\theta \in [1, \infty)$ to obtain a completely monotone generator. The theoretical Kendall's τ for this family is $(\theta - 1)/\theta =: f(\theta)$, so we have a strictly increasing mapping f from $[1, \infty)$ onto the range $[0, 1)$ for Kendall's τ. The inverse of this mapping is $f^{-1}(x) = 1/(1 - x)$. Given a set of data we estimate Kendall's τ as $\hat{\tau}_{1000} = 0.508945$, which results in the estimate[2] $\hat{\theta}_{1000} = f^{-1}(\hat{\tau}_{1000}) = 2.036432$. The influence of the sample size n and the asymptotic behavior are illustrated in Figure 6.1.

---

[1] Note that the assumption of continuous marginals is convenient, since we do not have to consider ties in the data, and that no further assumptions on the marginal laws are needed since ranks (and the copula) are invariant under strictly monotone transformations. Moreover, identifiability issues are circumvented.

[2] The dataset was a sample of 1000 observations generated with a true value of $\theta = 2$.

6.1.1 Some Theoretical Background

If some estimation strategy is proposed, one is typically interested in its finite sample and asymptotic properties. In the above case using the empirical Kendall's τ, one has a consistent sequence of estimates for Kendall's τ, meaning that if the sample size n goes to infinity, the sequence of estimates $\hat{\tau}_n$ converges to the true value of Kendall's τ with probability one. This can be shown for the empirical Kendall's τ using the theory of so-called U-statistics, see [Hoeffding (1961)]. If f^{-1} is continuous, then $f^{-1}(\hat{\tau}_n)$ is also a consistent sequence of estimators for $f^{-1}(\tau) = \theta$, which follows from the continuous mapping theorem, see [van der Vaart, Wellner (1996), Theorems 1.3.6, 1.9.5]. But one has even more: the empirical Kendall's τ is asymptotically normal, that is, $\sqrt{n}(\hat{\tau}_n - \tau)$ converges in distribution to a normal distribution with zero mean and some standard deviation $\sigma_C > 0$ that depends on the chosen copula family. Then, by the so-called delta-method, see [van der Vaart, Wellner (1996), Theorem 3.9.4], we have that $\sqrt{n}(f^{-1}(\hat{\tau}_n) - f^{-1}(\tau))$ converges to a standard normal distribution with zero mean and variance given by $(f^{-1})'(\tau)\sigma_C^2$. These observations are useful in many regards. First of all, they provide evidence that the method works in the limit. Then, they show that strong slopes in the function f^{-1} near τ might substantially increase the variance of the estimate. Moreover, they allow us to construct confidence bounds and tests for the parameters. Since the limiting distribution depends on the chosen family of copulas, careful case-by-case investigations are necessary. Such treatments are found in [Dengler (2010), Genest et al. (2011)]. Similar considerations that we exemplarily made for Kendall's τ also apply to Spearman's ρ_S and other measures of dependence. The interested reader is referred to [Schmid, Schmidt (2007)].

FAQ 6.1.2 (What are the pros and cons of this method?)
An obvious advantage of the method of moments is its simplicity and its well-studied asymptotic behavior. For most one-parametric families of bivariate copulas, Kendall's τ and Spearman's ρ_S are known and indeed increasing functions of the parameter.[3] Clearly, if this assumption is violated, the methodology breaks down. Moreover, if we have a two-dimensional parameter space we have to adapt the method. In this case one might compute two different empirical dependence measures and must solve a (typically non-linear) system of two equations. In the best case, a solution exists and is unique, but this depends on the chosen example. Moreover, multivariate extensions require multivariate dependence measures[4] and the solution of high-dimensional equation systems. A multivariate example where the method of moments is still easily applicable is the Gaussian copula with correlation matrix $\Sigma = (\rho_{j,k})_{j,k=1,\dots,d}$. Here, one has the relation $\tau_{C_{jk}} = 2/\pi \arcsin(\rho_{j,k})$, see Section 4.1.1, where C_{jk} is the bivariate Gaussian copula associated with the sub-matrix restricted to the components $j \neq k$. This example is especially convenient, since all bivariate pairs fully specify the dependence structure, which is an exception rather than the rule.

---

[3] A sufficient condition that is often easy to check is that the ordering $\theta \leq \eta$ implies $C(u_1, u_2; \theta) \leq C(u_1, u_2; \eta)$ for all $(u_1, u_2) \in [0,1]^2$, see [Nelsen (1998), Theorems 1.5.3, 1.5.9].
[4] See [Schmid et al. (2011)] for a survey.

6.2 Maximum-likelihood Methods

Like the method of moments, the maximum-likelihood method starts from the assumption of having a parametric model for the distribution in concern. To recall the rough idea in the univariate case, one assumes that the sample $X = (X^{(1)}, \ldots, X^{(n)})$ comes from a distribution with density $f(\cdot; \alpha)$, where α is the parameter (possibly a vector) of the density. Then, one computes the so-called 'likelihood function'

$$L(X; \alpha) := \prod_{i=1}^{n} f(X^{(i)}; \alpha)$$

and maximizes this expression as a function of α. The product stems from $X^{(1)}, \ldots, X^{(n)}$ being independent and the idea to maximize this expression over α is motivated by finding the parameter (vector) α that is in 'best agreement' with the observed data. Clearly, the logarithm being a strictly increasing transform, one can alternatively maximize the so-called 'log-likelihood function' given by

$$\ell(X; \alpha) := \log(L(X; \alpha)) = \sum_{i=1}^{n} \log(f(X^{(i)}; \alpha)),$$

which is in many cases numerically more convenient to handle, because sums are often more convenient than products. The resulting estimates are very well studied in the literature and turn out to have convenient properties (for example asymptotic normality) under mild technical assumptions.

Naturally, one tries to extend this approach to the multivariate case. We consider the bivariate case for notational simplicity. We take as given a sample of the form $X = ((X_1^{(1)}, X_2^{(1)}), \ldots, (X_1^{(n)}, X_2^{(n)}))$ and assume the underlying bivariate distribution function has the bivariate density $f(x_1, x_2; \alpha)$, where α is again the parameter (vector) of the model. In principle, the above steps can be repeated one-by-one. The big difference lies in two issues that we need to overcome in the following. (i) The computational effort typically increases dramatically, since multivariate distribution functions are parameterized in most cases by a parameter vector that can have considerable dimension.[5] Hence, in many cases we need numerical routines to identify the maximum-likelihood estimates which can be numerically expensive and one might be stuck in a local maximum when carrying out the optimization step. (ii) Classical multivariate distribution functions may not be adequate for the data set we look at. For instance, the marginal laws might come from completely different parametric families. For both issues, the separation of the multivariate law into marginal laws and copula can be advantageous. We assume the joint distribution to be given as $F(x_1, x_2) = C(F_1(x_1; \alpha_1), F_2(x_2; \alpha_2); \theta)$, that is, the univariate marginal law F_j has

---

[5] Take the d-variate normal distribution as an example, which is parameterized by a d-dimensional location vector μ and a covariance matrix Σ with d^2 entries, where (by symmetry) only the $d(d+1)/2$-entries on and above the diagonal have to be specified.

parameter (vector) α_j and the copula comes from a parametric family with parameter (vector) θ. Taking the bivariate normal case as an example, this corresponds to $\alpha_j = (\mu_j, \sigma_j)$, $j = 1, 2$, and $\theta = \rho_{1,2}$. Assuming marginal laws and copula to both have a density, denoted f_1, f_2, and c, we obtain (by taking the partial derivatives with respect to x_1 and x_2) for the bivariate density

$$\frac{\partial^2}{\partial x_1 \, \partial x_2} F(x_1, x_2; \alpha_1, \alpha_2, \theta) = f(x_1, x_2; \alpha_1, \alpha_2, \theta) = \frac{\partial^2}{\partial x_1 \, \partial x_2} C(F_1(x_1; \alpha_1), F_2(x_2; \alpha_2); \theta)$$

$$= f_1(x_1; \alpha_1) f_2(x_2; \alpha_2) c(F_1(x_1; \alpha_1), F_2(x_2; \alpha_2); \theta).$$

Applying the log-transform, we find $\log f(x_1, x_2; \alpha_1, \alpha_2, \theta) = \cdots$

$$\cdots = \underbrace{\log f_1(x_1; \alpha_1)}_{\text{depends only on } \alpha_1} + \underbrace{\log f_2(x_2; \alpha_2)}_{\text{depends only on } \alpha_2} + \underbrace{\log c(F_1(x_1; \alpha_1), F_2(x_2; \alpha_2); \theta)}_{\text{depends on } \alpha_1, \alpha_2, \text{ and } \theta}, \qquad (6.1)$$

and it is worth noting that the problem splits into a sum of terms that are alike in the univariate maximum-likelihood procedure (for each of the marginal laws) and a term that depends on both: parameters of the marginal laws and parameters of the dependence structure.

6.2.1 Perfect Information about the Marginal Laws

The most convenient (but at the same time the least realistic) situation would be knowing the marginal laws for sure, that is, knowing α_1, α_2. In this case, we can apply the transform $F_j(\cdot; \alpha_j)$ to the respective coordinate of the sample and end up with the new sample $((F_1(X_1^{(1)}; \alpha_1), F_2(X_2^{(1)}; \alpha_2)), \ldots, (F_1(X_1^{(n)}; \alpha_1), F_2(X_2^{(n)}; \alpha_2))) =:$ $((U_1^{(1)}, U_2^{(1)}), \ldots, (U_1^{(n)}, U_2^{(n)}))$, and the $(U_1^{(i)}, U_2^{(i)}) =: U^{(i)}$ are independent and distributed according to the copula $C(\cdot, \cdot; \theta)$. In this case, no ambiguity about the marginal laws 'distorts' our sample U and the only thing we have to estimate is θ. Looking at the logarithm of the joint density (6.1), we observe that when we set up our log-likelihood function, this is precisely

$$\ell(X; \alpha_1, \alpha_2, \theta) = \sum_{i=1}^{n} \sum_{j=1}^{2} \log f_j(X_j^{(i)}; \alpha_j) + \sum_{i=1}^{n} \log c(F_1(X_1^{(i)}; \alpha_1), F_2(X_2^{(i)}; \alpha_2); \theta)$$

$$= \sum_{i=1}^{n} \sum_{j=1}^{2} \log f_j(X_j^{(i)}; \alpha_j) + \sum_{i=1}^{n} \log c(U_1^{(i)}, U_2^{(i)}; \theta). \qquad (6.2)$$

Maximizing ℓ over θ (recall that α_1, α_2 are assumed to be known) is equivalent to only maximizing the last sum over θ, that is, yields the same maximizer. This has been implemented for many copula densities in most statistical software packages. Note that the problem is considerably simplified as only the copula parameters must be treated.

Let us denote the maximizer obtained in this way by $\hat{\theta}_n$. It is an asymptotically efficient estimate, which heuristically means that it uses the available information better than other estimates do.

6.2.2   Joint Maximization Over α and θ: Full Maximum-Likelihood

Without any additional information about the marginal laws (resp. parameters α_j) we face the problem of having to maximize

$$\ell(X; \alpha_1, \alpha_2, \theta) = \sum_{i=1}^{n} \sum_{j=1}^{2} \log f_j(X_j^{(i)}; \alpha_j) + \sum_{i=1}^{n} \log c(F_1(X_1^{(i)}; \alpha_1), F_2(X_2^{(i)}; \alpha_2); \theta) \quad (6.3)$$

jointly over $\alpha_1, \alpha_2, \theta$. Only in very rare cases does the structure of c, f_j, and F_j simplify this task. Mostly, this is a highly non-trivial optimization problem, given the typically large dimension of the parameter vector $(\alpha_1, \alpha_2, \theta)$. One has to be aware of the risk of ending up in a local maximum instead of the global one. From a theoretical point of view, however, the resulting estimates $\hat{\alpha}_{1,n}, \hat{\alpha}_{2,n}, \hat{\theta}_n$ have convenient properties like asymptotic normality[6] and asymptotic efficiency.

6.2.3   Inference Functions for Margins (IFM) Method

This method, which is at the heart of copula modeling, goes back to [Joe, Xu (1996)] and is studied further in [Joe (2005)]. The idea behind this method relies on the decomposition of the joint distribution into marginal laws and copula and tries to overcome the numerical problems associated with the full maximum-likelihood procedure explained in the previous paragraph. It consists of the following two steps. (i) Consider all marginal laws separately and perform a maximum-likelihood procedure to estimate the parameters α_1 and α_2. Denote the resulting estimates by $\tilde{\alpha}_{1,n}$ and $\tilde{\alpha}_{2,n}$. (ii) Plug the marginal maximum-likelihood estimates into the marginal distribution functions $F_j(\cdot; \tilde{\alpha}_{j,n})$ and use these to convert the observations $X_j^{(i)}$ to $[0,1]$ via the transform $U_j^{(i)} := F_j(X_j^{(i)}; \tilde{\alpha}_{j,n})$, $j = 1, 2$. It is important to note that the $U_j^{(i)}$ obtained in this way are only approximately distributed as $\mathcal{U}[0,1]$, since in general $\tilde{\alpha}_{j,n}$ is not perfectly equal to the true but unknown parameter α_j. Moreover, the estimates $\tilde{\alpha}_{j,n}$ contain information from the full sample X, so the pairs $(U_1^{(i)}, U_2^{(i)})$, $i = 1, \ldots, n$, are not independent. Hence, U is only approximately an iid sample from $C(\cdot, \cdot; \theta)$, the influence of the unknown marginal laws has distorted it. Nevertheless, in the IFM method we continue with U and maximize $\ell(\tilde{\alpha}_{1,n}, \tilde{\alpha}_{2,n}, \theta)$ as a function of θ, which ultimately yields the estimate $\tilde{\theta}_n$.

Clearly, the so-obtained estimate $\tilde{\theta}_n$ most likely differs from $\hat{\theta}_n$. But [Joe, Xu (1996)] succeeded in showing that (under some regularity conditions) asymptotically the

---

[6] Asymptotic normality means that the distance between the estimates $\hat{\alpha}_{j,n}, \hat{\theta}_n$ and the true values α_j, θ, $j = 1, 2$, when multiplied with $\sqrt{n}$ converges (in distribution) to a multivariate normal distribution with zero mean and some covariance matrix Σ. This means that the sequence of estimates converges in n to the true parameters, a property we call consistency, and the asymptotic distribution when scaled by $\sqrt{n}$ is known.

IFM method also provides a consistent and normally distributed estimate for θ. Moreover, in many practical studies the method has shown to perform very well. The striking advantage is the reduction of numerical complexity. The high-dimensional optimization over the full parameter space is replaced by separate optimizations for each marginal law and one for the dependence parameters. It is also possible to take these estimates as the starting values for a joint maximization in (6.1).

6.3   Using a Rank Transformation to Obtain (Pseudo-)Samples

We might also completely avoid parametric assumptions on the marginal laws, and only assume the marginal laws F_1, F_2 to be continuous. Our aim, again, is to transform the sample X from the joint distribution F to a (pseudo-)sample of the copula C, denoted U. This might be achieved via rank statistics or, in other words, the empirical distribution function (of each marginal law) is applied to the respective component. Let us start by recalling the empirical distribution function in the univariate case.

Definition 6.3.1 (Univariate empirical distribution function)
Consider a sample $X = (X^{(1)}, \ldots, X^{(n)})$ from a univariate random variable whose distribution function is denoted F. We define the empirical distribution function via

$$\hat{F}_n(x) := \frac{1}{n} \sum_{i=1}^{n} \mathbf{1}_{\{X^{(i)} \leq x\}}, \quad n \in \mathbb{N}, x \in \mathbb{R}.$$

Concerning an interpretation, we simply count how often $X^{(i)}$ is less than or equal to x and divide by the sample size. Note that $\mathbf{1}_{\{X^{(i)} \leq x\}}$ can be interpreted as a Bernoulli experiment with success probability $F(x)$.

For each fixed $x \in \mathbb{R}$ it is clear, by the strong law of large numbers applied to the sequence of Bernoulli experiments $\{\mathbf{1}_{\{X^{(i)} \leq x\}}\}_{i \in \mathbb{N}}$, that $\hat{F}_n(x)$ converges almost surely to $F(x)$ as n tends to infinity. But we even understand the rate of convergence via the central limit theorem: consider $G_n(x) := \sqrt{n}(\hat{F}_n(x) - F(x))$ and observe that it converges in distribution to a normally distributed random variable with zero mean and variance $F(x)(1 - F(x))$. This is illustrated in Figure 6.2 for a uniform distribution on $[-1, 1]$. One can even show stronger statements about uniform convergence, but this requires more involved notions beyond the scope of this introduction. Heuristically speaking, even the supremum (taken over all x) of $|\hat{F}_n(x) - F(x)|$ tends to zero as n tends to infinity and $\{G_n\}_{n \in \mathbb{N}}$ converges to a so-called generalized Brownian bridge, a very useful result for hypothesis tests of the form $\mathcal{H}_0 : F = F_0$ for a certain given distribution function F_0. It is beyond the scope of this introduction to go into more details here and we refer the interested reader to the book [van der Vaart, Wellner (1996)] instead.

To conclude with consequences for the estimation of the marginal laws $F_1, \ldots, F_d$: irrespectively of the shape of the (continuous) marginal distribution functions F_j, the empirical distribution function $\hat{F}_{j,n}$ is a plausible estimate for F_j with nice asymptotic properties. Hence, it is clearly tempting to use the estimated functions $\hat{F}_{j,n}$ to

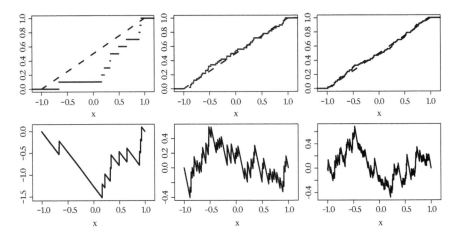

Figure 6.2   Illustration of the processes $\{\hat{F}_n(x)\}_{n\in\mathbb{N}}$ (top) and $\{G_n(x)\}_{n\in\mathbb{N}}$ (bottom) for $n = 10, 50, 100$. The true distribution function is that of a $\mathcal{U}[-1,1]$ distribution; it is illustrated in the above plots using a dotted line.

transform the observations $X_j^{(i)}$ to $[0,1]$, for $j = 1,\ldots,d$. For continuous marginal laws (where we have ties in the observations only with probability zero) empirical distribution functions are closely related to rank statistics. This is intuitively clear, since counting how many of the $X_j^{(i)}$ are below some x_j is equivalent to checking which rank is the last to be below x_j. So we have $\hat{F}_{j,n}(X_j^{[i]}) = i/n$, where $X_j^{[1]} \leq X_j^{[2]} \leq \cdots \leq X_j^{[n]}$ is the order statistic of $(X_j^{(1)},\ldots,X_j^{(n)})$, the j-th components of the observations X, providing us with a convenient formula to compute the (pseudo-)observations. For each component $j = 1,\ldots,d$ we separately derive the rank statistics and set the respective (pseudo-)observations as $U_j^{(i)} := \mathrm{rank}(X^{(i)})/n = \hat{F}_{j,n}(X_j^{(i)})$.

Closely related to the univariate case, we can consider a multivariate analogue of the empirical distribution function. Given the sample $X = (X^{(1)},\ldots,X^{(n)})$, where $X^{(i)}$ is distributed according to the d-variate distribution function F, this is defined below and illustrated in Figure 6.3.

Definition 6.3.2 (Multivariate empirical distribution function)
Consider a sample $X = (X^{(1)},\ldots,X^{(n)})$, drawn from a multivariate distribution function F. We can then define the (multivariate) empirical distribution function via

$$\hat{F}_n(\boldsymbol{x}) := \hat{F}_n(x_1,\ldots,x_d) := \frac{1}{n}\sum_{i=1}^{n}\mathbf{1}_{\{X_1^{(i)}\leq x_1,\ldots,X_d^{(i)}\leq x_d\}}, \quad n\in\mathbb{N},\, x_1,\ldots,x_d\in\mathbb{R}, \quad (6.4)$$

and the empirical process as

$$\hat{G}_n(\boldsymbol{x}) := G_n(x_1,\ldots,x_d) := \sqrt{n}(\hat{F}_n(x_1,\ldots,x_d) - F(x_1,\ldots,x_d)),$$
$$n\in\mathbb{N},\, x_1,\ldots,x_d\in\mathbb{R}.$$

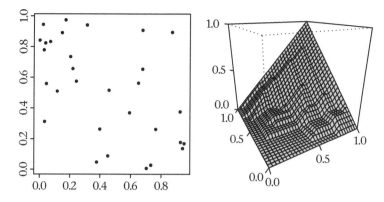

Figure 6.3 Scatter plot (left) of $n = 30$ observations drawn from a Gaussian copula with $\rho = -0.5$ (C_ρ serving as distribution function F) and corresponding empirical distribution function $\hat{F}_n$ (right). This was computed using the function C.n() from the R-package copula and plotted with persp().

Similarly to the univariate case, when the sample size n tends to infinity one has (for some fixed $\boldsymbol{x} \in \mathbb{R}^d$) almost sure convergence of $\hat{F}_n(\boldsymbol{x})$ to $F(\boldsymbol{x})$ and convergence in distribution of $G_n(\boldsymbol{x})$ to a normally distributed random variable with zero mean and variance $F(\boldsymbol{x})(1 - F(\boldsymbol{x}))$. Moreover, uniformly in $\boldsymbol{x}$, $\hat{F}_n$ tends almost surely to F and $\{G_n\}_{n\in\mathbb{N}}$ converges to a so-called tight Gaussian process. Again, we omit technical details and invite the interested reader to study [van der Vaart, Wellner (1996)].

The empirical distribution function is typically defined via the scaling factor $1/n$, see (6.4). In the copula context, however, this has the disadvantage that the biggest entry is assigned to the boundary value $n/n = 1$, which might create problems in the implementation later on when the copula density is only defined in the interior of $[0, 1]^d$. Hence, the scaling factor $1/(n+1)$ is typically used instead of $1/n$ to circumvent this problem. Asymptotically, clearly, the two choices are equivalent, as $(n+1)/n \to 1$ for $n \to \infty$. One must also be aware of the fact that the $\boldsymbol{U}^{(i)}$, $i = 1, \ldots, n$, obtained in this way are not a true sample from the copula $C(\cdot, \cdot; \theta)$. Again, the fact that ranks are computed from all observations jointly makes them stochastically dependent and the scaling by $1/(n+1)$ slightly shifts them from being $\mathcal{U}[0, 1]$ distributed. Both are only a problem for very small sample sizes n.

Example 6.3.3 (Constructing a (pseudo-)sample)
In Table 6.1, a simple example for a (pseudo-)sample obtained from a rank transformation is given. The scaling of the ranks is done by $1/(n+1)$ to force the (pseudo-)observations inside $(0, 1)$. The sample size is $n = 9$.

After this short introduction to empirical distribution functions, let us use for the remaining section the scaling factor $1/(n+1)$ and define our (pseudo-)observations as $U_j^{(i)} := n/(n+1) \hat{F}_{j,n}(X_j^{(i)})$, $j = 1, \ldots, d$ and $i = 1, \ldots, n$. We now assume a parametric form of the copula density (to simplify notation let $d = 2$), denoted $c(\cdot, \cdot; \theta)$. If we plug our (pseudo-)observations into the log-likelihood function, we are left with the

Table 6.1. *Observations* $(X_1^{(i)}, X_2^{(i)})$ *from a bivariate standard normal distribution with correlation* $\rho = 0.5$ *and the resulting (pseudo-)observations with scaling* $1/(n+1)$.

i	1	2	3	4	5	6	7	8	9
$X_1^{(i)}$	−0.103	−1.041	−2.478	−0.121	1.168	0.324	−2.115	−1.966	−0.993
$X_2^{(i)}$	−0.721	−1.786	−3.577	0.492	1.426	−0.170	−1.640	−1.428	−1.367
$U_1^{(i)}$	0.7	0.4	0.1	0.6	0.9	0.8	0.2	0.3	0.5
$U_2^{(i)}$	0.6	0.2	0.1	0.8	0.9	0.7	0.3	0.4	0.5

maximization of

$$\ell(\boldsymbol{X};\theta) = \sum_{i=1}^{n} \log c \left(\underbrace{\frac{n}{n+1} \hat{F}_{1,n}(X_1^{(i)})}_{U_1^{(i)}}, \underbrace{\frac{n}{n+1} \hat{F}_{2,n}(X_2^{(i)})}_{U_2^{(i)}}; \theta \right). \tag{6.5}$$

The maximizing argument $\bar{\theta}_n$ of this objective function can be used as an estimate for θ. The estimate obtained in this way is investigated in [Genest et al. (1995)]. Among others, they show that, given some regularity conditions on $c(\cdot, \cdot; \theta)$, this estimate is consistent and asymptotically normally distributed, see also [Shih, Louis (1995)] and [Tsukahara (2005)].

6.3.1 Visualization of the Methods

Let us now experiment with the presented estimation methods to gain a deeper understanding. To do so, we artificially construct a bivariate[7] distribution function by means of Sklar's Theorem 1.2.4; combining a Clayton copula (with parameter $\theta = 2$) with marginal laws being log-normal (with parameters $\mu = 5$ and $\sigma = 0.25$) in the case of X_1 and exponential (with rate $\lambda = 0.1$) in the case of X_2. One might think of two companies' default times. Having specified this distribution ourselves, we can simulate $n = 100$ times from the model. The resulting sample $\boldsymbol{X}$ is displayed in Figure 6.4 (upper left). Based on this scatter plot we can now compare the three methods to obtain (pseudo-)observations $\boldsymbol{U}$. In the simplest (but in real situations most unrealistic) case we assume the marginal laws to be fully known and directly compute the observations $\boldsymbol{U}$ by applying the true marginal distribution functions to the components of $\boldsymbol{X}$. This yields the well-known scatter plot of a Clayton copula, see Figure 6.4 (upper right). It is now interesting to compare this true copula scatter plot to the (pseudo-)observations. In the first case (IFM method) we have given the parametric form of the marginal laws, but have to estimate the parameters (μ, σ)

---

[7] An extensive multivariate study is presented in [Embrechts, Hofert (2013b)].

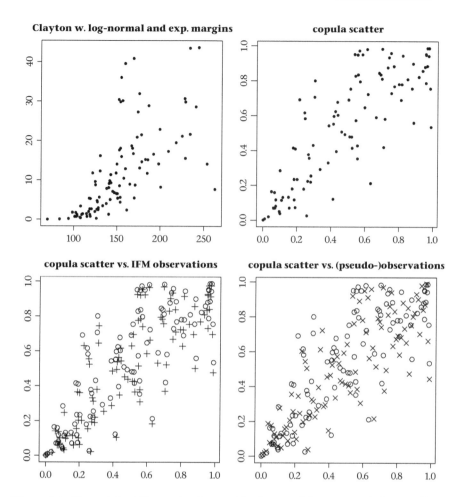

Figure 6.4 Upper left: 100 samples from a bivariate model constructed from a Clayton copula and log-normal, respectively exponential, marginals. Upper right: the true copula scatter plot. Lower left: marginals are estimated via maximum-likelihood and the so-obtained marginal distribution functions have been used to derive (pseudo-)observations. These (marked with a plus sign) are compared to the true copula scatter (circles). Lower right: the (pseudo-)observations (cross sign) coming from the rank transformation are compared with the true copula scatter (circles).

and λ using an initial maximum-likelihood method. The so-obtained estimates are used to specify the marginal distribution functions that are then applied to X. The resulting (pseudo-)observations are compared to the true values in Figure 6.4 (lower left). We find that these are quite close, but the quality worsens when the sample size decreases. Finally, we compute as described above our (pseudo-)observations from the empirical distribution functions of the marginal laws, where we do not need to know that these are log-normal and exponential, respectively. This is compared to the true copula sample in Figure 6.4 (lower right). We are again quite close to the true sample.

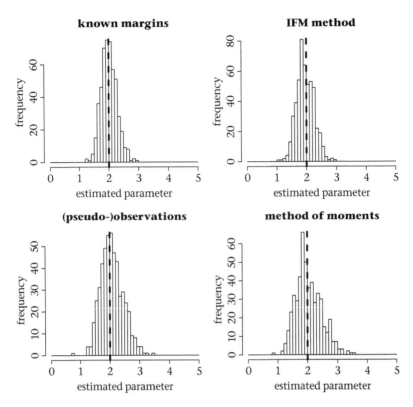

Figure 6.5 Distribution of the obtained copula parameter when the four methods are repeated $m = 500$ times with $n = 100$ observations in each case. The true parameter of the Clayton copula is $\theta = 2$. An extensive numerical study where different estimation methods are compared is provided in [Kojadinovic, Yan (2010)].

Finally, we can estimate the unknown copula parameter θ. In all cases, this corresponds to a maximization over θ of the log-likelihood function of the copula density, the difference being the observations U (respectively (pseudo)-observations) plugged into this density. Alternatively, one could use the method of moments and estimate θ via the empirical version of Kendall's τ, that is, $\hat{\tau}_n$. All methods are run $m = 500$ times (for the same sample size $n = 100$) and the distribution of the resulting estimates is presented in Figure 6.5. One observes that in all four cases the peak is roughly around the true parameter value $\theta = 2$, but we still have a considerable variance. The variance is, not surprisingly, decreasing in the available amount of information about the marginal laws. So the smallest variance corresponds to the case of perfectly known marginals, followed by knowing their parametric family, followed by not having any prior information at all.

6.4 Estimation of Specific Copula Families

In principle, the method of moments as well as the maximum-likelihood methods that have been presented in earlier sections can be applied to an arbitrary parametric family of copulas. On the one hand, the method of moments only requires analytical closed-form expressions for the 'moments' in question. In the bivariate case, or even in larger dimensions via restricting oneself to the consideration of bivariate pairs of the multivariate samples, the appropriate moments are typically either Kendall's τ or Spearman's ρ_S; an example has already been presented in Section 6.1 for the Gumbel copula, cf. Example 6.1.1. These two most prominent concordance measures are known in closed form for virtually all parametric copula families, see Chapter 4. On the other hand, the maximum-likelihood method is not always as straightforward as the method of moments, and can only be applied easily when the density of the copula in question exists,[8] is available in closed form, and can be evaluated efficiently. When feasible, maximum-likelihood methods are typically the first choice because the resulting estimator does usually have better convergence properties than a method of moments based estimator. Typically, the maximum-likelihood method works only in small dimensions, for some families of copulas only in dimension $d = 2$, and it is primarily used for Gaussian copulas, t-copulas, Archimedean copulas, and some extreme-value copulas with existing densities. For Archimedean copulas in higher dimensions, [Hofert et al. (2012)] tackle the issue of numerically evaluating the required density.

6.4.1 Taylor-made Estimation Strategies for Extreme-value Copulas

For extreme-value copulas there exist some quite specialized estimation algorithms, which are not of the general kinds described so far and which deserve to be mentioned briefly here. In the bivariate case there exists a non-parametric approach to estimate the parameterizing function A, due to [Pickands (1981)]. The underlying idea is to make use of the fact that a random vector (X_1, X_2) with extreme-value survival copula and unit exponential marginal laws is min-stable multivariate exponential, that is, $\min\{X_1/(1 - x), X_2/x\}$ has an exponential distribution with parameter $A(x)$ for arbitrary $x \in (0, 1)$, cf. Exercise 6. Given an iid sample $(U_1^{(i)}, U_2^{(i)})$, $i = 1, \ldots, n$, from the extreme-value copula C associated with A, the transformed sample $(X_1^{(i)}, X_2^{(i)}) := (-\log(U_1^{(i)}), -\log(U_2^{(i)}))$, $i = 1, \ldots, n$, has survival copula C and unit exponential marginals. Hence, the random variables $\min\{X_1^{(i)}/(1 - x), X_2^{(i)}/x\}$, $i = 1, \ldots, n$, are iid exponentially distributed with rate $A(x)$. By one-dimensional estimation theory it is well known that the exponential rate $A(x)$ may be estimated from

$$\hat{A}_n(x) := n \left(\sum_{i=1}^{n} \min\left\{ \frac{X_1^{(i)}}{1 - x}, \frac{X_2^{(i)}}{x} \right\} \right)^{-1}, \quad x \in (0, 1). \tag{6.6}$$

This is called the '*Pickands estimator*', named after [Pickands (1981)], which is thoroughly studied and improved in [Deheuvels (1991)]. Further important contributions in the same direction comprise [Genest, Segers (2009), Bücher et al. (2011)]. Unfortunately, extensions of this idea to larger dimensions are not easy to achieve.

---

[8] Marshall–Olkin copulas are a prominent example for copulas without density, see Section 4.3.1. In this case, one has to generalize the maximum-likelihood method to allow for dominating measures other than the Lebesgue measure, which is outside the scope of this book. The interested reader is referred to [Proschan, Sullo (1976), Peña (1991), Hanagal (1993)].

However, within a parametric setup a similar idea can be applied to the estimation of the subclass of Marshall–Olkin copulas, even in larger dimensions, which is described in Example 6.4.1 below.

Another non-parametric estimator for the function A, which is based on a similar idea and typically outperforms the Pickands estimator, is introduced in [Capéraà et al. (1997)], and called a 'CFG-estimator'. The underlying idea is to estimate the one-dimensional distribution function of $\log(U_1)/\log(U_1 U_2)$, which is given in terms of the function A, as

$$F(x) := \mathbb{P}(\log(U_1)/\log(U_1 U_2) \leq x) = x + x(1-x)\frac{A'(x)}{A(x)}, \quad x \in [0,1). \quad (6.7)$$

Replacing the distribution function F in (6.7) with its empirical counterpart $\hat{F}_n$ and solving the respective differential equation for A yields an estimator $\hat{A}_n$, which is shown in [Segers (2007)] to equal

$$\hat{A}_n(x) = \exp\left(-\frac{1}{n}\sum_{i=1}^{n}\log\left(\min\left\{\frac{X_1^{(i)}}{1-x}, \frac{X_2^{(i)}}{x}\right\}\right)\right.$$
$$\left. -(1-x)\sum_{i=1}^{n}\log(X_1^{(i)}) - x\sum_{i=1}^{n}\log(X_2^{(i)})\right), \quad (6.8)$$

$x \in (0,1)$. Unfortunately, the functions $\hat{A}_n$, obtained via (6.6) or (6.8), are not guaranteed to satisfy the characterizing properties of Corollary 4.3.3. However, this open problem has been investigated by many researchers for quite some time and as a result there exist diverse techniques to project the obtained function $\hat{A}_n$ onto the set of admissible functions without destroying the consistency of the estimator, see [Pickands (1981), Smith et al. (1990), Deheuvels (1991), Abdous, Ghoudi (2005), Hall, Tajvidi (2000), Jiménez et al. (2001), Fils-Villetard et al. (2008)]. However, it appears to be quite a challenging problem to extend this to larger dimensions, because the characterizing conditions on the stable tail dependence function become complicated in $d \geq 3$. Work in this direction is presented in [Berghaus et al. (2013)] and the references therein.

Example 6.4.1 (Estimating Marshall–Olkin copulas)

The Marshall–Olkin distribution, formally introduced in Section 4.3.1, is characterized by the multivariate lack-of-memory property and of such a natural extension of the exponential law. The stochastic model of [Marshall, Olkin (1967)] leading to this distribution is a frailty model with independent exponential shocks that affect certain subgroups of the components, see FAQ 4.3.4. This makes a 'classical' estimation (based on densities that are absolutely continuous with respect to the Lebesgue measure) somewhat delicate, since the Marshall–Olkin distribution has no copula density in the classical sense. But, why not make use of the aforementioned stochastic model for the estimation as well? Consider the bivariate case where

$$X_1 = \min\{E_{\{1\}}, E_{\{12\}}\}, \quad X_2 = \min\{E_{\{2\}}, E_{\{12\}}\},$$

and the random variables $E_{\{1\}}$, $E_{\{2\}}$, and $E_{\{12\}}$ are independent and exponentially distributed with rates $\lambda_{\{1\}}$, $\lambda_{\{2\}}$, and $\lambda_{\{12\}}$. The following estimation strategy is presented in [Arnold (1968)]. Following the steps that lead to the derivation of these estimates sheds some light on the Marshall–Olkin distribution itself, and we recommend going through the exposition below. We only present the bivariate case, extensions to $d > 2$ are conceptually straightforward, but the required computation time increases with the number of parameters (that is $2^d - 1$). Exploiting the min-stability of the univariate exponential distribution, we find $X_1 \sim \mathcal{E}(\lambda_{\{1\}} + \lambda_{\{12\}})$, $X_2 \sim \mathcal{E}(\lambda_{\{2\}} + \lambda_{\{12\}})$, and $\min\{X_1, X_2\} \sim \mathcal{E}(\lambda_{\{1\}} + \lambda_{\{2\}} + \lambda_{\{12\}})$. Moreover, defining the events $Y_{\{1\}} := \{X_1 < X_2\}$, $Y_{\{2\}} := \{X_2 < X_1\}$, and $Y_{\{12\}} := \{X_1 = X_2\}$ that indicate which of the shock arrival times E_I happens first, we have $\mathbb{P}(Y_I) = \lambda_I / \Lambda$, where $\Lambda = \lambda_{\{1\}} + \lambda_{\{2\}} + \lambda_{\{12\}}$, $I \in \{\{1\}, \{2\}, \{12\}\}$. Now we have all the ingredients collected to formulate the estimate. Given a sample $X = ((X_1^{(1)}, X_2^{(1)}), \dots, (X_1^{(n)}, X_2^{(n)}))$, the idea is to count how often the respective events Y_I occur in the sample. Let these numbers be denoted $N_{\{1\}}$, $N_{\{2\}}$, and $N_{\{12\}}$. Then, we observe the almost sure convergence

$$\frac{N_I}{n} \to \mathbb{P}(Y_I) = \frac{\lambda_I}{\lambda_{\{1\}} + \lambda_{\{2\}} + \lambda_{\{12\}}}, \quad \text{as } n \to \infty, \quad \forall I \in \{\{1\}, \{2\}, \{12\}\},$$

so N_I/n provides a consistent sequence of estimates for λ_I / Λ. To get rid of the denominator, we estimate Λ as well. Take $\hat{M}_n := (n - 1)/\sum_{i=1}^{n} \min\{X_1^{(i)}, X_2^{(i)}\}$ as a consistent estimate for Λ and obtain as estimates for the parameters of the Marshall–Olkin law λ_I, again consistent by the continuous mapping theorem,

$$\hat{M}_n \frac{N_I}{n} \to \lambda_I, \quad \text{as } n \to \infty, \quad \forall I \in \{\{1\}, \{2\}, \{12\}\}.$$

A deeper investigation of the properties of this estimate is presented in [Arnold (1968)]. From a numerical point of view the condition $X_1 = X_2$ has to be checked carefully if rounding errors are possible. It might be numerically advantageous to replace it by $|X_1 - X_2| < \epsilon$, where ϵ is the precision at which the X_i can be measured.

Further literature on the estimation of the Marshall–Olkin law is [Proschan, Sullo (1976), Peña (1991), Hanagal (1993)].

6.5 A Note on Positive Semi-definiteness

This section briefly touches the problem of estimated correlation matrices that are symmetric but not positive semi-definite, which clearly is a contradiction (since a proper correlation matrix is positive semi-definite). So how can such a situation occur and what can we do to overcome it?

(a) Consider the situation that we have time series of stock returns for d stocks. The problem with our data now is that some of the time series are not available for certain periods of time. Reasons might be data problems, composition changes in an index, the default of some company, companies that are newly listed (or de-listed) on the stock markets, and so on. Now we face the dilemma of using only a small time window on which we have information of all stock returns, versus the possibility of estimating the different pairwise correlations from the longest overlapping data window of the respective two firms. The former is more appropriate with respect to statistical properties, while the latter makes use of more data. If one opts for the latter, it might happen that the resulting 'correlation matrix' B that has as entry at position j, k (and k, j by symmetry) the estimated correlation of stock returns j and k is not positive semi-definite. Hence, it is not a real correlation matrix.

(b) The second situation often appears if no data is available at all. Consider, for example, yearly losses in the different business lines in a multi-line insurance company. In such a situation, one can expect data of at most a few years, if at all. Then, it is usually a matter of 'expert judgment' how the business lines are assumed to be correlated. If the expert judgments on all pairwise correlations are combined to a matrix, this might not be positive semi-definite. One example is the matrix

$$B = \begin{pmatrix} 1 & -0.25 & 0.50 \\ -0.25 & 1 & 0.75 \\ 0.50 & 0.75 & 1 \end{pmatrix}$$

having eigenvalues $1.80, 1.23, -0.03$ (rounded to two digits), where the smallest eigenvalue is negative, so B is not positive semi-definite.

In both situations, we are trying to find the 'closest' true correlation matrix to the matrix B and continue working with this one. The meaning of 'closest' needs to be made mathematically precise and various matrix norms $|| \cdot ||$ to measure the distance between two matrices are plausible. Mathematically speaking, we need to find

$$\underbrace{\hat{B}}_{\text{solution}} := \operatorname{argmin} \left\{ \underbrace{||B - \Sigma||}_{\text{distance between } B \text{ and } \Sigma} \quad : \underbrace{\Sigma \text{ is a correlation matrix}}_{\text{required property}} \right\}.$$

For a weighted version of the so-called 'Frobenius norm', this problem has been solved in [Higham (2002)] and is implemented in R, see Section 6.6. In the above example, we get

$$\hat{B} = \begin{pmatrix} 1.0000000 & -0.2379309 & 0.4865819 \\ -0.2379309 & 1.0000000 & 0.7327730 \\ 0.4865819 & 0.7327730 & 1.0000000 \end{pmatrix},$$

with non-negative eigenvalues $1.78, 1.22, 0$ (again rounded to two digits).

6.6   Some Remarks Concerning the Implementation

Most of the methods presented in this chapter are implemented in R for popular families of copulas. The R-package `copula` provides an extremely valuable toolbox for the simulation (via the command `rCopula()`), estimation (the function call is `fitCopula()`), and actual work with copulas (density and distribution function are evaluated using `dCopula()` and `pCopula()`). It also contains methods for the computation of (pseudo-)observations (command `pobs()`) and the empirical copula (command `C.n()`). The R-package `Kendall` evaluates the empirical Kendall's τ and computes p-values for a test of independence based on this dependence measure. The function `nearPD()` from the `Matrix` package allows finding the 'closest' positive semi-definite matrix given some non-positive semi-definite matrix.

EXERCISES

1. Derive a method of moments estimator for the bivariate Clayton copula based on the closed-form expression for Kendall's τ.

2. Simulate n iid samples from a d-dimensional Clayton copula. Use the estimator from the previous exercise in order to estimate the parameter θ based on each available pair of components. Notice that there are $d(d-1)/2$ pairs. Compare the estimate based on the pair of the first two components with the estimate obtained by averaging over all estimates of available pairs for different $d \geq 3$ and $n \in \mathbb{N}$. How do these two estimates compare? Can you explain this?

3. Consider the bivariate Cuadras–Augé copula C_α with parameter $\alpha \in [0,1]$, cf. Table 4.3 with $\theta = \alpha$.

    a. For $(U_1, U_2) \sim C_\alpha$ compute $\mathbb{E}[U_1 U_2]$. Hint: Use the fact that

    $$\iint_{[0,1]^2} \bar{C}(u_1, u_2)\, du_1\, du_2 = \mathbb{E}[U_1 U_2].$$

    b. Use part a. to derive a method of moments estimator for the parameter α. Notice that this estimator basically corresponds to an estimator based on the expression for Spearman's ρ_S.

    c. Derive a method of moments estimator for α based on the expression for Kendall's τ of C_α.

    d. Compare the estimators of part b. and part c.

4. Consider the univariate $\mathcal{E}(\lambda)$ distribution with density $f(x; \lambda) = \lambda \exp(-\lambda x)\mathbf{1}_{\{x>0\}}$. Derive the maximum-likelihood estimate and the moment-estimator. Compare the obtained formulas.

5. Derive the maximum-likelihood estimator for $(\mu_1, \mu_2, \sigma_1, \sigma_2, \rho)$ in case of the bivariate normal distribution. Do the same when $\mu_1 = \mu_2 = 0$ and $\sigma_1 = \sigma_2 = 1$ are known, that is, derive the maximum-likelihood estimator for ρ in case of a standardized bivariate normal law. Compare the two resulting estimators for ρ qualitatively.

6. Let C be an extreme-value copula with parameterizing function A, and denote by (X_1, X_2) a random vector with joint survival function

    $$\bar{F}(x_1, x_2) = C(\exp(-x_1), \exp(-x_2)), \quad x_1, x_2 \geq 0.$$

    Prove that the random variable $\min\{X_1/(1-x), X_2/x\}$ has an exponential distribution with rate $A(x)$.

7 How to Deal with Uncertainty Concerning Dependence?

Which copula should we use in situations where we have no, or only limited, historical data? In other words, a classical estimation is not feasible and we are exposed to uncertainty concerning the dependence structure. This is not at all an academic question: consider a financial institution that wants to assess its overall risk across different pillars such as market risk, operational risk, credit risk, and so on. If these risk figures are measured on a yearly basis only, then classical estimation strategies are hopeless due to insufficient observations. So what is done in such a situation? In most cases, it is a matter of experience to understand the nature and stylized facts of the risks one faces and a good financial engineer can try to translate those considerations into a suitable parametric family of copulas. But still, the parameters of this family need to be specified. The next step would typically be to stress the parameters of the chosen model to the extremes, which reflects the hope of also understanding the extremes of the application one has in mind. In principle, this is a good idea. The weak point, however, is that the chosen family of copulas need not contain the worst-case scenario across all possible copulas and the extremes within the constructed model might be significantly smaller than the extremes across all copulas. A typical fallacy, which we encounter below, is the mis-belief that the comonotonicity copula implies the biggest risk in many cases. In the following we discuss two important applications where in both cases the worst-case dependence structure is not the comonotonicity copula. Moreover, we introduce valuable tools to solve the respective optimization problems across all possible copulas. Section 7.1 is an excursion to risk aggregation under model uncertainty concerning the dependence structure. Section 7.2 considers the worst-case dependence structure for two default times with given marginal laws when the risk considered is a joint default.

Let us start with the first example. In many situations one observes a battery of financial risks, denoted $L_1, \ldots, L_d$ and interpreted as losses, and one is interested in the aggregated loss $L := L_1 + \cdots + L_d$. Examples are the aggregated portfolio loss resulting from individual claims in different insurance policies, losses resulting from credit events of d firms, the overall operational loss of some company aggregated over the different lines of operational losses, or the aggregated loss within some stock portfolio. In the latter example, loss is simply defined as the negative of (portfolio) returns.

Despite its well-documented shortcomings[1] we use the '*Value-at-Risk*' (VaR) at some confidence level $\alpha \in (0, 1)$ (typical numbers of interest are $\alpha \in [0.90, 0.999)$) to

---

[1] The VaR is not sub-additive. This means that diversification is not rewarded in all situations, see the example in [McNeil et al. (2005), p. 241].

measure risk, which formally is defined by[2]

$$\mathrm{VaR}_\alpha(L) := \inf\{x \in \mathbb{R} : \mathbb{P}(L \leq x) > \alpha\}. \tag{7.1}$$

The well-known interpretation of this risk measure is that given the chosen confidence level α (which is typically chosen close to one), the loss L exceeds the VaR_α only with probability $1 - \alpha$ (which is then close to zero). It is intuitively clear that this quantile depends on the joint distribution of the individual risks $(L_1, \ldots, L_d)$, since L is defined as the sum of the individual risks. In many cases it is plausible to assume that we have a sound understanding of the marginal distribution functions $L_1 \sim F_1, \ldots, L_d \sim F_d$ and we assume these to be continuous. It remains to specify, by Sklar's Theorem 1.2.4, the copula C that joins the marginal laws. Taking the copula as known, however, is a brave assumption. Consider, for instance, some holding company that tries to assess its overall yearly loss resulting from the individual losses in its business lines. In such a situation one can hardly expect more than 10 years of historical data and the past may not be meaningful for an estimation of the loss in the upcoming year. So estimating the copula from data is not feasible in this situation. On a more abstract level, [Knight (1921)] distinguished the following situations that we adapt to dependence modeling:

(a) **Model 'risk' with respect to the dependence structure**: One knows the possible outcomes of some experiment and their probabilities. In the above situation, this could be interpreted as knowing the copula C. In this (quite convenient) situation one can either try to compute $\mathrm{VaR}_\alpha(L)$ explicitly, which typically is not possible in closed form as soon as we have inhomogeneous marginals, or estimate it via a Monte-Carlo simulation. This is possible in all situations where we have a simulation strategy for $(L_1, \ldots, L_d)$ available. We simply have to simulate the joint losses sufficiently often and estimate $\mathrm{VaR}_\alpha(L)$ by the empirical α-quantile, see FAQ 7.1.7 for details.

(b) **Model 'uncertainty' with respect to the dependence structure**: One knows only the possible outcomes of some experiment but not their probabilities. In our situation, this corresponds to not knowing the copula. The most conservative ansatz we can pursue in such a situation is trying to find an upper (and lower) bound for $\mathrm{VaR}_\alpha(L)$, varying over all possible copulas C. Clearly, this is a non-trivial optimization problem. A numerical algorithm that allows us to solve this problem is the '*Rearrangement Algorithm*' introduced below.

---

[2] Sometimes, the VaR is alternatively defined as $\mathrm{VaR}_\alpha(L) := F_L^{-1}(\alpha)$, where F_L denotes the distribution function of L. A careful reader might have spotted the difference between (7.1) and the definition of the generalized inverse in Definition 1.2.6, where we use '$\geq$' instead of '$>$'. Clearly, when the distribution function of L is continuous, the two formulations agree. In case of jumps in $\mathbb{P}(L \leq x)$, however, there are subtle differences to acknowledge, see [Embrechts, Hofert (2013a)]. So why is Definition (7.1) more convenient for this chapter? Formulated in this way, the supremum we consider in (7.2) is actually attained by a suitable dependence structure. For practical considerations this difference in notation might be negligible, but for theoretical results that 'live on the edge of α' one has to be careful which version to use. You might want to test both formulations in Example 7.1.1.

A somewhat related question is addressed in Section 7.2. Here, we assume as given the marginal laws of two default times X_1, X_2 but again have no reliable information about their dependence. We then derive an upper bound for the probability of a default of both firms at the same moment in time. This has important applications in the field of counterparty credit risk.

7.1 Bounds for the VaR of a Portfolio

Above, we have introduced our problem informally, so let us now be mathematically precise. We assume the marginal distribution functions of our risks $L_1 \sim F_1, \ldots, L_d \sim F_d$ to be continuous and fixed and we denote the joint distribution function by $F(x_1, \ldots, x_d) := \mathbb{P}(L_1 \leq x_1, \ldots, L_d \leq x_d)$. Separating the joint distribution into (unknown) copula C and (known) marginal laws $F_1, \ldots, F_d$, we define the extremes of possible VaR_α by

$$\mathrm{VaR}_\alpha(L)^\oplus := \sup_{\text{copula } C} \{\mathrm{VaR}_\alpha(L_1 + \cdots + L_d) : F(\cdot) = C(F_1(\cdot), \ldots, F_d(\cdot))\}, \quad (7.2)$$

$$\mathrm{VaR}_\alpha(L)^\ominus := \inf_{\text{copula } C} \{\mathrm{VaR}_\alpha(L_1 + \cdots + L_d) : F(\cdot) = C(F_1(\cdot), \ldots, F_d(\cdot))\}.$$

In the following we only focus on the (for applications more important) upper bound $\mathrm{VaR}_\alpha(L)^\oplus$ and refer the interested reader to [Embrechts et al. (2013)] for a treatment of the lower bound. It is tempting to believe, at least for the upper bound, that the maximizing copula could be the comonotonicity copula, since it reflects the strongest possible positive dependence. This is, however, not the case, as Example 7.1.1 illustrates.

Example 7.1.1 (Comonotonicity $\not\Rightarrow$ maximal VaR)
(i) Consider two losses L_1 and L_2, both being $\mathcal{U}[0,1]$-distributed for the sake of simplicity of this educational example. Now join them via the comonotonicity copula as dependence structure, so $(L_1, L_2) \sim M_2$, $L_1 = L_2$ almost surely, and we get for the sum $L := L_1 + L_2 = 2L_1$. In this case, the distribution function of L is easily found to be $F_L(x) = 0.5x$, for $x \in [0,2]$. Computing the VaR at the level $\alpha = 0.9$ yields $\mathrm{VaR}_\alpha(L) = F_L^{-1}(0.9) = 1.8$.
(ii) Next, we construct an alternative copula to be used as dependence structure (the $\mathcal{U}[0,1]$-distribution of the marginals remains the same) that implies a higher VaR_α. We start with $\tilde{L}_1 \sim \mathcal{U}[0,1]$ and define $\tilde{L}_2$ by

$$\tilde{L}_2 := \begin{cases} \tilde{L}_1 & \text{if } \tilde{L}_1 < 0.9 \\ 1.9 - \tilde{L}_1 & \text{if } \tilde{L}_1 \geq 0.9 \end{cases}.$$

One verifies that $\tilde{L}_2 \sim \mathcal{U}[0,1]$, see Exercise 5, and one can identify the copula behind $(\tilde{L}_1, \tilde{L}_2)$, which looks somewhat strange on the first view. It equals precisely the comonotonicity copula in the lower-left rectangle $[0,0.9] \times [0,0.9]$, but in the upper-right rectangle $[0.9,1] \times [0.9,1]$ it looks like the countermonotonicity copula, see Figure 7.1 (right). Clearly, this implies

$$\tilde{L} := \tilde{L}_1 + \tilde{L}_2 = \begin{cases} 2\tilde{L}_1 & \text{if } \tilde{L}_1 < 0.9 \\ 1.9 & \text{if } \tilde{L}_1 \geq 0.9 \end{cases}.$$

The distribution function of $\tilde{L}$ in this situation is given by

$$\mathbb{P}(\tilde{L} \leq x) = \begin{cases} 0 & \text{if } x \in (-\infty, 0) \\ 0.5x & \text{if } x \in [0, 1.8) \\ 0.9 & \text{if } x \in [1.8, 1.9) \\ 1 & \text{if } x \in [1.9, \infty) \end{cases}.$$

And in this case, the $\text{VaR}_{0.9}(\tilde{L})$ is given by 1.9. This is larger than the respective $\text{VaR}_{0.9}(L)$ in the comonotonicity case (i). This example is further illustrated in Figure 7.1.

The bivariate case with identical marginal laws is one of the rare cases where $\text{VaR}_\alpha(L)^\oplus$ can explicitly be derived (we need some assumptions on the density of $F_1 = F_2$). This result is given in [Embrechts et al. (2013), Proposition 2], where it is stated that $\text{VaR}_\alpha(L)^\oplus = 2F_1^{-1}((1+\alpha)/2)$, which in our setup is precisely 1.9. So the case (ii) with $(\tilde{L}_1, \tilde{L}_2)$ is actually a maximizer for the problem of finding an upper bound for the VaR.

FAQ 7.1.2 (What changes, if I use expected shortfall instead of VaR?)

If the expected shortfall (synonyms are Average-VaR or CVaR) to some given α-level is used as risk measure instead of VaR (as will most likely be the case in the upcoming Basel framework), then it is indeed the comonotonicity copula that maximizes this risk measure applied to the sum of individual losses. This result is shown (without explicitly mentioning the expected shortfall) in [Müller (1997), Kusuoka (2001),

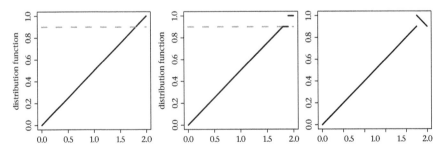

Figure 7.1 The distribution function of $L = L_1 + L_2$ in the comonotonic case (left) and of $\tilde{L} = \tilde{L}_1 + \tilde{L}_2$ (middle) where the copula of $(\tilde{L}_1, \tilde{L}_2)$ has probability mass as displayed to the right.

Ogryczak, Ruszczynski (2002)]. The rearrangement algorithm, however, can still be applied for the computation, see [Puccetti (2013)]. So do we circumvent all problems by replacing VaR with the expected shortfall? Unfortunately not, as discussed in [Embrechts et al. (2014)].

So what to conclude from Example 7.1.1? First of all, comonotonicity need not be the worst-case dependence scenario when the measure of risk is the VaR. Moreover, it looks advantageous (for trying to increase the VaR) to have some sort of negative dependence above the respective quantile level, which is indeed the case and made precise below. However, we have learned that it is not clear how to extend the notion of negative dependence to higher dimensions. In the present case it is important that the sum of the two risks (above the α-quantile) always admits a constant value. Via this construction, we can 'squeeze' as much mass behind the VaR level as possible. And this is precisely the motivation of 'negative dependence' that we must lift to higher dimensions. We are now trying to construct a dependence structure such that (above the α-quantile) the sum of d risks is (as close as possible to) a constant. A distribution satisfying

$$\mathbb{P}(L_1 + \cdots + L_d = \text{constant}) = 1$$

is called 'd-completely mixable'. The rearrangement algorithm manages to (approximate) the dependence structure behind some discrete random variables such that this 'd-completely mixable' condition is achieved as well as possible.

Example 7.1.3 (d-completely mixable)

Consider some holding company with $d = 4$ lines of business, indexed by $j = 1, \ldots, 4$. By expert judgment, the management defines six equally likely scenarios $\omega_1, \ldots, \omega_6$, where the following operational losses $L_j(\omega_i)$ are expected. Note that the ordering in the left matrix corresponds to the idea that ω_1 is the best-case scenario where hardly any losses are observed, and so on. The matrix on the left, where all the columns are similarly ordered, corresponds to the comonotonic case. It does not correspond to a d-completely mixable distribution, as the sum of losses is not constant. After rearranging the entries, which corresponds to changing the dependence structure, since then different events take place jointly, we find that in all scenarios the aggregated loss is the same, so the resulting distribution of $(L_1, \ldots, L_4)$ is d-completely mixable. Finding such rearrangements can be done via Algorithm 7.1.4. Please note that this example shall explain the notion of d-complete mixability. Later on, when the rearrangement algorithm is used to find the worst-case VaR$_\alpha$ to some given level α, we only apply it to the upper $(1 - \alpha)$-fraction of the ordered losses. This will be made more precise in FAQ 7.1.5(b).

	L_1	L_2	L_3	L_4	$\sum_{j=1}^{4} L_j$
ω_1	0	0	0	1	1
ω_2	1	2	0	3	6
ω_3	1	5	1	14	21
ω_4	8	15	60	19	102
ω_5	49	60	80	30	219
ω_6	80	90	101	40	311

$\overset{\text{Alg. 7.1.4}}{\rightsquigarrow}$

	L_1	L_2	L_3	L_4	$\sum_{j=1}^{4} L_j$
ω_1	8	2	60	40	110
ω_2	80	15	1	14	110
ω_3	49	60	0	1	110
ω_4	1	5	101	3	110
ω_5	0	0	80	30	110
ω_6	1	90	0	19	110

We will now introduce the rearrangement algorithm. It is, however, beyond the scope of this introduction to go into more details on how/why this approach solves the present problem of maximizing/minimizing the VaR over all copulas. This non-trivial theory is found in [Rüschendorf (1982), Rüschendorf (1983), Puccetti, Rüschendorf (2012), Puccetti, Rüschendorf (2014), Embrechts et al. (2013), Wang et al. (2013)] and the references therein.

Algorithm 7.1.4 (The '*Rearrangement Algorithm*')
This formulation of the rearrangement algorithm is taken from [Embrechts et al. (2013)]. We first have to initiate the algorithm. This means defining a matrix $M \in \mathbb{R}^{N \times d}$ and some exit tolerance level $\epsilon > 0$. We comment below on how M can be chosen in FAQ 7.1.5.

$$M_{\text{new}} = M$$

REPEAT

$$M_{\text{old}} = M_{\text{new}}$$

$$M_{\text{new}} = \text{REORDERING}(M_{\text{old}})$$

$$\text{UNTIL } (s(M_{\text{new}}) - s(M_{\text{old}}) < \epsilon)$$

$$\text{OUTPUT } (M_{\text{new}}, s(M_{\text{new}}))$$

The main function to be repeatedly called, until the stopping criteria is met, is the function `REORDERING( · )`. It takes a matrix $M = (m_1, \ldots, m_d)$ as input and runs through all of its d columns $m_1, \ldots, m_d$. For each column m_j, the 'rowSums'[3] of the reduced matrix where column m_j is removed, that is, $M \backslash \{m_j\} := (m_1, \ldots, m_{j-1}, m_{j+1}, \ldots, m_d)$, are computed and column m_j is reordered such that it is precisely in the opposite order[4] to rowSums$(M \backslash \{m_j\})$. The function $s(M)$ is defined as $s(M) := \min \{\text{rowSums}(M)\}$, that is, it returns the smallest of the n row sums. Since the stopping criterion is typically not met after the first round of reordering, a single column can be reordered many times. Also note that instead of the stopping criterion used above the repeat loop might be replaced by a simple loop that is run a given number of times.

FAQ 7.1.5 (How to select the matrix M in Algorithm 7.1.4?) (a)   Consider the situation that we have given marginal laws $L_1 \sim F_1, \ldots, L_d \sim F_d$ and some α-level for VaR$_\alpha$. Recall that we are only interested in a reordering behind the α-quantile of the distribution functions $F_1, \ldots, F_d$. We thus partition only the range $[\alpha, 1]$ in N equidistant bins and define for $i = 1, \ldots, N$ and $j = 1, \ldots, d$

$$M_{i,j}^{\text{lower}} := F_j^{-1}(\alpha + (1 - \alpha)(i - 1)/N), \quad M_{i,j}^{\text{upper}} := F_j^{-1}(\alpha + (1 - \alpha)i/N).$$

---

[3] Formally defined as rowSums$(M \backslash \{m_j\}) := (\sum_{i=1, i \neq j}^{d} m_{1,i}, \ldots, \sum_{i=1, i \neq j}^{d} m_{n,i})$.
[4] Providing an example: the columns $(1, 3, 5, 7)$ and $(10, 8, 6, 4)$ are oppositely ordered.

Some caution is requested when setting the last values $M_{N,j}^{\mathrm{upper}}$, since this might be defined as infinity when F_j has unbounded support. If your programming language does not support working with the symbol ∞, some big number strictly above $M_{N-1,j}^{\mathrm{upper}}$ must be taken. We then apply the rearrangement algorithm to both matrices M^{lower}, M^{upper} and obtain the respective minima of the rowSums. These form an interval that shrinks to $\mathrm{VaR}_\alpha(L)^\oplus$ when N tends to infinity.

(b)   Another situation might be that we have empirical observations $(L_1^{(i)},\ldots,L_d^{(i)})$ of our losses given, where $i=1,\ldots,n$. In this case, we order the observations of each loss L_j separately, where we denote the ordered observations by $L_j^{[1]} \le L_j^{[2]} \le \ldots \le L_j^{[n]}$. Then, we fill column j of the matrix M with the largest $[(1-\alpha)\cdot n]$ losses $L_j^{[\alpha\cdot n+1]} \le \ldots \le L_j^{[n]}$. The α-fraction of small losses $L_j^{[1]} \le \ldots \le L_j^{[\alpha\cdot n]}$ is not relevant for the upper bound of the VaR_α. Giving an example, if we take $\alpha = 0.9$ and have $n = 1000$ observations, then the biggest $N = n(1-\alpha) = 100$ are considered in M for each marginal. In short, we do the following:

(i)   Collect n observations of the losses $(L_1,\ldots,L_d)$, denoted $L_j^{(i)}$, $i=1,\ldots,n$, $j=1,\ldots,d$.

(ii)   Sort the observed losses in each component in increasing order $L_j^{[1]} \le L_j^{[2]} \le \cdots \le L_j^{[n]}$, $j=1,\ldots,d$.

(iii)   Create the matrix $M = (m_1,\ldots,m_d)$ by taking as its columns the biggest $n(1-\alpha)$ of the observed losses, that is,

$$\underbrace{L_j^{[1]} \le L_j^{[2]} \le \cdots \le L_j^{[\alpha\cdot n]}}_{\text{needed only for } \mathrm{VaR}_\alpha^\ominus} \le \underbrace{L_j^{[\alpha\cdot n+1]} \le \cdots \le L_j^{[n]}}_{\text{defines } m_j \text{ to find } \mathrm{VaR}_\alpha^\oplus}.$$

Before Algorithm 7.1.4 is started, it might be useful to randomly reorder the columns of M, as there are potential situations in which the rearrangement algorithm might be stuck, otherwise.

Example 7.1.6 (Case study: daily losses in an asset portfolio)
We illustrate estimated VaR numbers (for a one-day holding period) of a small asset portfolio and compare these to the upper bound derived from the rearrangement algorithm. We consider a stock portfolio containing (equally weighted and normed, such that the portfolio has total value of 1 unit of currency) stocks of Adidas, SAP, and Deutsche Bank. We define $L_{\mathrm{Adi},t_i} := -(S_{\mathrm{Adi},t_i} - S_{\mathrm{Adi},t_{i-1}})/S_{\mathrm{Adi},t_{i-1}}$, where S_{Adi,t_i} is the stock price of Adidas at time t_i, and the very same is done for the other two stocks. We are interested in the VaR_α of our portfolio for a one day period, which is

$$\mathrm{VaR}_\alpha\left(\frac{1}{3}(L_{\mathrm{Adi},t} + L_{\mathrm{SAP},t} + L_{\mathrm{DB},t})\right).$$

We have available a data set containing stock values of each trading day, ranging from October, 26, 2010 until November, 26, 2013. This set of data is now exploited in many ways.

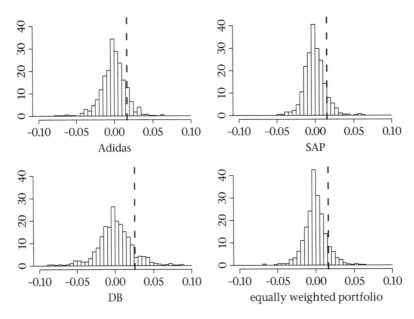

Figure 7.2   Empirical daily losses (negative of discrete returns) for the three stocks and the equally weighted portfolio. The respective empirical VaR$_\alpha$ at the $\alpha = 90\%$ level is reported via a vertical bar in each plot.

(a)   First of all, we can compute the resulting loss (negative of the return) for each day in the observation period. This is done for each stock and for the equally weighted portfolio. This gives us a list of $n = 805$ observed losses. We order these losses and take the $[\alpha\,n]$-biggest as our estimate for the empirical VaR$_\alpha$ of our portfolio. Using $\alpha = 0.9$, we obtain the empirical value VaR$_\alpha(L) = 1.617\%$. This means that historically, in 90% of all cases the daily portfolio loss was below 1.617%, see Figure 7.2 for a visualization.

(b)   We can now compare the empirical VaR$_\alpha(L)$ from (a) to the one computed with the same historical marginal distributions but with an independence assumption (resp. comonotonicity copula) as dependence structure. We evaluate both using a Monte-Carlo simulation with $1,000,000$ scenarios. We obtain for the independence case VaR$_\alpha(L) = 1.241\%$ and for the comonotonic case VaR$_\alpha(L) = 1.931\%$, which are below the historical value for the independence case and above for the comonotonic case.

(c)   In the present situation with $n = 805$ observations we can try to estimate the copula behind the returns. For simplicity, we assume the daily returns to be iid.[5] Plotting the (pseudo-)observations of the daily losses, see Figure 7.3, we decide to use a t-copula to fit the dependence structure. We obtain as pairwise entries of Σ

[5] Clearly, this is not consistent with volatility clusters and other well-documented stylized facts that are not compatible with the iid assumption. However, we do not want to over-complicate the example by introducing a non-trivial time-series model. A much more involved case study is presented in [Aas, Puccetti (2013)].

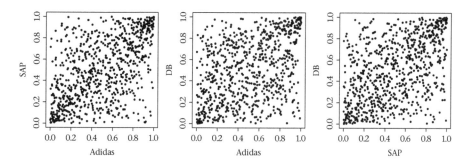

Figure 7.3 Scatter plots of the (pseudo-)observations of all pairs of empirical daily losses (negative of discrete returns) for the three stocks. The shape of the scatter plots makes a t-copula plausible.

the values 0.54 (Adidas vs. SAP), 0.46 (Adidas vs. DB), and 0.51 (SAP vs. DB) and as degrees of freedom $\nu = 6.45$. Having specified the copula model, we can then perform a Monte-Carlo simulation with this estimated dependence structure and the historical marginal laws. We again use one million simulation runs and obtain as estimated $\mathrm{VaR}_\alpha(L)$ the number $1.642\,\%$. This is, as expected, very close to the historical value derived in (a). Let us remark that in this three-dimensional example, one might avoid the use of Monte-Carlo and use the AEP algorithm instead, see [Arbenz et al. (2011)].

(d)   Finally, we start the rearrangement algorithm. The matrix M contains in its three columns the respective largest $1 - \alpha = 10\%$ of the observed daily losses of the three stocks. We obtain $\mathrm{VaR}_\alpha(L)^{\oplus} = 3.021\,\%$ as an upper bound in the worst-case scenario. We note that this is far above the empirical value from (a) and even far above the comonotonic case from (b). So relying on those values alone, one might have a deceiving feeling of being conservative enough.

FAQ 7.1.7 (How to implement the simulation in Example 7.1.6?)
Assume as given n empirical losses $L_j^{(1)},\ldots,L_j^{(n)}$ for each marginal $j = 1,\ldots,d$. These are ordered for each marginal as $L_j^{[1]} \le L_j^{[2]} \le \cdots \le L_j^{[n]}$, $j = 1,\ldots,d$. Next, we assume a certain copula C to be used as dependence structure and we select the number of Monte-Carlo runs n_{runs}. In each run $i = 1,\ldots,n_{\mathrm{runs}}$, we have to draw a sample from the copula C, denoted $(U_1^{(i)},\ldots,U_d^{(i)})$. We multiply $U_j^{(i)}$, which is in $(0,1)$, with n and apply the ceiling function to the result,[6] obtaining a number within $\{1,\ldots,n\}$. This number $k_j^{(i)} := \mathrm{ceiling}(U_j^{(i)}\,n)$ is the rank in our empirical loss observations. The total loss $L^{(i)}$ in scenario i is then given by

$$L^{(i)} := L_1^{[k_1^{(i)}]} + \cdots + L_d^{[k_d^{(i)}]}.$$

[6] The ceiling function of x returns the largest integer equal to or bigger than x, so $\mathrm{ceiling}(2.71) = 3$.

The so-obtained losses $L^{(1)}, \ldots, L^{(n_{\text{runs}})}$ of each scenario are again ordered in increasing order and the $(\alpha\, n_{\text{runs}})$-largest of them is the estimated VaR at the α-level.

7.2 What Is the Maximal Probability for a Joint Default?

We have learned about the rearrangement algorithm in Section 7.1. This algorithm provides a tool to maximize (resp. minimize) certain functionals, for example the VaR, of a multivariate distribution function when the marginal laws are fixed. Closely related, this section considers an example of a very special functional in the bivariate case, which is of paramount interest in counterparty credit-risk modeling. Section 7.2.1 provides a motivation for the problem and Section 7.2.2 provides a mathematical solution.

7.2.1 Motivation

Consider an aircraft that can land safely as long as at least one of its two engines is working. Here, the joint default of both engines constitutes a major source of risk which we would like to control. Less drastic, but relevant from a financial perspective, the same risk as in the aircraft occurs frequently in counterparty credit-risk modeling. To this end, we assume that we have bought CDS insurance on an underlying reference entity A from a counterparty B, with maturity T years.

FAQ 7.2.1 (What is a credit default swap?)
A 'credit default swap' (CDS) is an insurance contract between two parties. The insurance buyer makes periodic premium payments, typically quarterly, until the maturity of the contract or the default of the reference entity, whichever happens first. The annualized premium payment to be made is quoted in basis points of the contract's notional and called the 'CDS spread'. In return, the insurance seller makes a compensation payment to the protection buyer if a contractually specified credit event happens during the lifetime of the contract. Such a credit event refers to a third party, the so-called reference entity, and can be a failure to pay, a due coupon, or a bankruptcy. Such contracts are used, for example, by banks in order to secure parts of their loan books. For the assessment of a fair insurance premium a mathematical model is required for the unknown future time point at which the credit event occurs, which we call 'default time' of the reference entity. Furthermore, the solvency of the protection seller is also important to the protection buyer, because an insurer that cannot pay in case of a credit event is undesired.

Denoting by X_1 the default time of the reference entity A and by X_2 the default time of our counterparty, what are the major sources of default risk for us as insurance buyer? There are three possible scenarios that have different levels of severity:

⊕⊕ $\{X_1 < \min\{T, X_2\}\}$: In this case, the CDS deal ends at X_1 and we receive the compensation payment from our counterparty B. This is an event which is okay for us. Indeed, we have bought our CDS insurance precisely for that event.

⊕⊖ $\{X_2 < \min\{T, X_1\}\}$: In this case, our CDS insurance becomes worthless at time X_2, because our counterparty cannot make any compensation payments anymore if the reference entity defaults at a later time point. We therefore have to replace the CDS deal with a novel counterparty. This need not be problematic; however, we might have problems finding a new counterparty, for example because the default of our original counterparty was the result of a macroeconomic event that affected all CDS protection sellers, so that CDS protection has become more expensive.

⊖⊖ $\{X_2 = X_1 \leq T\}$: This event is the worst-case scenario for us, because we need our CDS protection due to the default of the reference entity A, but our counterparty cannot make the due compensation payments. Moreover, we cannot replace the CDS with a new counterparty, because nobody is willing to insure an event that has already happened.

As a consequence, the probability of the event $\{X_1 = X_2 \leq T\}$ is an important counterparty credit-risk measure for us, because it is the probability of the only event whose probability we would like to keep really small. Unfortunately, this probability depends both on the marginal distributions F_1, F_2 of the default times of A and B, respectively, and on the copula C of X_1 and X_2. We therefore denote it by

$$p(T; C, F_1, F_2) := \mathbb{P}(X_1 = X_2 \leq T)$$

for the sake of clarity. In practical situations, we can typically infer F_1 and F_2 pretty well from observed CDS spreads or bond data referring to A and B, but little, perhaps even nothing, is known about the interrelation between A and B. The question is: what can we do? Interestingly, it is possible to derive an upper bound on $p(T; C, F_1, F_2)$, namely

$$0 \leq p(T; C, F_1, F_2) \leq \sup_{\text{copula } C} \{p(T; C, F_1, F_2)\} \leq 1,$$

where the supremum is taken over all bivariate copulas. We show in Section 7.2.2 that this supremum is actually a maximum and can be computed in closed form. It depends strongly on the marginals F_1 and F_2. This is a conservative upper bound for the present situation of uncertainty concerning the copula.

7.2.2   Maximal Coupling

The solution to our problem can be retrieved from the literature on a well-developed theory called 'maximal coupling', which typically appears in a completely different context (Markov chain theory). The proof of Theorem 7.2.2 can be found in [Thorisson (2000), p. 9], where the statement is formulated without the notion of copulas. Rewriting it in terms of copulas, it can be formulated as follows.

Theorem 7.2.2 (The maximal probability of a joint default given the marginals)
Assume that X_1, X_2 have densities f_1, f_2 on $(0, \infty)$, and denote by $F_j(x) := \int_0^x f_j(s)\, ds$, $j = 1, 2$, the marginal distribution functions.

(a) For each $0 \leq T \leq \infty$ it follows that

$$\sup_{\text{copula } C} \{p(T; C, F_1, F_2)\} = \int_0^T \min\{f_1(s), f_2(s)\} ds =: p_T. \qquad (7.3)$$

(b) Moreover, the supremum is actually a maximum and we can provide a probabilistic construction for the maximizer. If $f_1 \equiv f_2$, then $p_\infty = 1$; if the supports of f_1 and f_2 are disjoint, then $p_\infty = 0$. In all other cases we have $p_\infty \in (0,1)$ and a maximizing copula C_{F_1,F_2}, which strongly depends on the marginals, is given by

$$C_{F_1,F_2}(u_1, u_2) = \int_0^{\min\{F_1^{-1}(u_1), F_2^{-1}(u_2)\}} \min\{f_1(s), f_2(s)\} ds$$
$$+ \frac{1}{1 - p_\infty} \left(\int_0^{F_1^{-1}(u_1)} f_1(s) - \min\{f_1(s), f_2(s)\} ds \right) \left(\int_0^{F_2^{-1}(u_2)} f_2(s) - \min\{f_1(s), f_2(s)\} ds \right).$$

There are several important aspects that we can conclude from this result:

(i) A simulation algorithm for the maximizing copula C_{F_1,F_2} in Theorem 7.2.2 can be retrieved directly from the proof of the theorem (which was not given). The interested reader is referred to [Mai, Scherer (2014)] for details, see also Exercise 3.

(ii) The 'more inhomogeneous' the marginal laws F_1, F_2 are, the smaller the maximal probability p_∞ for a joint default becomes. In other words, p_∞ serves as a good measure for homogeneity of the marginals. Translating this into our CDS example, this means, for example, if we buy CDS protection on a highly risky reference entity from a solid counterparty (meaning that $F_1 \gg F_2$), then the likelihood of our worst-case scenario cannot become too big, even within the most adverse bivariate stochastic model for (X_1, X_2). In typical situations, however, the upper bound from Theorem 7.2.2 is higher than one's expectation for this joint default probability and only provides a model-independent range for the risk measure $p(T; C, F_1, F_2)$.

(iii) Since the maximizing copula is highly dependent on the marginal distributions, the present example, similar to the explanation in FAQ 4.1.3, shows that one has to be very careful when plugging inhomogeneous marginals into an exchangeable copula. The maximizing copula in general is by no means exchangeable, and therefore the interpretation 'larger concordance measure of the copula $\Rightarrow$ larger probability of a joint default' needs not hold, even though this might be one's intuition.

To provide a numeric example, if F_1, F_2 are exponential distributions with rate parameters λ_1, λ_2, respectively, it follows that

$$
p_\infty = \begin{cases} 1 - \left(\dfrac{\min\{\lambda_1,\lambda_2\}}{\max\{\lambda_1,\lambda_2\}}\right)^{\frac{\min\{\lambda_1,\lambda_2\}}{|\lambda_2-\lambda_1|}} + \left(\dfrac{\min\{\lambda_1,\lambda_2\}}{\max\{\lambda_1,\lambda_2\}}\right)^{\frac{\max\{\lambda_1,\lambda_2\}}{|\lambda_1-\lambda_2|}}, & \lambda_1 \neq \lambda_2, \\ 1, & \lambda_1 = \lambda_2 \end{cases}
$$

cf. Exercise 1.

EXERCISES

1. Compute p_∞ in (7.3) if F_1, F_2 are exponential distributions with rate parameters λ_1, λ_2, respectively. Then consider two companies with five year CDS spreads of 70 basis points and 250 basis points, respectively. Use the 'credit triangle': CDS spread$_j = (1 - R)\lambda_j$ with recovery rate $R = 40\%$ to approximate the intensities λ_j, assuming the default times to be exponentially distributed. What is the maximal probability of the resulting companies defaulting jointly? What is the maximal probability of defaulting jointly within the first five years?

2. Derive the credit triangle mentioned in the previous exercise, by carrying out the following steps:

   a. Compute the expected discounted payments of the CDS protection buyer to the seller by the formula $s \int_0^T e^{-rt} \mathbb{P}(\tau > t)\, dt$, where $r > 0$ is a flat interest rate parameter, s is the CDS spread, T is the CDS maturity, and the default time τ is assumed to be exponential with parameter λ.

   b. Compute the expected discounted payments of the CDS protection seller to the buyer by the formula $(1 - R)\mathbb{E}[e^{-r\tau} 1_{\{\tau \leq T\}}]$, where R is a constant recovery rate, giving the fraction of CDS notional to be received in case of a default.

   c. If the values obtained in a) and b) agree, this means that the CDS value at inception is fair in the sense that no party (neither seller nor buyer) makes a systematic gain by entering into the CDS deal. Show that this is the case if and only if $s = (1 - R)\lambda$.

3. Let f_1 and f_2 be two densities on $(0, \infty)$ and assume that

$$
p_\infty = \int_0^\infty \min\{f_1(x), f_2(x)\}\, dx \in (0, 1).
$$

   a. Show that $h_{\min} := \min\{f_1, f_2\}/p_\infty$, $h_1 := (f_1 - p_\infty h_{\min})/(1 - p_\infty)$, and $h_2 := (f_2 - p_\infty h_{\min})/(1 - p_\infty)$ are also densities of positive random variables.

   b. Consider four independent random variables $H_{\min} \sim h_{\min}, H_1 \sim h_1, H_2 \sim h_2$, and X a dichotomous random variable with $\mathbb{P}(X = 1) = p_\infty = 1 - \mathbb{P}(X = 0)$. Define the random vector

$$
(X_1, X_2) = \begin{cases} (H_{\min}, H_{\min}) & \text{if } X = 1 \\ (H_1, H_2) & \text{if } X = 0 \end{cases}
$$

   and show that $X_1 \sim f_1, X_2 \sim f_2$, as well as $\mathbb{P}(X_1 = X_2) = p_\infty$.

4. Use the stochastic model of the previous exercise in order to simulate from the copula C_{F_1,F_2} in the case of F_1, F_2 being two (different) exponential distributions. Verify the validity of the algorithm by comparing the theoretical formula derived in Exercise 1 with its empirical counterpart obtained from n independent simulations.

5. Compute the copula of $(\tilde{L}_1, \tilde{L}_2)$ from Example 7.1.1.

6. Consider two dice, D_1 and D_2, and consider their sum $D_1 + D_2$. Assume you can freely choose the dependence structure among them. Show that $\text{VaR}_{2/3}(D_1 + D_2)^\oplus = 11$.

7. Implement the rearrangement algorithm. As a control result to check your implementation, taken from [Embrechts et al. (2013)], verify that for $d = 3$ risks L_j, all of them having Pareto(2) distribution, the portfolio VaR at the $\alpha = 0.99$ level is around 46.

8   How to Construct a Portfolio-default Model?

We discuss different possibilities how models for dependent default times can be constructed. Such models are required for many tasks, examples are the pricing of portfolio-credit derivatives, the risk management of credit portfolios, and computations in the context of counterparty credit risk. It also illustrates how copulas can be used to create dependence between pre-specified marginal laws, which is one of the core applications of Sklar's Theorem 1.2.4.

FAQ 8.0.1 (What about individual default probabilities?)

In financial applications one often has a pretty good understanding of the marginal laws. In credit-risk modeling valuable information about individual default probabilities are CDS spreads and bond prices, information taken from balance sheets, and ratings. Such information provides us with (via, for example, structural-, intensity-, or scoring-models) the term structure of default probabilities of some given company. Since individual default risk is not the focus of our book,[1] let us assume the marginal default probabilities to be given and denote them by $t \mapsto \mathbb{P}(X_j \leq t) =: F_j(t)$, where X_j is the default time of company j, $j = 1, \ldots, d$.

8.1   The Canonical Construction of Default Times

Aiming at the possibility of drawing samples from X_j, we first need a stochastic model for the default times. Ideally, this model is simple enough to allow for meaningful generalizations later on. One such model is the 'canonical construction of default times', given by

$$X_j := \inf\{t \geq 0 : F_j(t) \geq U_j\}, \quad U_j \sim \mathcal{U}[0,1], \tag{8.1}$$

and illustrated in Figure 8.1. Simulating from this model is conveniently simple: one only has to sample the univariate trigger U_j from the $\mathcal{U}[0,1]$-distribution[2] and then determine X_j as the first point in time t where $F_j(t) \geq U_j$. Note that if F_j has inverse function[3] F_j^{-1}, this corresponds to setting $X_j := F_j^{-1}(U_j)$. Construction (8.1)

---

[1] Good textbooks on default risk are [Bielecki, Rutkowski (2002), Schönbucher (2003)].

[2] This is implemented in all programming languages, for example the command `runif()` in R.

[3] The inverse F_j^{-1} exists, for example, if F_j has positive density on $(0,\infty)$, which is an innocent assumption from an economic perspective. If a proper inverse does not exist, one simply replaces it by the generalized inverse (see Definition 1.2.6) and everything else remains the same (but requires some careful considerations in the derivation of the statements).

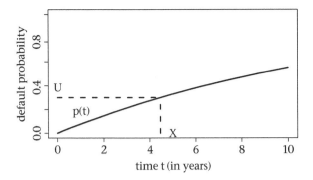

Figure 8.1 The 'canonical construction' of a default time X, see Equation (8.1). Default happens the first time the (deterministic) term structure of default probabilities $t \mapsto p(t) = \mathbb{P}(X \leq t)$ exceeds the (random) trigger variable $U \sim \mathcal{U}[0,1]$.

is convenient because it holds true for arbitrary marginals F_j, that is, the 'derivation' of F_j plays no role.

Construction (8.1) can be generalized in many ways. One popular way is to randomize F_j, that is, to replace it by a non-decreasing stochastic process, for example, driven by an intensity process. This constitutes the class of intensity-based models. The corresponding stochastic model is

$$X_j := \inf\{t \geq 0 : \underbrace{\int_0^t \lambda_j(s) \, ds}_{\text{intensity process}} \geq \epsilon_j\}, \quad \epsilon_j \sim \mathcal{E}(1),$$

$$= \inf\{t \geq 0 : \underbrace{1 - e^{-\int_0^t \lambda_j(s)ds}}_{=:F_{j,t} \text{ a randomized distribution function}} \geq \underbrace{1 - e^{-\epsilon_j}}_{=:U_j \sim \mathcal{U}[0,1]}\}, \quad (8.2)$$

so X_j defaults at the first time the integrated intensity process exceeds the unit exponential trigger level ϵ_j. Note from the second line that this might be interpreted as the canonical construction with a randomized distribution function $F_{j,t}$ replacing $F_j(t)$. Such a generalization is required, e.g., when one needs to model not only the default time, but additionally the fluctuations of the associated credit spread over time.

FAQ 8.1.1 (How to include dependence?)

There is vast literature on possible portfolio-default models, all of them concerned with a vector of dependent default times $(X_1, \ldots, X_d)$. Most of the proposed approaches can be related to the canonical construction of default times and their motivation for introducing dependence can be classified in one of the following two ways.

(a) **Dependent trigger variables** $(U_1, \ldots, U_d)$: One considers a vector of d default times $(X_1, \ldots, X_d)$, all of them defined as in construction (8.1). In this basic form with deterministic distribution functions $F_1, \ldots, F_d$ the only random quantities in a multivariate extension of (8.1) are the univariate trigger variables $U_1, \ldots, U_d$.

Hence, a natural idea is to model them as dependent random variables. Their dependence then introduces dependence among the default times. It is extremely convenient that all marginals of a copula are $\mathcal{U}[0,1]$-distributed: the simple assumption $(U_1,\ldots,U_d) \sim C$ preserves the marginal laws and dependence to the vector $(X_1,\ldots,X_d)$ is introduced via the choice of copula C, see [Schönbucher, Schubert (2000)]. This approach is investigated in more detail in Section 8.2.

(b) **Random distribution functions** $(F_{1,t},\ldots,F_{d,t})$: Instead of taking dependent trigger variables, one can alternatively use randomized (and dependent) distribution functions $(F_{1,t},\ldots,F_{d,t})$. The model for $(X_1,\ldots,X_d)$ is then

$$X_j := \inf\{t \geq 0 : F_{j,t} \geq U_j\}, \quad U_j \overset{iid}{\sim} \mathcal{U}[0,1], \quad j=1,\ldots,d. \tag{8.3}$$

Popular choices to specify such an approach are dependent intensity processes in a formulation as introduced in (8.2). Generally speaking, with approach (b) it is simpler to define dynamic models, but it is more complicated to investigate dependence properties of $(X_1,\ldots,X_d)$ than it is in (a). An important subclass of models with randomized distribution functions is obtained when the processes $F_{j,t} = F_t$ do not depend on the company j, that is, are the very same for all companies. Then one might speak of a one-factor model with a stochastic distribution function F_t as joint factor. Such models enjoy a great level of analytical tractability. One example, driven by an α-stable subordinator, is introduced in Section 8.3. A systematic overview on such models is provided in [Mai et al. (2013)].

It is interesting to know that, when suitably formulated, many popular models can be derived in both ways. For instance, the Gaussian copula model can be formulated as in (a) with a Gaussian copula connecting $(U_1,\ldots,U_d)$. Alternatively, a certain random distribution function involving a normally distributed mixture variable leads to the same distribution of $(X_1,\ldots,X_d)$ via (b), see Examples 8.2.5 and 8.3.2, as well as Exercise 2.

8.2 Classical Copula Models for Dependent Default Times

We now discuss the approach of FAQ 8.1.1(a) in more detail, that is, we consider multivariate extensions of the canonical construction of default times where dependence is introduced via trigger variables having some copula C as joint distribution function. In most multivariate applications, the quantities one is interested in (like the portfolio VaR or the price of some portfolio-credit derivative) can hardly ever be computed analytically. Hence, a Monte-Carlo simulation is often the method of choice. In this context, we need to be able to simulate the vector of dependent default times. Such a sampling scheme is conveniently simple, at least as long as one is able to simulate from the selected copula C. Hence, the possibility to efficiently sample from C might be a requirement on the model from the perspective of numerical tractability. This might interfere with requirements from model building, especially when the portfolio size is large.

Algorithm 8.2.1 (Sampling dependent default times)
Let n be the number of independent scenarios to be drawn. In each Monte-Carlo run $i = 1, \ldots, n$ perform the following steps:

(1) Simulate (dependent) trigger variables from the selected copula, that is, $\mathbf{U}^{(i)} := (U_1^{(i)}, \ldots, U_d^{(i)}) \sim C$.

(2) Derive the resulting default times $\mathbf{X}^{(i)} := (X_1^{(i)}, \ldots, X_d^{(i)})$ from Equation (8.1).

It is important to notice that each choice of copula C implies a (mathematically) valid model for $(X_1, \ldots, X_d)$. However, it is not said that this model is realistic from an economic perspective. For an adequate selection of the copula C it is crucial to understand how properties of C translate to properties of the vector of default times. Some comments in this regard are given in FAQ 8.2.2. For instance, C need not be compatible with the marginals, see FAQ 4.1.3.

FAQ 8.2.2 (What are interesting properties for dependent default times?)
(a) **Tail dependence:** An interesting property for (two) default times (X_j, X_k) is positive lower-tail dependence, see Definition 3.3.1. Heuristically speaking, this corresponds to a positive probability of joint early defaults. This scenario is a major risk in many applications and should thus be considered within the model.[4] To achieve this, consider a (bivariate) copula connecting $(U_j, U_k) \sim C$ with positive lower-tail dependence $\lim_{u \searrow 0} C(u, u)/u = LTD_C > 0$. One then observes for homogeneous[5] marginal laws $t \mapsto p(t) := F_j(t) = F_k(t)$ with $\lim_{t \searrow 0} p(t) = 0$ that

$$\lim_{t \searrow 0} \mathrm{Cor}\left(\mathbf{1}_{\{X_j \leq t\}}, \mathbf{1}_{\{X_k \leq t\}}\right) = \lim_{t \searrow 0} \frac{C(p(t), p(t)) - p(t)^2}{p(t)(1 - p(t))} = LTD_C.$$

This means that the lower-tail dependence coefficient of the involved copula plays a major role for the risk of joint early defaults measured in terms of default correlation. Recall from Section 4.1.1 that the Gaussian copula is tail independent. Hence, the Gaussian copula model might underestimate the risk of joint early defaults, which makes it difficult to calibrate it to, for example, quoted CDO tranches.

(b) **Hierarchies:** A property that is often realistic from an economic perspective is hierarchical structure. To see the motivation behind this property consider a big loan portfolio and assume that, for example, the geographic region and/or the industry sector of each loan is known. It is then reasonable to believe that companies from the same industry sector share similar risk factors and are thus more strongly associated than firms from different industries. The same applies to geographic regions, where it is plausible to assume that a time of

---

[4] The symmetric scenario corresponding to positive upper-tail dependence, namely extraordinary long joint survival times, is usually not a risky scenario for default times, but might be one for pension plans if one models mortality events.

[5] The case of inhomogeneous marginals is related but notationally more involved.

Figure 8.2   Illustration of a possible hierarchical classification of a loan portfolio.

prosperity/depression hits all companies in one region alike. Such a model is implied by, for example, hierarchical copulas (see [Hofert, Scherer (2011)] for an application of hierarchical Archimedean copulas to CDO pricing), an illustration is given in Figure 8.2.

(c) **Scalability in** d: Finally, a very practical requirement is scalability of the model in the dimension. This means that the model can be increased (resp. decreased) in portfolio size d whenever required, without violating the structure of the model. This is a very natural requirement in practice, since very often credits are removed from the portfolio or new credits enter the portfolio. Factor models especially enjoy a great level of flexibility with respect to such changes in d, see [Mai, Scherer (2012)] for a deeper study.

8.2.1   The Portfolio-loss Distribution

For many applications in the field of portfolio credit-risk management the quantity that is ultimately required is the portfolio-loss distribution. Considering a portfolio with d credits, having associated default times $X_1, \ldots, X_d$, outstanding notionals $N_1, \ldots, N_d$, and (possibly random) recovery rates $R_1, \ldots, R_d$, the portfolio-loss process is defined as

$$L_{d,t} := \sum_{j=1}^{d} (1 - R_j)\, N_j \, \mathbf{1}_{\{X_j \leq t\}}, \quad t \geq 0. \tag{8.4}$$

The portfolio-loss process starts at $L_{d,0} = 0$, meaning that no default has been observed, yet. Whenever a default event takes place, which happens at $X_1, \ldots, X_d$, the process steps up. The size of the jump is determined by the observed loss in notional corresponding to the defaulted name. The difficulty we face is to construct a model that explains the above objects as realistically as possible, while it is still analytically tractable enough so that we can compute the probability distribution of $L_{d,t}$. This requires a careful balance of simplifying assumptions.

FAQ 8.2.3 (How to model stochastic recovery rates?)

The recovery rate R_j denotes the fraction of notional N_j that is lost at the time of default X_j of company j. A common assumption is to model it as a random variable with support $[0, 1]$, for example using a so-called Beta distribution. The empirical density of realized recoveries is often described as U-shaped with a mean slightly above 40%. There is some empirical evidence that recoveries tend to be high (low) in times of prosperity (depression). So not only are $(R_1, \ldots, R_d)$ dependent, they are even (negatively) associated with $(X_1, \ldots, X_d)$. A model that concerns such observations and contains references for empirical studies on realized recovery rates is [Höcht, Zagst (2010)].

Obviously, the problem of finding the probability distribution of $L_{d,t}$ simplifies if fewer random objects are considered/modeled. In some cases, like the pricing of certain portfolio-credit derivatives, the simplification of a homogeneous notional might actually be part of the contractual specification and thus natural. In this case, the notional is standardized to $N_j = 1$. The simplifying assumptions of a constant recovery rate, $R = 40\%$ say, is usually a tribute to the mathematical complexity of the problem and the reason for accepting it is rooted in mathematical needs. In this case, the portfolio-loss process is simplified to

$$L_{d,t} = (1 - R) \sum_{j=1}^{d} \mathbf{1}_{\{X_j \le t\}}, \quad t \ge 0. \tag{8.5}$$

An even stronger assumption is called 'large homogeneous portfolio assumption'. This is introduced, discussed, and applied in Section 8.3, see Definition 8.2.6.

FAQ 8.2.4 (Pros and cons of $R_j = 40\%$?)

Obviously, the level of mathematical difficulty is massively reduced if fixed recovery rates are assumed. But there is another advantage. If both default risk and recovery risk are modeled, one faces an identifiability problem when estimating the model from CDS spreads or bond prices, since both risks influence the respective spread levels. The danger of fixing recovery rates is that, especially in periods with many defaults, recovery rates tend to be small. So these scenarios are not present when recovery rates are fixed and thus one underestimates the risk of big losses in the portfolio.

We now review four methods to obtain the probability distribution of $L_{d,t}$. These require different levels of simplification.

(a) The first method is an explicit computation, which is only possible for some factor-copula models and additionally requires the simplifications in (8.5). The numerical advantage of factor-copula models is the possibility to first condition on the factor(s) that introduce dependence and to subsequently work with conditionally independent quantities. In a second step, one integrates out the distribution of the factor(s) to obtain the unconditional quantities. This approach is especially convenient for identical marginal laws, as a great level of symmetry can be exploited with combinatoric considerations.[6] Let us illustrate this in the context of the Gaussian one-factor model.

[6] If the marginal laws are inhomogeneous, recursion schemes can be applied. The seminal paper by [Panjer (1981)] has been generalized and improved in different directions, for example, by [Gerhold et al. (2010)].

Example 8.2.5 (The Gaussian one-factor model)

The standard 'one-factor Gaussian copula model', also notorious for being 'the formula that killed Wall street', quoting [Salmon (2009)], has become the industry standard for the pricing of CDOs and dates back to the influencing publications [Vasicek (1987), Li (2000)]. In this framework one has a very simplistic dependence structure, namely a Gaussian copula with equi-correlation. This means that all off-diagonal entries of the correlation matrix Σ are identically given by $\rho \in [0,1]$. Such a dependence structure can be constructed using a one-factor model, where we consider for $j = 1,\ldots,d$ the variables

$$Y_j := \sqrt{\rho}\,M + \sqrt{1-\rho}\,\epsilon_j, \quad U_j := \Phi(Y_j).$$

The market factor M and the idiosyncratic factors ϵ_j are independent and standard normally distributed. Clearly, the pairwise correlation (and covariance, since the variance is standardized to one) between Y_j and Y_k is ρ and the Y_j, $j = 1,\ldots,d$, are all standard normal, so the joint distribution of $(Y_1,\ldots,Y_d)$ is multivariate normal with mean vector zero and covariance matrix Σ. A transformation of the marginal laws via the univariate standard normal cumulative distribution function Φ yields $(U_1,\ldots,U_d)$, which is distributed according to the respective homogeneous Gaussian copula. Further transforming the marginal laws via the quantile transform $X_j := F_j^{-1}(U_j)$, cf. (8.1), yields a representation of $(X_1,\ldots,X_d)$ with a Gaussian copula as dependence structure and marginal laws $X_j \sim F_j$. Note that both transformations are strictly increasing, so the copula remains unaltered by Lemma 2.3.1. Checking whether company j has defaulted before time t corresponds to testing if $F_j(t) \geq U_j = \Phi(Y_j)$, which is equivalent to $(\Phi^{-1}(F_j(t)) - \sqrt{\rho}\,M)/\sqrt{1-\rho} \geq \epsilon_j$. The factor-model representation can now be exploited by conditioning on the market factor M, so that $\mathbb{P}(X_j \leq t|M = m) = \Phi((\Phi^{-1}(F_j(t)) - \sqrt{\rho}\,m)/\sqrt{1-\rho})$. The individual default indicators $\mathbf{1}_{\{X_j \leq t\}}$ are independent given $M = m$ and have a Bernoulli distribution with the above conditional default probability as success probability.

If, further, all marginal laws are identical, that is, $F_j(t) = p(t)$, for $j = 1,\ldots,d$, then the conditional probability of having exactly k out of d defaults is that of a binomial distribution with d trials, so for $k = 0,\ldots,d$:

$$\mathbb{P}\left(\frac{L_{d,t}}{1-R} = k\Big|M = m\right) = \binom{d}{k}\mathbb{P}(X_j \leq t|M = m)^k\,(1 - \mathbb{P}(X_j \leq t|M = m))^{d-k}.$$

Note that this formula is only applicable for moderate d, as otherwise the binomial coefficient cannot be evaluated. For large d, however, limit theorems might be applicable to handle the law of $L_{d,t}$ approximately, as illustrated in Example 8.3.2 below. The unconditional distribution is finally obtained by numerically integrating out the conditional distribution against the standard normal density of M, that is,

$$\mathbb{P}\left(\frac{L_{d,t}}{1-R}=k\right)=\int_{-\infty}^{\infty}\mathbb{P}\left(\frac{L_{d,t}}{1-R}=k\Big|M=m\right)\frac{1}{\sqrt{2\pi}}e^{-\frac{1}{2}m^2}\,dm.$$

Approaches in the very same spirit are possible for various one-factor copula models, see [Burtschell et al. (2009), Mai et al. (2013)] and the references therein for an overview. Essentially, they only differ in the conditional default probabilities that have to be computed.

(b)   Second, one might approximate the portfolio-loss distribution numerically. Quite popular are so-called '*saddle-point approximations*' in combination with a latent one-factor structure. In the present context, this has been used in, for example, [Gordy (2002), Yang et al. (2006), Huang et al. (2007)]. In contrast to (a), this method is also feasible with inhomogeneous portfolio weights and recovery rates.

(c)   The third method is to perform a Monte-Carlo simulation. This approach is very flexible; simplifying assumptions are conceptually not needed but might improve the runtime. Its drawback lies in the required computation time, which is larger compared to the other techniques. To estimate the portfolio-loss distribution via a Monte-Carlo engine, we only have to run Algorithm 8.2.1 and in each run $i=1,\dots,n$ we derive the respective portfolio loss up to time t given the simulated default times of this run. A histogram of the loss samples $L_{d,t}^{(1)},\dots,L_{d,t}^{(n)}$ then provides the empirical distribution of $L_{d,t}$.

(d)   The last methodology yields a convenient approximation for the probability distribution of $L_{d,t}$ in (8.5), but requires a battery of simplifying assumptions. Its motivation is to rely on stochastic limit theorems, applied to conditionally independent and identically distributed components. Required assumptions are a 'large homogeneous portfolio' combined with a 'one-factor copula model' as dependence structure, conditions that we formally define in Definition 8.2.6 below. Note that this approach is closely related to method (a). We illustrate this method via classical Archimedean copulas, following the derivation in [Schönbucher (2002)], a more involved factor model in the same spirit is presented in Section 8.3. Recall from Section 4.2 that samples from Archimedean copulas with completely monotone generator φ can be represented as

$$(U_1,\dots,U_d):=\big(\varphi(\epsilon_1/M),\dots,\varphi(\epsilon_d/M)\big),$$

where $\epsilon_1,\dots,\epsilon_d$ are independent standard exponential random variables and M is a positive random variable with Laplace transform $\varphi(x)=\mathbb{E}[\exp(-xM)]$. Further, we assume a homogeneous portfolio with marginal default probabilities $t\mapsto p(t)$. One then has for $X_j:=p^{-1}(U_j)=p^{-1}(\varphi(\epsilon_j/M))$ that

$$\mathbf{1}_{\{X_j\leq t\}}=\mathbf{1}_{\{\varphi(\epsilon_j/M)\leq p(t)\}}=\mathbf{1}_{\{\varphi^{-1}(p(t))\,M\leq\epsilon_j\}}$$

and we have convergence (in distribution) of

$$\frac{1}{d} \sum_{j=1}^{d} 1_{\{X_j \leq t\}} \longrightarrow e^{-\varphi^{-1}(p(t))M}, \quad \text{as } d \to \infty. \tag{8.6}$$

The unconditional large homogeneous portfolio approximation of the distribution of $\frac{1}{d} L_{d,t}$ in (8.5) is hence given by

$$\mathbb{P}\left(\frac{1}{d} L_{d,t} \leq x\right) \approx 1 - F_M\left(-\log\left(\frac{x}{1-R}\right)\middle/\varphi^{-1}(p(t))\right), \quad x \in [0, 1-R],$$

where $F_M(x) = \mathbb{P}(M \leq x)$ is the distribution function of M. The density is then easily obtained by differentiating, if required. This asymptotic density is illustrated in Figure 8.3. The assumptions needed for the presented approximation strategy are similar in different factor models, hence we formally define them.

Definition 8.2.6 (Large homogeneous portfolio assumption (LHP))
  (i)   The portfolio is very large, $d \gg 100$ say, and all portfolio weights N_j are the same.
 (ii)   The recovery rates R_j of all portfolio constituents are deterministic and identical to some $R \in [0, 1]$.
(iii)   All X_j have the same marginal distribution function, which we denote by $t \mapsto p(t)$, that is, $F_1(t) = \cdots = F_d(t) =: p(t)$ for all $t \geq 0$.
(iv) $(X_1, \ldots, X_d)$ are conditionally independent given a latent market factor.

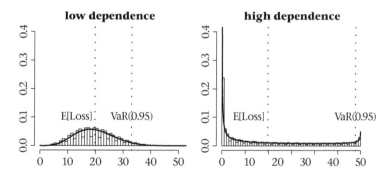

Figure 8.3   The portfolio-loss distribution at time $t = 5$ of a model in dimension $d = 125$, where the homogeneous marginal laws satisfy $p(5) = 0.33$ and the dependence is implied by a Clayton copula, a member of the Archimedean family. Finally, we set $R = 40\%$. The loss distribution is obtained via a Monte-Carlo simulation with $n = 50,000$ simulation runs and via the large homogeneous portfolio approximation. The resulting histogram and the approximated density are displayed; they are very close. Moreover, the expected loss and the VaR at the 95% level are displayed. This illustrates that while the expected loss is independent of the choice of copula, the VaR differs significantly.

8.3   A Factor Model for CDO Pricing

Our last journey is an excursion to the formulation and calibration of collateralized debt obligation (CDO) pricing models based on different copulas. This application is chosen, as copulas were introduced to the world of finance, among others, with the intention of building portfolio-default models, see [Schönbucher, Schubert (2000)] for an early reference. Also, there is a lot of public debate about the (mis-)pricing of CDO tranches and we want to comment on this as well.

8.3.1   An Excursion to CDO Pricing

A model for the pricing of CDO tranches is discussed in which dependence between companies is induced by a latent market factor with α-stable distribution. Being primarily intended for a quick access to CDO pricing and daily tracking of market prices in front-office systems, the model relies on the simplifying large homogeneous portfolio assumption, see Definition 8.2.6. It arises as a special case of the Lévy-frailty model developed in [Mai, Scherer (2009a)]. Being parameterized by a single parameter $\alpha \in [0,1]$, it can be compared to the well-known Gaussian one-factor model from Example 8.2.5. We review numerical techniques that render the implementation of the α-stable model as straightforward and efficient as for the Gaussian model, although the calibration capacity to CDO data is much better.

FAQ 8.3.1 (Interested in a brief introduction to CDOs?)
CDOs are credit derivatives, whose (market) value depends on the creditworthiness of an underlying basket of credit-risky assets. This basket can contain various credit-risky assets such as bonds, CDS, mortgages, loans, and so on. CDOs work like insurance contracts between two parties. The insurance buyer pays a periodic premium, s called 'tranche spread', to the protection seller. In return, the protection seller compensates the protection buyer for losses in the underlying pool of assets. In a CDO deal, compensation payments are only due in the case when the losses affect a certain tranche of the portfolio. More precisely, the contract specifies a lower (resp. upper) attachment point l (resp. u), serving as entrance and exit barriers for the relative portfolio loss. Table 8.1 depicts a typical specification of these attachment points.

Table 8.1. *Standard tranche definitions of the iTraxx Europe indices.*

lower attachment l	upper attachment u	tranche name
0%	3%	equity
3%	6%	junior mezzanine
6%	9%	senior mezzanine
9%	12%	senior
12%	22%	super senior
22%	100%	super super senior

The lowest tranche, called 'equity tranche', bears the highest default risk, because already the first default in the underlying reference basket causes a default compensation payment to be made by the insurance seller, who is sometimes also called an 'investor' into the tranche. A 'principal tranche' is a tranche with lower attachment point 0%. Besides the equity tranche, an investor might also invest into other principal tranches by investing into several tranches at the same time, for example into the equity and mezzanine tranches, leaving him with an investment into tranche [0%, 9%] in the example of Table 8.1. It is market standard that the tranche spread s, which the insurance buyer has to pay periodically, is standardized, for example to 100, 300, or 500 bps.[7] In order to make the CDO deal fair, both contractual parties agree on a so-called 'upfront payment' (denoted upf in the following) to be made at inception. If it is positive, this corresponds to a payment of the protection buyer to the protection seller, and vice versa if it is negative. This upfront payment is essentially the market value of the contract, which fluctuates on a daily basis, because it is the money amount at which the contract can be unraveled in the marketplace. Regarding the mathematical evaluation, the expected discounted sum of all payments of the insurance buyer to the insurance seller (the so-called 'premium leg') is approximately[8] given by

$$EDPL := \mathrm{upf} + s\mathbb{E}\left[\sum_i DF(t_i)\,(t_i - t_{i-1})\left(u - l - L_{d,t_i}^{(l,u)}\right)\right],$$

where the sum is taken over all premium payment dates t_i of the contract, $DF(t)$ denotes a discount factor for the future time point t, and the relative tranche loss $L_{d,t}^{(l,u)}$ is defined by

$$L_{d,t}^{(l,u)} := \min\left\{\max\left\{0, \frac{1}{d}L_{d,t} - l\right\}, u - l\right\}.$$

In particular, the relative tranche loss is zero if the relative portfolio loss is below l, and it is capped at $u - l$ when the relative portfolio loss exceeds u. The so-called 'protection leg' or 'default leg', that is, the sum of the expected discounted payments to be made by the protection seller to the buyer, is accordingly given by

$$EDDL := \mathbb{E}\left[\sum_i DF(t_i)\left(L_{d,t_i}^{(l,u)} - L_{d,t_{i-1}}^{(l,u)}\right)\right].$$

The market value of the tranche contract, that is, the upfront payment upf, is determined as the money amount which implies $EDPL = EDDL$, an equality implying that neither of the parties makes a systematic gain and that the contract can be considered fair. Regarding the economic use, a CDO tranche contract allows investors

---

[7] Recall that one basis point (bp) equals 10^{-4}, that is, $1\% = 100$ basis points.
[8] Ignoring accrued interest due to defaults happening between two premium payment dates.

to trade interesting risk-return profiles. However, to assess the true credit risk one is entering into is a non-trivial task, because the dependence structure between the assets of the underlying pool plays a dominant role. Moreover, one should be aware of spread risk (mark-to-market risk) associated with CDOs.

An 'index CDS' contract is similar to a CDO tranche contract with attachment points $l = 0$ and $u = 1$. It is also an insurance contract between two parties on a reference basket of credit-risky assets. Moreover, the expected discounted sum of all payments to be made by the insurance seller coincides precisely with $EDDL$ in the case of a CDO with $l = 0$ and $u = 1$. Only the premium leg is slightly different, being given by

$$EDPL := \mathrm{upf} + s \sum_i DF(t_i)\,(t_{i+1} - t_i) \left(1 - \mathbb{E}\left[\frac{1}{d} \sum_{j=1}^d N_j \mathbf{1}_{\{X_j \le t_i\}} \right] \right).$$

The periodic insurance premium s is called the 'index CDS spread'. Having a close look at this premium leg in comparison to the premium leg of a CDO with tranche attachment points $l = 0$ and $u = 1$ reveals that the recovery rates do not enter the formula, meaning that the full notional associated with a defaulted asset leaves the basket. All else is equal to the CDO contract, in particular the maturities and the payment dates are typically standardized in such a way that they coincide with the respective dates in a CDO contract on the same reference basket. From a mathematical point of view, however, there is a significant difference between a CDO tranche contract and an index CDS contract. For the computation of $EDDL$ and $EDPL$ in an index CDS contract, we only require expectation values of the form $\mathbb{E}[\mathbf{1}_{\{X_j \le t\}}] = F_j(t)$, which are completely independent of the underlying copula of the default times. In other words, there is no need for a dependence model when pricing index CDS contracts. However, under the large homogeneous portfolio assumption, market quotes for index CDS may be used to infer the (homogeneous) marginal default probabilities $t \mapsto p(t) = F_j(t)$, see Section 8.3.2.

From a mathematical viewpoint, there are at least two challenges: (i) the dependence between the default times of the underlying assets has a strong effect on the market value of CDOs, and (ii) the number d of underlying assets is large, for example $d = 125$ is a standard contract specification. One has to build high-dimensional models with an intuitive dependence structure that are still simple enough to guarantee viability.

What is required for a model to be viable? For the pricing of CDOs, a stochastic model is required for the random vector $(X_1, \ldots, X_d)$ of default times such that the probability distribution of the portfolio-loss process $\{L_{d,t}\}_{t \ge 0}$, defined in (8.5), is given in convenient form. More specifically, we need the computational resources to efficiently compute expectations of the form

$$TE_{l,u}(t) := \mathbb{E}\left[L_{d,t}^{(l,u)}\right] = \mathbb{E}\left[\min\left\{ u - l, \max\left\{ 0, \frac{1}{d} L_{d,t} - l \right\} \right\} \right], \tag{8.7}$$

for lower and upper tranche attachment points l, u with $0 \leq l < u \leq 1$. Assume the default times $(X_1, \ldots, X_d)$ to have the joint distribution function $F(x_1, \ldots, x_d) := \mathbb{P}(X_1 \leq x_1, \ldots, X_d \leq x_d)$, for $x_1, \ldots, x_d \geq 0$, with continuous marginal distribution functions $F_j(t) := \mathbb{P}(X_j \leq x_j)$, $x_j \geq 0$. Sklar's Theorem 1.2.4 provides a decomposition of the joint distribution F into marginal laws $F_1, \ldots, F_d$ and copula C. In the context of CDO pricing this is a powerful tool, as it allows us to determine the marginal laws in a first step, which is a standard exercise in practice. In a subsequent step a dependence model, in the form of a parametric copula family, is imposed on the pre-determined marginals.

Here, we discuss models in which the distribution of $\frac{1}{d} L_{d,t}$ can be approximated by a density f_{L_t} on $[0,1]$, so that the expectation value (8.7) approximately equals the one-dimensional integral

$$TE_{l,u}(t) \approx \int_0^1 \min\{u - l, \max\{0, x - l\}\} f_{L_t}(x) \, dx, \tag{8.8}$$

which can be evaluated easily on a standard PC. Such an approximation relies on a battery of simplifying assumptions which are summarized in Definition 8.2.6 under the terminology 'large homogeneous portfolio assumption (LHP)'. Notice that the definition of $L_{d,t}$ in the simplified form of (8.5) already applies the assumption (ii) of identical and deterministic recovery rates as well as the assumption (i) of identical portfolio weights. LHP-models are typically used by traders in order to conveniently track market prices in their front-office systems, as well as for efficient computation of hedge ratios. Both tasks require a huge amount of mathematical viability, which is available for LHP-models. More complicated models with non-homogeneous pools and hierarchical dependence structures must typically rely on time-consuming Monte-Carlo techniques.

Example 8.3.2 (The Gaussian one-factor model; continuing 8.2.5)
With pre-determined marginal distribution function $t \mapsto p(t)$, the vector of default times $(X_1, \ldots, X_d)$ is formally defined as

$$X_j := p^{-1} \left(\underbrace{\Phi(\sqrt{\rho}\, M + \sqrt{1 - \rho}\, \epsilon_j)}_{=:U_j \sim \mathcal{U}[0,1]} \right), \quad j = 1, \ldots, d,$$

where $M, \epsilon_1, \ldots, \epsilon_d$ are iid random variables with standard normal distribution function Φ. Assuming (i) and (ii) to hold, this model satisfies (LHP). The validity of assumption (iii) is readily verified, since for arbitrary $j = 1, \ldots, d$

$$\mathbb{P}(X_j \leq t) = \mathbb{P}\left(\Phi(\sqrt{\rho}\, M + \sqrt{1 - \rho}\, \epsilon_j) \leq p(t)\right) = p(t),$$

where the second equality follows from $\sqrt{\rho}\,M + \sqrt{1-\rho}\,\epsilon_j$ having distribution function Φ, due to the stability of the normal distribution under independent addition, and hence $\Phi(\sqrt{\rho}\,M + \sqrt{1-\rho}\,\epsilon_j)$ is uniformly distributed on $[0,1]$. Assumption (iv) is satisfied, since conditioned on the random variable M, interpreted as market factor, the random variables $X_1, \ldots, X_d$ are iid. The copula behind $(X_1, \ldots, X_d)$ is a one-factor Gaussian copula with pairwise correlation coefficient $\rho \in [0,1]$. In case $\rho = 0$ all default times are independent, and in case $\rho = 1$ we have $X_1 = \cdots = X_d$, that is, we observe a global joint default event almost surely.

Assuming LHP, the stochastic process $\{\frac{1}{d}L_{d,t}\}_{t\geq 0}$ tends almost surely (and uniformly in $t \geq 0$) to a stochastic process $\{L_{\infty,t}\}_{t\geq 0}$, when the portfolio size d tends to infinity. Typically, the probability distribution of the limiting process is more convenient to work with than the required probability law of $\{\frac{1}{d}L_{d,t}\}_{t\geq 0}$. For instance, in the Gaussian one-factor copula model, the limiting process is

$$ L_{\infty,t} = (1-R)\,\Phi\left(\frac{\Phi^{-1}(p(t)) - \sqrt{\rho}\,M}{\sqrt{1-\rho}}\right), \quad t \geq 0, $$

see [Mai et al. (2013)]. For fixed $t > 0$, $L_{\infty,t}$ is a random variable with closed-form density f_{L_t} on $[0,1]$, as opposed to the numerically more burdensome discrete probability distribution of the random variable $\frac{1}{d}L_{d,t}$. Consequently, the approximation $\frac{1}{d}L_{d,t} \approx L_{\infty,t}$, justified under assumptions (i)–(iv), allows one to compute $TE_{l,u}(t)$ via the approximation formula (8.8) within the Gaussian one-factor copula model. The Gaussian one-factor copula model, however, suffers from theoretical and practical shortfalls. These can roughly be explained by the Gaussian copula (being tail independent) not assigning enough probability mass to the tails of the distribution of $\frac{1}{d}L_{d,t}$, respectively $L_{\infty,t}$. From a practical point of view, the model cannot explain observed market prices well and tends to underestimate hedge ratios when CDO tranches are hedged with an index CDS position. From a theoretical point of view, combining a Gaussian copula with marginal laws on the positive half-axis (default times are positive) is unnatural, as the multivariate normal distribution originally has components which may also take negative values.

It is the authors' conviction that a dependence concept which extends the univariate idea of an exponential distribution to the multivariate case is more natural, because 'the exponential [distribution] occupies as commanding a position in life testing as does the normal [distribution] elsewhere in parametric theory', quoting [David, Nagaraja (1970), p. 121]. In order to overcome the aforementioned weaknesses of the Gaussian copula, one core idea is to replace the underlying normal distribution by a (heavy-tailed) α-stable distribution. If constructed appropriately, the dependence structure will then be inherited from a multivariate exponential distribution, namely a Marshall–Olkin law.

Remark 8.3.3 (The positive stable law)
Every probability distribution on $(0, \infty)$ is characterized by its Laplace transform, that is, for a positive random variable M the function $u \mapsto \mathbb{E}[\exp(-uM)]$ determines its distribution. The density of the positive stable distribution is complicated, but its

Laplace transform is simple, hence this way of characterizing it. A positive random variable M is said to have a stable distribution with stability index $\alpha \in [0,1]$ and time parameter $t > 0$, denoted $\mathcal{S}(t,\alpha)$, if its Laplace transform is $\mathbb{E}[\exp(-uM)] = \exp(-t\,u^\alpha)$, for $u \geq 0$. The distribution $\mathcal{S}(t,\alpha)$ has a density that cannot be written down in terms of simple algebraic functions. Nevertheless, there exist numerical algorithms which evaluate the density efficiently, which is sufficient for our purpose, see [Nolan (1997)]. As the nomenclature suggests, the stable distribution has a stability property, which it shares with the normal distribution: if $M \sim \mathcal{S}(t,\alpha)$, then for each $n \in \mathbb{N}$ the distribution of M equals that of the sum of iid random variables $M_1,\ldots,M_n$ with distribution $\mathcal{S}(t/n,\alpha)$. For a given equidistant grid $0 < T/n < 2T/n < \cdots < (n-1)T/n < T$ this allows us to construct a stochastic process $S^{(n)} = \{S^{(n)}_{kT/n}\}_{k=0,\ldots,n}$ from n iid $\mathcal{S}(T/n,\alpha)$-distributed random variables $M_1,\ldots,M_n$ via:

$$S^{(n)}_0 := 0, \quad S^{(n)}_{kT/n} := M_1 + \cdots + M_k, \quad k = 1,\ldots,n.$$

As $n \to \infty$ this construction converges to a time-continuous stochastic process $S = \{S_t\}_{t \in [0,T]}$, called the '$\alpha$-stable Lévy subordinator'. Such a process constitutes a fundamental building block of the CDO pricing model presented in the following subsection.

Definition 8.3.4 (The α-stable Lévy-frailty model)
The (homogeneous) marginal distribution function $t \mapsto p(t)$ is transformed to $h(t) := -\log(1-p(t))$, $t \geq 0$, which starts at $h(0) = 0$ and increases to infinity as t does. The function $t \mapsto h(t)$ can be thought of as a clock, that is, an increasing function which serves as a replacement of the time argument t. The vector of default times $(X_1,\ldots,X_d)$ is formally defined by

$$X_j := \inf\{t \geq 0 : S_{h(t)} \geq \epsilon_j\}, \quad j = 1,\ldots,d,$$

where $\epsilon_1,\ldots,\epsilon_d$ are iid unit exponential random variables and $S = \{S_t\}_{t \geq 0}$ is an independent, $(1-\alpha)$-stable Lévy subordinator.[9] This might also be interpreted from the point of view of the canonical construction in (8.2). The difference is that the integrated intensity is replaced by a stochastic process with upward jumps – the $(1-\alpha)$-stable Lévy subordinator. The consequence, on the portfolio level, is that these jumps might create joint defaults.

Recalling Definition 8.2.6, it can be shown that (LHP) is satisfied for this model setup, provided we assume (i) and (ii). Assumption (iii) is observed from

$$\mathbb{P}(X_j \leq t) = \mathbb{P}(\epsilon_j \leq S_{h(t)}) = 1 - \mathbb{E}\left[e^{-S_{h(t)}}\right] = 1 - e^{-h(t)^{1-\alpha}} = p(t),$$

where the second equality follows from the independence of ϵ_j and S, and the third equality uses the definition of the stable distribution via its Laplace transform.

---

[9] The so-called Lévy-frailty model, developed in [Mai, Scherer (2009a)], allows for an arbitrary Lévy subordinator. Taking a $(1-\alpha)$-stable Lévy subordinator constitutes a special case of this model.

Moreover, assumption (iv) is satisfied, since $X_1, \ldots, X_d$ are iid conditioned on the whole path of the process S, which serves as the market factor inducing dependence. The implied copula behind the default times is known in closed form and is of Lévy-frailty kind, see the first family in Table 4.4 with $\theta = 1 - \alpha$. The Marshall–Olkin distribution, being a reasonable multivariate analogue of the univariate exponential distribution, constitutes a natural model for lifetimes of credit-risky assets. Similar to the Gaussian one-factor copula model, for $\alpha = 0$ the default times are independent and for $\alpha = 1$ we have $X_1 = \cdots = X_d$. Hence, like the correlation parameter ρ in the Gaussian model, the dependence parameter $\alpha \in [0, 1]$ interpolates between the extreme cases of independence and maximal dependence. However, for the interesting cases $\alpha \in (0, 1)$ the dependence structure differs significantly from the respective Gaussian models for $\rho \in (0, 1)$.

Like in the Gaussian model, when $d \to \infty$ the stochastic process $\{\frac{1}{d} L_{d,t}\}_{t \geq 0}$ converges uniformly in $t \geq 0$ to a limiting stochastic process given by

$$L_{\infty,t} := (1 - R)(1 - e^{-S_{h(t)}}), \quad t \geq 0.$$

This is striking, because the distribution of the random variable $L_{\infty,t}$ is just a transformation of $S(h(t), 1 - \alpha)$, and hence numerically tractable. Even better, the following algorithm shows that the computational effort for approximately evaluating the required expectations $TE_{l,u}(t)$ is comparable to the effort in the one-factor Gaussian copula model. It is an application of a result formally derived in [Bernhart et al. (2014)]. The integrals appearing in Algorithm 8.3.5 can be evaluated by standard quadrature routines, for example a simple trapezoidal rule, and are numerically robust. The required quadrature algorithms, as well as the appearing imaginary part operator Im(z), are pre-implemented in most statistical software packages, the function call in R is Im().

Algorithm 8.3.5 (Computation of $TE_{l,u}(t)$)
(0) Input: Tranche attachment points $0 \leq l < u \leq 1$, recovery rate $R \in [0, 1]$, dependence parameter[10] $\alpha \in (0, 1)$, time parameter t (resp. $h(t)$).
(1) Initialize certain numerical constants:

$$K_l := 1 - l/(1 - R); \quad K_u := 1 - u/(1 - R)$$
$$a_l := -1/\log(K_l); \quad a_u := -1/\log(K_u)$$
$$\text{IF } (\alpha \geq 0.5)$$
$$\qquad b_l := 2 a_l; \quad b_u := 2 a_u$$
$$\text{ELSE}$$
$$\qquad b_l := \tan(\pi/(1 - \alpha)(0.5 - \alpha)); \quad b_u := b_l$$
$$\text{END}$$

---

[10] For the two boundary cases $\alpha \in \{0, 1\}$, the tranche expectation $TE_{l,u}(t)$ is known in closed form, cf. Exercise 5.

(2) Compute the so-called '*lower call*' C_l and '*upper call*' C_u via the following code for $x \in \{l, u\}$: If $(K_x < 1)$, then $C_x = 0$, otherwise set

$$C_x := \frac{3 K_x^{1-a_x}}{\pi}$$

$$\times \int_0^1 \mathrm{Im} \left(\frac{e^{3 \log(K_x) \log(v) (b_x i - a_x) - h(t)(a_x - 3 \log(v)(b_x i - a_x))^{1-\alpha}} (b_x i - a_x)}{(a_x - 3 \log(v)(b_x i - a_x))(a_x - 1 - 3 \log(v)(b_x i - a_x))} \right) \frac{dv}{v}$$

(3) Finally, compute the required tranche expectation via:

$$\text{IF } (u < (1 - R))$$

$$TE_{l,u}(t) := u - l + (1 - R)(C_l - C_u)$$

$$\text{ELSE}$$

$$TE_{l,u}(t) := (1 - R)(1 - e^{-h(t)}) - l + (1 - R) C_l$$

$$\text{END}$$

We'd like to end this section by highlighting an important word of warning.

FAQ 8.3.6 (Are CDO prices one-to-one with copulas?)
It is one of the classical tasks of a financial analyst to re-engineer (risk-neutral) probability distributions from observed market prices of financial products. For instance, under mild assumptions the probability density of a future stock price can be extracted from an observed implied volatility (or price) curve, see [Breeden, Litzenberger (1978), Dupire (1994), Derman, Kani (1994)]. CDOs are financial products which depend critically on the dependence structure between the default times of the underlying assets of the referenced portfolio. Therefore, it has become market standard to convert these prices into dependence measures, for example into so-called base correlation curves, see below, and [O'Kane, Livesey (2004)] for a more detailed introduction. However, it must be pointed out that the copula behind a vector of default times is a very complex object. In particular, it cannot be fully re-engineered from observed CDO tranche prices. Let us illustrate this statement with an example. It is possible to write down a completely different model than we did in this section, based on the Gumbel copula, as explained in the derivation leading to approximation (8.6). The resulting limiting process $\{L_{\infty,t}\}_{t \geq 0}$ for the Gumbel model is different from the one derived in the α-stable model above. However, for each fixed time point $t > 0$ the distribution of the random variable $L_{\infty,t}$ is identical to the one in the α-stable model, hence so are all CDO tranche prices. This means that there exist completely different dependence models (resp. copulas) implying precisely the same CDO prices. In other words, CDO prices cannot fully determine the underlying copula! Put more dramatically, there is always a huge amount of model risk when dealing with (high-dimensional) dependence structures, simply due to the fact that the observed data is not sufficient to determine a unique copula.

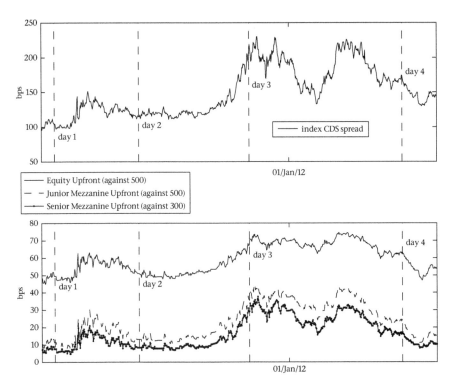

Figure 8.4   Time series of CDO tranche data, and visualization of the four selected dates, for which base correlations, respectively base α's, are visualized in Figure 8.5. The spreads for the equity and junior mezzanine tranche are 500 bps. The spread for the senior mezzanine tranche is 300 bps.

8.3.2   Calibrating the Two Portfolio-default Models

The Gaussian one-factor copula model and the α-stable Lévy-frailty model are fitted to market data. Available market data comprises index CDS spread as well as CDO tranche spreads (resp. upfront payments) for the standard tranches $[0,3\%]$, $[3\%,6\%]$, $[6\%,9\%]$, $[9\%,12\%]$, $[12\%,22\%]$ of the iTraxx Europe index (Series 9 with maturity 10 years), ranging from April 2010 to January 2013. The index CDS spread, as well as the upfront payments for equity, junior, and senior mezzanine tranches, are visualized in Figure 8.4. The marginal distribution function is defined to be exponential with parameter $\lambda > 0$, that is, $p(t) = 1 - \exp(-\lambda t)$. At each day of the time series, the following steps are carried out.

(a)   **Marginal laws:** The parameter λ is chosen such that the observed index CDS spread, which depends solely on $p(t)$, is matched perfectly.

(b1) **Base correlations:** For each of the principal tranches $[0,3\%]$, $[0,6\%]$, $[0,9\%]$, $[0,12\%]$, $[0,22\%]$, the dependence parameter ρ in the Gaussian one-factor model is calibrated to the observed tranche quote, so that it is explained

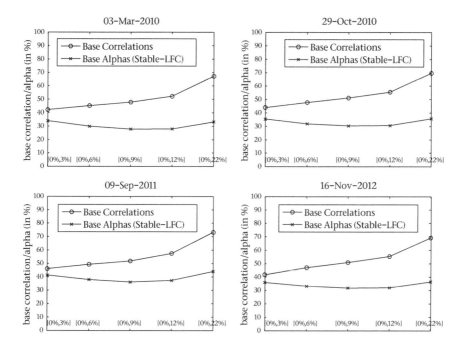

Figure 8.5 Selected dates of the time series of base correlations, respectively α's.

perfectly. In total, this yields a sequence of five dependence parameters, which is called a '*base correlation curve*'.

(b2) **Base α's:** For each of the principal tranches $[0, 3\%]$, $[0, 6\%]$, $[0, 9\%]$, $[0, 12\%]$, $[0, 22\%]$, the dependence parameter α in the model based on the $(1 - \alpha)$-stable Lévy subordinator is calibrated to the observed tranche quote, so that it is explained perfectly. In total, this yields a sequence of five dependence parameters which we call a '*base α curve*'.

The obtained time series of base correlation curves, respectively base α curves, are visualized in Figure 8.5 for the four selected days that are depicted in Figure 8.4.

The crucial observation in Figure 8.5 is that the base correlation curve is much more skewed than the base α curve, meaning that the model based on the α-stable distribution can explain the observed market prices for CDO tranches better. In particular, dependence parameters within the range of $\alpha \in [30\%, 45\%]$ seem to explain all observed CDO tranches across the whole considered time period. In contrast, for the Gaussian one-factor model the dependence parameter ρ varies in $[40\%, 75\%]$. For both underlying copulas we can convert the parameters ρ and α into Kendall's τ and Spearman's ρ_S, and then compare those. This is illustrated in Figure 8.6. In particular, for both models the dependence measure Spearman's ρ_S is almost linear in the respective dependence parameters, which implies that the parameters ρ and α can be compared pretty well.

For September 9, 2011, the bottom row of Figure 8.6 depicts the density of $L_{\infty, t}$ for the final maturity time point t of the index CDS and CDO tranche contracts. We

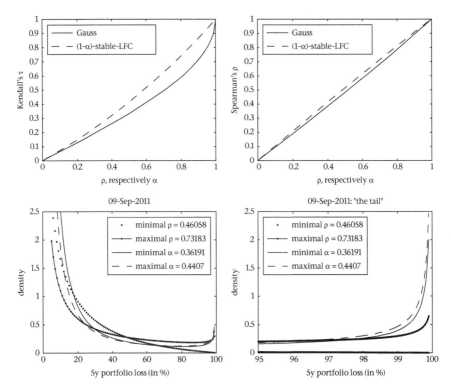

Figure 8.6 Top row: dependence measures Kendall's τ and Spearman's ρ_S for the Gaussian copula and the Marshall–Olkin copula induced by the $(1 - \alpha)$-stable law, in dependence on the parameters. Bottom row: visualization of the density for the approximated portfolio loss $L_{\infty,t}$ for one specific date of the time series. For both the Gaussian and the α-stable model the two densities with highest, respectively lowest, dependence (measured in terms of base correlation/base α) are plotted.

chose this specific date, because both models exhibit the biggest skew in their respective base correlation/α curve on that date, that is, the model fit is worst on that date of the time series. For both models, we chose the smallest and the largest dependence parameter of the respective curve, and plotted the aforementioned density of $L_{\infty,t}$. There are two interesting aspects which should be observed in this picture: (i) the general shape of the densities is such that the model based on the α-stable distribution has a heavier tail, compared with the Gaussian model, and (ii) the difference between the density corresponding to the smallest dependence parameter and the one with the largest dependence parameter, for instance measured in terms of area between the two densities, is much more significant in the Gaussian one-factor model. In particular the second observation strengthens the empirical evidence that the Gaussian model cannot explain all tranches simultaneously very well, because in order to explain the senior tranches, a completely different density shape is required compared with the equity tranche. In contrast, the densities for the model based on the α-stable distribution appear to be quite similar.

EXERCISES

1. Let $\{H_t\}_{t\geq 0}$ be a non-decreasing stochastic process with $H_0 = 0$ and $\lim_{t\to\infty} H_t = \infty$, and, independently thereof, let $\epsilon_1, \epsilon_2, \ldots$ be a list of unit exponential random variables. Define the sequence of random variables $X_1, X_2, \ldots$ via $X_j := \inf\{t \geq 0 : H_t \geq \epsilon_j\}$, $j = 1, 2, \ldots$. Show that the stochastic process $\frac{1}{d}\sum_{j=1}^d 1_{\{X_j \leq t\}}$ converges almost surely and uniformly in t to the stochastic process $1 - \exp(-H_t)$, as $d \to \infty$.

2. Applying Exercise 1, what is the process $\{H_t\}_{t\geq 0}$ in the Gaussian one-factor model?

3. Compute the density of $L_{\infty,t}$ in the case of the Gaussian one-factor copula model and visualize it for different values of the dependence parameter ρ.

4. Implement Algorithm 8.3.5. For the standard tranche definitions in Table 8.1, under the assumption of all marginal distributions being exponential with parameter $\lambda = 0.08$ and a recovery assumption of $R = 0.4$, visualize the values $TE_{l,u}(T)$ for varying values of the dependence parameter α, when $T = 4$. How can the behavior of the different tranches in dependence on α be explained intuitively?

5. Compute $TE_{l,u}(t)$ for the boundary cases $\alpha \in \{0,1\}$ in the initial step of Algorithm 8.3.5. To this end, first show that when $C = \Pi_d$,

$$\frac{1}{d} L_{d,t} \overset{(d\to\infty)}{\longrightarrow} (1-R)\,p(t),$$

and when $C = M_d$,

$$\frac{1}{d} L_{d,t} \overset{(d\to\infty)}{\longrightarrow} (1-R)\,1_{\{X_1 \leq t\}}.$$

References

K. Aas, C. Czado, A. Frigessi, H. Bakken, Pair-copula constructions of multiple dependence, *Insurance: Mathematics and Economics* **44**(2) (2009) pp. 182–198.

K. Aas, G. Puccetti, Bounds for total economic capital: the DNB case study, *working paper* (2013).

B. Abdous, K. Ghoudi, Non-parametric estimators of multivariate extreme dependence functions, *Journal of Nonparametric Statistics* **17**(8) (2005) pp. 915–935.

L.M. Adler, A modification of Kendall's tau for the case of arbitrary ties in both rankings, *Journal of the American Statistical Association* **52**(277) (1957) pp. 33–35.

A. Ang, J. Chen, Asymmetric correlations of equity portfolios, *Journal of Financial Economics* **63**(3) (2002) pp. 443–494.

P. Arbenz, P. Embrechts G. Puccetti, The AEP algorithm for the fast computation of the distribution of the sum of dependent random variables, *Bernoulli* **17**(2) (2011) pp. 562–591.

B. Arnold, Parameter estimation for a multivariate exponential distribution, *Journal of the American Statistical Association* **63**(323) (1968) pp. 848–852.

B. Ash, Lectures on Statistics, University of Illinois, Lecture 21. The multivariate Normal distribution, 21.6: 'Individually Gaussian versus jointly Gaussian' (2007).

B. Berghaus, A. Bücher, H. Dette, Minimum distance estimators of the Pickands dependence function and related tests of multivariate extreme-value dependence, *Journal de la Société Française de Statistique* **154**(1) (2013) pp. 116–137.

G. Bernhart, M. Escobar-Anel, J.-F. Mai, M. Scherer, Default models based on scale mixtures of Marshall–Olkin copulas: properties and applications, *Metrika* **76** (2013) pp. 179–203.

G. Bernhart, J.-F. Mai, S. Schenk, M. Scherer, The density for distributions of the Bondesson class, *Journal of Computational Finance (to appear)* (2014).

S. Bernstein, Sur les fonctions absolument monotones, *Acta Mathematica* **52**(1) (1929) pp. 1–66.

P.J. Bickel, K.A. Docksum, Mathematical Statistics: Basic Ideas and Selected Topics, Vol. 1, 2nd ed., *Prentice Hall*, London (2006).

T. Bielecki, M. Rutkowski, Credit Risk: Modeling, Valuation and Hedging, *Springer* (2002).

P. Billingsley, Probability and Measure, third edition, *Wiley Series in Probability and Statistics* (1995).

N. Bingham, R. Kiesel, Risk-neutral valuation: pricing & hedging of financial derivatives, second edition, *Springer* (2003).

N. Blomqvist, On a measure of dependence between two random variables, *The Annals of Mathematical Statistics* **21**(4) (1950) pp. 593–600.

T. Bouezmarni, J.-M. Rolin, Bernstein estimator for unbounded density function, *Journal of Nonparametric Statistics* **19**(3) (2007) pp. 145–161.

D.T. Breeden, R.H. Litzenberger, Prices of state-contingent claims implicit in option prices, *Journal of Business* **51**(4) (1978) pp. 621–651.

D. Brigo, F. Mercurio, Interest Rate Models – Theory and Practice, *Springer*, Berlin, (2001).

D. Brigo, K. Chourdakis, Counterparty Risk for Credit Default Swaps: Impact of Spread Volatility and Default Correlation, *International Journal of Theoretical and Applied Finance* **12**(7) (2009) pp. 1007–1026.

D. Brigo, M. Morini, A. Pallavicini, Counterparty Credit Risk, Collateral and Funding with Pricing Cases for all Asset Classes, *Wiley*, Chicester, (2013).

D. Brigo, A. Capponi, A. Pallavicini, Arbitrage-free bilateral counterparty risk valuation under collateralization and application to credit default swaps, *Mathematical Finance* **24**(1) (2014) pp. 125–146.

A. Bücher, H. Dette, S. Volgushev, New estimators of the Pickands dependence function and a test for extreme-value dependence, *Annals of Statistics* **39**(4) (2011) pp. 1963–2006.

A. Bücher, H. Dette, S. Volgushev, A test for Archimedeanity in bivariate copula models, *Journal of Multivariate Analysis* **110** (2012) pp. 121–132.

A. Bücher, S. Volgushev, Empirical and sequential empirical copula processes under serial dependence, *Journal of Multivariate Analysis* **119** (2013) pp. 61–70.

X. Burtschell, J. Gregory, J.P. Laurent, A comparative analysis of CDO pricing models, *The Journal of Derivatives* **16**(4) (2009) pp. 9–37.

P. Capéraà, A.L. Fougères, C. Genest, A nonparametric estimation procedure for bivariate extreme value copulas, *Biometrika* **84**(3) (1997) pp. 567–577.

P. Capéraà, A.-L. Fougères, C. Genest, Bivariate distributions with given extreme value attractor, *Journal of Multivariate Analysis* **72**(1) (2000) pp. 30–49.

P. Carr, V. Linetsky, A jump to default extended CEV model: an application of Bessel processes, *Finance and Stochastics* **10**(3) (2006) pp. 303–330.

P. Carr, D.B. Madan, Local volatility enhanced by a jump to default, *SIAM Journal on Financial Mathematics* **1**(1) (2010) pp. 2–15.

P. Carr, L. Wu, Stock options and credit default swaps: a joint framework for valuation and estimation, *Journal of Financial Econometrics* **8**(4) (2009) pp. 409–449.

J.M. Chambers, C.L. Mallows, B.W. Stuck, A method for simulating stable random variables, *Journal of the American Statistical Association* **71**(354) (1976) pp. 340–344.

A. Charpentier, A.-L. Fougères, C. Genest, J. Genest, Multivariate Archimax copulas, *Journal of Multivariate Analysis* **126** (2014) pp. 118–136.

A. Charpentier, J. Segers, Tails of multivariate Archimedean copulas, *Journal of Multivariate Analysis* **100**(7) (2009) pp. 1521–1537.

X. Chen, Y. Fan, Estimation and model selection of semiparametric copula-based multivariate dynamic models under copula misspecification, *Journal of Econometrics* **135**(1–2) (2006) pp. 125–154.

U. Cherubini, E. Luciano, W. Vecchiato, Copula Methods in Finance, *John Wiley and Sons, London* (2004).

U. Cherubini, F. Gobbi, S. Mulinacci, S. Romagnoli, Dynamic Copula Methods in Finance, *John Wiley and Sons, London* (2012).

C.M. Cuadras, J. Augé, A continuous general multivariate distribution and its properties, *Communications in Statistics – Theory and Methods* **10**(4) (1981) pp. 339–353.

H.A. David, H.N. Nagaraja, Order statistics, *Wiley Series in Probability and Statistics* (1970).

P. Deheuvels, On the limiting behavior of the Pickands estimator for bivariate extreme-value distributions, *Statistics and Probability Letters* **12**(5) (1991) pp. 429–439.

S. Demarta, A.J. McNeil, The t-copula and related copulas, *International Statistical Review* **73**(1) (2005) pp. 111–129.

B. Dengler, On the asymptotic behaviour of the estimator of Kendall's tau, *PhD thesis, Technische Universität Wien* (2010).

E. Derman, I. Kani, Riding on a smile, *Risk* **7** (1994) pp. 32–39.

L. Devroye, Non-uniform Random Variate Generation, *Springer, New York* (1986).

B. Dupire, Pricing with a smile, *Risk* **7** (1994) pp. 18–20.

F. Durante, J.J. Quesada-Molina, M. Úbeda-Flores, On a family of multivariate copulas for aggregation processes, *Information Sciences* **177**(24) (2007) pp. 5715–5724.

F. Durante, G. Salvadori, On the construction of multivariate extreme value models via copulas, *Environmetrics* **21**(2) (2010) pp. 143–161.

P. Embrechts, A. McNeil, D. Straumann, Correlation and dependence in risk management: properties and pitfalls, in: *Risk Management: Value at Risk and Beyond*, ed. M.A.H. Dempster, *Cambridge University Press, Cambridge* (2002) pp. 176–223.

P. Embrechts, G. Puccetti, L. Rüschendorf, Model uncertainty and VaR aggregation, *Journal of Banking and Finance* **37**(8) (2013) pp. 2750–2764.

P. Embrechts, G. Puccetti, L. Rüschendorf, R. Wang, A. Beleraj, An academic response to Basel 3.5, *Risks* **2**(1) (2014) pp. 25–48.

P. Embrechts, M. Hofert, A note on generalized inverses, *Mathematical Methods of Operations Research* **77**(3) (2013) pp. 423–432.

P. Embrechts, M. Hofert, Statistical inference for copulas in high dimensions: A simulation study, *ASTIN Bulletin* **43**(2) (2013) pp. 81–95.

K.-T. Fang, S. Kotz, K.-W. Ng, Symmetric multivariate and related distributions, *Chapman and Hall, London* (1990).

D.G.J. Farlie, The performance of some correlation coefficients for a general bivariate distribution, *Biometrika* **47** (1960) pp. 307–323.

A. Fils-Villetard, A. Guillou, J. Segers, Projection estimators of Pickands dependence functions, *The Canadian Journal of Statistics* **36**(3) (2008) pp. 369–382.

R.A. Fisher, Frequency distribution of the values of the correlation coefficient in samples of an indefinitely large population, *Biometrika* **10**(4) (1915) pp. 507–521.

G. Frahm, On the extremal dependence coefficient of multivariate distributions, *Statistics and Probability Letters* **76**(14) (2006) pp. 1470–1481.

M.J. Frank, On the simultaneous association of $F(x, y)$ and $x + y - F(x, y)$, *Aequationes Math* **21** (1979) pp. 37–38.

M. Fréchet, Sur les tableaux de corrélation dont les marges sont données, *Annales de l'Université de Lyon. Section A: Sciences mathématiques et astronomie* **9** (1951) pp. 53–77.

E.W. Frees, J. Carriere, E. Valdez, Annuity valuation with dependent mortality, *Journal of Risk and Insurance* **63** pp. 229–261.

J. Galambos, Order statistics of samples from multivariate distributions, *Journal of the American Statistical Association* **70**(351a) (1975) pp. 674–680.

C. Genest, Frank's family of bivariate distributions, *Biometrika* **74** (1987) pp. 549–555.

C. Genest, A. Carabarín-Aguirre, F. Harvey, Copula parameter estimation using Blomqvist's beta, *Journal de la Société Française de Statistique* **154**(1) (2013) pp. 5–24.

C. Genest, K. Ghoudi, L.-P. Rivest, A semiparametric estimation procedure of dependence parameters in multivariate families of distributions, *Biometrika* **82**(3) (1995) pp. 543–552.

C. Genest, K. Ghoudi, L.-P. Rivest, Comment on: understanding relationships using copulas, by E.W. Frees, E.A. Valdez, January 1998, *North American Actuarial Journal* **2** (1998) pp. 143–149.

C. Genest, M. Gendron, M. Bourdeau-Brien, The advent of copulas in finance, *European Journal of Finance* **15** (2009) pp. 609–618.

C. Genest, J. MacKay, The joy of copulas: Bivariate distributions with uniform marginals, *The American Statistician* **40**(4) (1986) pp. 280–283.

C. Genest, J. Nešlehová, A primer on copulas for count data, *Astin Bulletin* **37**(2) (2007) pp. 475–515.

C. Genest, J. Nešlehová, N. Ben Ghorbal, Estimators based on Kendall's tau in multivariate copula models, *Australian & New Zealand Journal of Statistics* **53**(2) (2011) pp. 157–177.

C. Genest, J. Nešlehová, J.-F. Quessy, Tests of symmetry for bivariate copulas, *Annals of the Institute of Statistical Mathematics* **64**(4) pp. 811–834.

C. Genest, L.-P. Rivest, A characterization of Gumbel's family of extreme value distributions, *Statistics and Probability Letters* **8**(3) (1989) pp. 207–211.

C. Genest, L.-P. Rivest, Statistical inference procedures for bivariate Archimedean copulas, *Journal of the American Statistical Association* **88**(423) (1993) pp. 1034–1043.

C. Genest, J. Segers, Rank-based inference for bivariate extreme value copulas, *Annals of Statistics* **37**(5B) (2009) pp. 2990–3022.

C. Genest, B.J.M. Werker, Conditions for the asymptotic semiparametric efficiency of an omnibus estimator of dependence parameters in copula models, in *Distributions with given marginals and statistical modelling*, Dordrecht: Kluwer Acad. Publ. (2002) pp. 103–112.

S. Gerhold, U. Schmock, R. Warnung, A generalization of Panjer's recursion and numerically stable risk aggregation, *Finance and Stochastics* **14**(1) (2010) pp. 81–128.

S. Ghosal, Convergence rates for density estimation with Bernstein polynomials, *The Annals of Statistics* **28**(5) (2001) pp. 1264–1280.

K. Ghoudi, A. Khoudraji, L.-P. Rivest, Propriétés statistiques des copules de valeurs extrêmes bidimensionelles, *Canadian Journal of Statistics* bf 26(1) (1998) pp. 187–197.

K. Giesecke, Correlated default with incomplete information, *Journal of Banking and Finance* **28**(7) (2004) pp. 1521–1545.

M.B. Gordy, Saddlepoint approximation of CreditRisk+, *Journal of Banking & Finance* **26**(7) (2002) pp. 1335–1353.

G. Gudendorf, J. Segers, Extreme-value copulas, in *Copula Theory and Its Applications – Lecture Notes in Statistics, Springer* (2010) pp. 127–145.

E.J. Gumbel, Bivariate exponential distributions, *Journal of the American Statistical Association* **55**(292) (1960) pp. 698–707.

P. Hall, N. Tajvidi, Distribution and dependence-function estimation for bivariate extreme-value distributions, *Bernoulli* **6**(5) (2000) pp. 835–844.

D.D. Hanagal, Some inference results in several symmetric multivariate exponential models, *Communications in Statistics – Theory and Methods* **22**(9) (1993) pp. 276–288.

C. Hering, M. Hofert, J.-F. Mai, M. Scherer, Constructing hierarchical Archimedean copulas with Lévy subordinators, *Journal of Multivariate Analysis* **101**(6) (2010) pp. 1428–1433.

P. Hieber, M. Scherer, Modeling credit portfolio derivatives, including both a default and a prepayment feature, *Applied Stochastic Models in Business and Industry* **29**(5) (2013) pp. 479–495.

N. Higham, Computing the nearest correlation matrix – a problem from finance, *IMA Journal of Numerical Analysis* **22**(3) (2002) pp. 329–343.

S. Höcht, R. Zagst, Pricing distressed CDOs with stochastic recovery, *Review of Derivatives Research* **13**(3) (2010) pp. 219–244.

W. Hoeffding, Scale-invariant correlation theory (1940), in *The collected works of Wassily Hoeffding*, N.I. Fisher, P.K. Sen (Eds.), pp. 57–107, *Springer-Verlag* (New York) (1994).

W. Hoeffding, The strong law of large numbers for U-statistics, *Technical Report*, Institute of Statistics Mimeograph Series **302** North Carolina State University, Department of Statistics (1961).

M. Hofert, Sampling Archimedean copulas, *Computational Statistics and Data Analysis* **52**(12) (2008) pp. 5163–5174.

M. Hofert, M. Mächler, A.J. McNeil, Likelihood inference for Archimedean copulas in high dimensions under known margins, *Journal of Multivariate Analysis* **110** (2012) pp. 133–150.

M. Hofert, I. Kojadinovic, M. Mächler, J. Yan, Copula: Multivariate dependence with copulas, *R-package version 0.999-7*
`http://CRAN.R-project.org/package=copula` (2013).

M. Hofert, M. Scherer, CDO pricing with nested Archimedean copulas, *Quantitative Finance* **11**(5) (2011) pp. 775–787.

X. Huang, C.W. Oosterlee, H. van der Weide, Higher-order saddlepoint approximations in the Vasicek portfolio credit loss model, *Journal of Computational Finance* **11**(1) (2007) pp. 93–113.

W. Hürlimann, Hutchinson-Lai's conjecture for bivariate extreme value copulas, *Statistics and Probability Letters* **61**(2) (2003) pp. 191–198.

J. Hüsler, R. Reiss, Maxima of normal random vectors: between independence and complete dependence, *Statistics and Probability Letters* **7**(4) (1989) pp. 283–286.

R.L. Iman, W.J. Conover, Approximations of the critical region for Spearman's rho with and without ties present, *Communications in Statistics – Simulation and Computation* **7**(3) (1978) pp. 269–282.

J.R. Jiménez, E. Villa-Diharce, M. Flores, Nonparametric estimation of the dependence function in bivariate extreme value distributions, *Journal of Multivariate Analysis* **76**(2) (2001) pp. 159–191.

H. Joe, Parametric families of multivariate distributions with given margins, *Journal of Multivariate Analysis* **46**(2) (1993) pp. 262–282.

H. Joe, Multivariate Models and Dependence Concepts, *Chapman & Hall, London* (1997).

H. Joe, Asymptotic efficiency of the two-stage estimation method for copula-based models, *Journal of Multivariate Analysis* **94**(2) (2005) pp. 401–419.

H. Joe, T. Hu, Multivariate distributions from mixtures of max-infinitely divisible distributions, *Journal of Multivariate Analysis* **57**(2) (1996) pp. 240–265.

H. Joe, J.J. Xu, The estimation method of inference functions for margins for multivariate models, *Technical Report* **166** Vancouver: University of British Columbia, Department of Statistics (1996).

M. Kendall, A new measure of rank correlation, *Biometrika* **30**(1–2) (1938) pp. 81–89.

J.F. Kenney, E.S. Keeping, Mathematics of Statistics Part Two, *D. van Nordstrand company Inc., Princeton, New Jersey* (1953).

A. Khoudraji, Contributions à l'étude des copules et à la modélisation des valeurs extrêmes bivariées, *Ph.D. thesis, Université Laval, Québec, Canada* (1995).

G. Kim, M.J. Silvapulle, P. Silvapulle, Comparison of semiparametric and parametric methods for estimating copulas, *Computational Statistics and Data Analysis* **51**(6) (2007) pp. 2836–2850.

F. H. Knight, Risk, Uncertainty, and Profit, *Boston, MA: Hart, Schaffner & Marx; Houghton Mifflin Company* (1921) .

I. Kojadinovic, J. Yan, Comparison of three semiparametric methods for estimating dependence parameters in copula models, *Insurance: Mathematics and Economics* **47**(1) (2010) pp. 52–63.

R. Korn, E. Korn, G. Kroisandt, Monte Carlo Methods and Models in Finance and Insurance, *Chapman and Hall/CRC press, London* (2010).

W.H. Kruskal, Ordinal measures of association, *Journal of the American Statistical Association* **53**(284) (1958) pp. 814–861.

D. Kurowicka, H. Joe, Dependence modeling: Vine copula handbook, *World Scientific Publishing Company* (2010).

S. Kusuoka, On law invariant coherent risk measures, in *Advances in Mathematical Economics*, Vol. 3, Tokyo, Springer, eds. S. Kusuoka, T. Maruyama (2001) pp. 83–95.

M. Larsson, J. Nešlehová, Extremal behavior of Archimedean copulas, *Advances in Applied Probability* **43**(1) (2011) pp. 195–216.

D.X. Li, On default correlation: a copula function approach, *Journal of Fixed Income* **9**(4) (2000) pp. 43–54.

H. Li, Orthant tail dependence of multivariate extreme value distributions, *Journal of Multivariate Analysis* **100**(1) (2009) pp. 243–256.

X. Li, P. Mikusinski, H. Sherwood, M.D. Taylor, Some integration-by-parts formulas involving 2-copulas, in *Distributions with given Marginals and Statistical Modelling*, ed. C.M. Cuadras, J. Fortiana, J.A. Rodríguez-Lallena, *Kluwer, Dordrecht* (2002) pp. 153–159.

E. Liebscher, Construction of asymmetric multivariate copulas, *Journal of Multivariate Analysis* **99**(10) (2008) pp. 2234–2250.

E. Liebscher, Erratum to ŞConstruction of asymmetric multivariate copulasŤ, *Journal of Multivariate Analysis* **102**(4) (2011) pp. 869–870.

F. Lindskog, A.J. McNeil, Common Poisson shock models: applications to insurance and credit risk modelling, *Astin Bulletin* **33**(2) (2003) pp. 209–238.

V. Linetsky, Pricing equity derivatives subject to bankruptcy, *Mathematical Finance* **16**(2) (2006) pp. 255–282.

C.H. Ling, Representation of associative functions, *Publicationes Mathematicae Debrecean* **12** (1965) pp. 189–212.

J.-F. Mai, M. Scherer, A tractable multivariate default model based on a stochastic time-change, *International Journal of Theoretical and Applied Finance* **12**(2) (2009a) pp. 227–249.

J.-F. Mai, M. Scherer, Lévy-frailty copulas, *Journal of Multivariate Analysis* **100**(7) (2009b) pp. 1567–1585.

J.-F. Mai, M. Scherer, Reparameterizing Marshall–Olkin copulas with applications to sampling, *Journal of Statistical Computation and Simulation* **81**(1) (2011a) pp. 59–78.

J.-F. Mai, M. Scherer, Bivariate extreme-value copulas with discrete Pickands dependence measure, *Extremes* **14**(3) (2011b) pp. 311–324.

J.-F. Mai, M. Scherer, Simulating Copulas: Stochastic Models, Sampling Algorithms and Applications, *Series of Quantitative Finance Vol. 4, Imperial College Press, London* (2012).

J.-F. Mai, M. Scherer, Simulating from the copula that generates the maximal probability for a joint default under given (inhomogeneous) marginals, *working paper* (2014).

J.-F. Mai, M. Scherer, R. Zagst, CIID frailty models and implied copulas, in *Copulae in Mathematical and Quantitative Finance* pp. 201–230, *Springer Berlin Heidelberg* (2013).

S.V. Malov, On finite-dimensional Archimedean copulas, in *Asymptotic Methods in Probability and Statistics with Applications, in Statistics for Industry and Technology, Birkhäuser, St. Petersburg, Boston, MA* (2001) pp. 19–35.

A.W. Marshall, Copulas, marginals and joint distributions, in *Distributions with fixed marginals and related topics*, edited by L. Rüschendorf, B. Schweizer, M.D. Taylor, *Hayward, CA Institute of Mathematical Statistics* (1996) pp. 213–222.

A.W. Marshall, I. Olkin, A multivariate exponential distribution, *Journal of the American Statistical Association* **62**(317) (1967) pp. 30–44.

A.W. Marshall, I. Olkin, Families of multivariate distributions, *Journal of the American Statistical Association* **83**(403) (1988) pp. 834–841.

A.J. McNeil, Sampling nested Archimedean copulas, *Journal of Statistical Computation and Simulation* **78**(6) (2008) pp. 567–581.

A.J. McNeil, R. Frey, P. Embrechts, Quantitative Risk Management, *Princeton University Press, Princeton, New Jersey* (2005).

A.J. McNeil, J. Nešlehová, Multivariate Archimedean copulas, d-monotone functions and l_1-norm symmetric distributions, *Annals of Statistics* **37**(5B) (2009) pp. 3059–3097.

C. Meyer, The bivariate normal copula, *Communications in Statistics – Theory and Methods* **42**(13) (2013) pp. 2402–2422.

T. Mikosch, Copulas: Tales and facts, *Extremes* **9**(1) (2006) pp. 3–20.

K.S. Miller, S.G. Samko, Completely monotonic functions, *Integral Transforms and Special Functions* **12**(4) (2001) pp. 389–402.

I. Molchanov, Convex geometry of max-stable distributions, *Extremes* **11**(3) (2008) pp. 235–259.

D. Morgenstern, Einfache Beispiele zweidimensionaler Verteilungen, *Mitteilungsblatt für Mathematische Statistik* **8** (1956) pp. 234–235.

P.M. Morillas, A method to obtain new copulas from a given one, *Metrika* **61**(2) (2005) pp. 169–184.

A. Müller, Stop-loss order for portfolios of dependent risks, *Insurance: Mathematics and Economics* **21**(3) (1997) pp. 219–223.

R.B. Nelsen, An Introduction to Copulas, first edition, *Springer, New York* (1998).

R.B. Nelsen, An Introduction to Copulas, second edition, *Springer, New York* (2006).

R.B. Nelsen, J.J. Quesada-Molina, J.A. Rodriíguez-Lallena, M. Úbeda-Flores, Bounds on bivariate distribution functions with given margins and measures of associations, *Communications in Statistics – Theory and Methods* **30**(6) (2001) pp. 1155–1162.

J.P. Nolan, Numerical calculation of stable densities and distribution functions, *Communications in Statistics – Stochastic Models* **13**(4) (1997) pp. 759–774.

G.L. O'Brien, The comparison method for stochastic processes, *The Annals of Probability* **3** (1975) pp. 80–88.

W. Ogryczak, A. Ruszczynski, Dual stochastic dominance and related mean-risk models, *SIAM Journal on Optimization* **13**(1) (2002) pp. 60–78.

D. O'Kane, M. Livesey, Base correlation explained, *Technical report, Lehman Brothers* (2004).

H.H. Panjer, Recursive evaluation of a family of compound distributions, *Astin Bulletin* **12**(1) (1981) pp. 22–26.

E.A. Peña, Improved estimation for a model arising in reliability and competing risks, *Journal of Multivariate Analysis* **36**(1) (1991) pp. 18–34.

J. Pickands, Multivariate extreme value distributions, in *Proceedings of the 43rd session of the International Statistical Institute, Vol. 2 (Buenos Aires)* **49** (1981) pp. 859–878.

G. Puccetti, Sharp bounds on the expected shortfall for a sum of dependent random variables, *Statistics and Probability Letters* **83**(4) (2013) pp. 1227–1232.

G. Puccetti, L. Rüschendorf, Computation of sharp bounds on the distribution of a function of dependent risks, *Journal of Computational and Applied Mathematics* **236**(7) (2012) pp. 1833–1840.

G. Puccetti, L. Rüschendorf, Sharp bounds for sums of dependent risks, *Journal of Applied Probability* **50**(1) (2013) pp. 42–53.

G. Puccetti, L. Rüschendorf, Asymptotic equivalence of conservative value-at-risk- and expected shortfall-based capital charges, *Journal of Risk* **16**(3) (2014) pp. 3–22.

F. Proschan, P. Sullo, Estimating the parameters of a multivariate exponential distribution, *Journal of the American Statistical Association* **71**(354) (1976) pp. 465–472.

R Core Team, R: A Language and Environment for Statistical Computing, R Foundation for Statistical Computing, Vienna, Austria, (2013), www.r-project.org.

B. Rémillard, N. Papageorgiou, F. Soustra, Copula-based semiparametric models for multivariate time series, *Journal of Multivariate Analysis* **110** (2012) pp. 30–42.

P. Ressel, Homogeneous distributions and a spectral representation of classical mean values and stable tail dependence functions, *Journal of Multivariate Analysis* **117** (2013) pp. 246–256.

L. Rüschendorf, Stochastically ordered distributions and monotonicity of the OC-function of sequential probability ratio tests, *Series Statistics* **12**(3) (1981) pp. 327–338.

L. Rüschendorf, Random variables with maximum sums, Advances in Applied Probability **14**(3) (1982) pp. 623–632.

L. Rüschendorf, Solution of a statistical optimization problem by rearrangement methods, *Metrika* **30**(1) (1983) pp. 55–61.

L. Rüschendorf, Fréchet-bounds and their applications, in *Advances in Probability Distributions with given Marginals*, Mathematics and Its Applications **67**, edited by G. Dall'Aglio, S. Kotz, G. Salinetti, *Kluwer, Dordrecht* (1991) pp. 151–187.

L. Rüschendorf, On the distributional transform, Sklar's theorem, and the empirical copula process, *Journal of Statistical Planning and Inference* **139**(11) (2009) pp. 3921–3927.

L. Rüschendorf, Mathematical Risk Analysis: Dependence, Risk Bounds, Optimal Allocations and Portfolios, *Springer* (2013).

F. Salmon, Recipe for disaster: the formula that killed Wall street, *Wired magazine* **17**(3) February 23 (2009).

C. Savu, M. Trede, Hierarchical Archimedean copulas, *Quantitative Finance* **10**(3) (2010) pp. 295–304.

M. Scarsini, On measures of concordance, *Stochastica* **8**(3) (1984) pp. 201–218.

R. Schilling, R. Song, Z. Vondracek, Bernstein Functions: Theory and Applications, *De Gruyter* (2010).

R. Schmidt, U. Stadtmüller, Non-parametric estimation of tail dependence, *Scandinavian Journal of Statistics* **33**(2) (2006) pp. 307–335.

F. Schmid, R. Schmidt, Multivariate extensions of Spearman's rho and related statistics, *Statistics & Probability Letters* **77**(4) (2007) pp. 407–416.

F. Schmid, R. Schmidt, T. Blumentritt, S. Gaißer, M. Ruppert, Copula-based measures of multivariate association, in Jaworski, Durante, Härdle, Rychlik, editors, *Copula theory and its applications: proceedings of the workshop held in Warsaw, 25-26 September 2009, Springer* **198** (2010) pp. 209–236.

P.J. Schönbucher, Taken to the limit: simple and not-so-simple loan loss distributions, *working paper*, available at SSRN 378640 (2002).

P.J. Schönbucher, Credit Derivatives Pricing Models, *John Wiley & Sons, New York* (2003).

P.J. Schönbucher, D. Schubert, Copula-dependent default risk in intensity models, *working paper* (2000).

B. Schweizer, A. Sklar, Operations on distribution functions not derivable from operations on random variables, *Studia Mathematica* **52**(1) (1974) pp. 43–52.

B. Schweizer, A. Sklar, Probabilistic Metric Spaces, *North-Holland/Elsevier, New York* (1983).

J. Segers, Non-parametric inference for bivariate extreme-value copulas, in *M. Ahsanulah, S. Kirmani (eds.) Extreme Value Distributions, Nova Science Publishers, Inc.* (2007) pp. 181–203.

J. Segers, R. van den Akker, B.J.M. Werker, Semiparametric Gaussian copula models: Geometry and rank-based efficient estimation, *arXiv:1306.6658* (2013).

J. Shao, Mathematical Statistics, *Springer, New York* (1999), second edition (2003).

W.J. Shih, W. Huang, Evaluating correlation with proper bounds, *Biometrics* **48** (1992) pp. 1207–1213.

J.H. Shih, T.A. Louis, Inferences on the association parameter in copula models for bivariate survival data, *Biometrics* **51**(4) (1995) pp. 1384–1399.

A. Sklar, Fonctions de répartition à *n* dimensions et leurs marges, *Publications de l'Institute de Statistique de l'Université de Paris* **8** (1959) pp. 229–231.

A. Sklar, Random variables, distribution functions, and copulas – a personal look backward and forward, in *L. Rüschendorf, B. Schweizer, M.D. Taylor, (eds.) Distributions with fixed marginals and related topics*, Hayward, CA: Institute of Mathematical Statistics (1996) pp. 1–14.

R.L. Smith, J.A. Tawn, H.K. Yuen, Statistics of multivariate extremes, *International Statistical Review/Revue Internationale de Statistique* **58** (1990) pp. 47–58.

Y. Sun, R. Mendoza–Arriaga, V. Linetsky, Marshall–Olkin multivariate exponential distributions, multidimensional Lévy subordinators, efficient simulation, and applications to credit risk, *working paper* (2012).

H. Thorisson: Coupling, Stationarity, and Regeneration, *Springer, New York* (2000).

H. Tsukahara, Semiparametric estimation in copula models, *Canadian Journal of Statistics* **33**(3) (2005) pp. 357–375.

A.W. van der Vaart, J.A. Wellner, Weak Convergence and Empirical Processes, *Springer, New York* (1996).

O. Vasicek, Probability of loss on loan portfolio, *working Paper, KMV Corporation* (1987).

W.N. Venables, D.M. Smith, R Core Team, An Introduction to R, (2012)
   `http://cran.r-project.org`.

R. Wang, L. Peng, J. Yang, Bounds for the sum of dependent risks and worst
   Value-at-Risk with monotone marginal densities, *Finance and Stochastics*
   17(2)(2013) pp. 395–417.

R.E. Williamson, Multiply monotone functions and their Laplace transforms, *Duke
   Mathematical Journal* **23**(2) (1956) pp. 189–207.

J. Yang, T.R. Hurd, X. Zhang, Saddlepoint approximation method for pricing CDOs,
   Journal of Computational Finance **10**(1) (2006) pp. 1–20.

Index